T0365118

Other books by Duane Acker

Back to Troublesome Creek: A Farm Boy's Encounters on the way to a University Presidency. 2013, iUniverse

Two at a Time: Revelations and Reflections of a Kansas State University Presidency and the Years that Followed. 2010, iUniverse

Can State Universities be Managed? A Primer for Presidents and Management Teams. 2006, American Council on Higher Education.

Animal Science and Industry. First Edition, 1963; seventh edition with co-authors, 2005, Prentice Hall

BACK TO TROUBLESOME CREEK

Encounters in Developing Countries, Washington's Bureaucracy, and on the Farm

Duane Acker

BACK TO TROUBLESOME CREEK
ENCOUNTERS IN DEVELOPING COUNTRIES, WASHINGTON'S BUREAUCRACY, AND ON THE FARM

Copyright © 2015 Duane Acker.

All rights reserved. No part of this book may be used or reproduced by any means, graphic, electronic, or mechanical, including photocopying, recording, taping or by any information storage retrieval system without the written permission of the publisher except in the case of brief quotations embodied in critical articles and reviews.

iUniverse books may be ordered through booksellers or by contacting:

iUniverse
1663 Liberty Drive
Bloomington, IN 47403
www.iuniverse.com
1-800-Authors (1-800-288-4677)

Because of the dynamic nature of the Internet, any web addresses or links contained in this book may have changed since publication and may no longer be valid. The views expressed in this work are solely those of the author and do not necessarily reflect the views of the publisher, and the publisher hereby disclaims any responsibility for them.

Any people depicted in stock imagery provided by Thinkstock are models, and such images are being used for illustrative purposes only.
Certain stock imagery © Thinkstock.

ISBN: 978-1-4917-6986-7 (sc)
ISBN: 978-1-4917-6987-4 (hc)
ISBN: 978-1-4917-6985-0 (e)

Library of Congress Control Number: 2015909899

Print information available on the last page.

iUniverse rev. date: 07/09/2015

Frontispiece

Photo of DA and wife dancing

After nearly two decades back on the farm, the author and wife continued to enjoy dancing. The community hall where they had first danced was long gone, and their more common dancing venue was the top floor of what had been, in their youth, the Omaha, Nebraska, Livestock Exchange. That structure, then holding the offices and related services of a major cattle, swine, and sheep market, had become largely an apartment and office building in the middle of a shopping and industrial complex.

Frontispiece

TABLE OF CONTENTS

ACKNOWLEDGEMENTS

So many have provided information and support for this book that it would be difficult to name all. First, though, I thank my wife, Shirley, and our two daughters, Diane Acker Nygaard and LuAnn Acker Deter, for their encouragement to "complete the story," to share encounters and lessons learned in the years that followed our university career, and also for reviewing manuscript sections and offering helpful suggestions.

Former USDA colleagues Allen Mustard, Chris Goldthwait, Val Mezainis, Gregg Young, and Catherine Bertini confirmed names of several persons in photos or that were key people in some of my encounters. Donna Rock, Tom Rial, and Chris Nissen, young USDA staff during my time in the department, each brought me up to date on their life and work. Jim Sears, a former Iowa State student that I had encountered while with USDA, did the same.

David Topel and Maynard Hogberg of Iowa State University told me what had happened or did not happen regarding a National Pork Research Facility, one of the "line items" funded during my time as assistant secretary of agriculture.

I owe special thanks to Steve Olsen and his wife, Laura, for being such enjoyable and appreciated partners and co-workers in our several-year farming operation. I also thank Steve Mathias, Clair Acker, and Gail Nelson, who helped us at critical times. Olsen and Rick Pellett, who owned and operated the large-square baler during our farming years, refreshed my memory of how they widened the time span for baling alfalfa without risk of later spoilage.

For the several sections on the Rural Development Action Committee, Garry Pellett provided valuable information, and for sections on the SouthWest Iowa Egg cooperative, Rich Hall, Frank Jones, and Dwight Bower reviewed drafts and provided information and suggestions. Christy Cunningham gave me current information on Milk Unlimited, Darrel Busby and Randy Euken helped complete the story of the Precision Beef Alliance, and Delbert Westphalen did the same for SouthWest Iowa Specialty Crops.

For considerable information on the continued work of the Iowa Agricultural Finance Corporation, especially SiouxPreme Pork, and for reviewing portions of my draft, I give special thanks to Reginald Clause. Also, Bill Richards and Bill Loughmiller helped refresh my memory of events in which they were involved.

I can not identify the photographer for all the photos from my files—most from our Washington work have been in my desk for two decades, but I do thank the late Betty Armstrong Boeck for photographing the Southwest Iowa Egg groundbreaking, Gary Maas for photos of the completed business, Ken Hammond and Thomas Witham for the aerial photo of USDA, Marilyn Paling for the photo of Florida golfers, and Kerry Barrett for the frontispiece photo of the dancers.

My special thanks to staff at Choice Printing and Rex Pharmacy for scanning photos and to Jason Hansen, Atlantic computer guru, who, by some remote magic kept my seven-year-old laptop running at good speed and free of disabling viruses until I could get these words and photos off to the publisher.

Most important, I would be remiss if I did not acknowledge the many home area citizens and professional people, some mentioned in stories told herein, who have helped this former academic and bureaucrat and his wife enjoy many wonderful years back in their home community.

INTRODUCTION

I begin this introduction with a condensed excerpt from a later chapter; it tells in a few words what triggered this book. I follow this pattern with each chapter, a brief or condensed excerpt, suggesting at least one type of encounter the reader may find in that chapter.

"After I planted the end-rows, the tractor lights and my familiarity with the land—I had worked every inch of this home farm in my youth—led me to the far end of the longest terrace, one my father had built with his Farmall F-20 and moldboard plow forty-five years earlier. That terrace would guide my side-hill planting pattern the balance of the night.

"This all-night work is not so bad," I thought. The tillage coulters were working well and the planter's monitor lights were blinking with regularity (each of the six monitor lights blinked as a seed dropped past a sensor in the tube below the planter box). The ten o'clock news, radio talk shows, and my watching both the monitor and trailing equipment kept me from getting sleepy.

It was late April, my first year operating our own Iowa farm, and I was living out one of several goals that my wife, Shirley, and I had written down early in my Kansas State University presidency.

We had had rich and diverse experiences before returning to Kansas State and its presidency. We were in our mid 40s and should have many years ahead. Beyond her duties as the University's "first lady" and insuring that every faculty member and spouse were welcomed in our "president's home," Shirley's list included international travel, especially to South America and Scandinavia, to eventually find a retirement location in a warm climate, and, especially, to learn to paint. She had dabbled in painting in her earlier years.

My list included:

1. Serve Kansas State for up to ten years. I was enjoying the challenges and experiences but, recognizing the perils of a presidency, I would tell my friends that I wanted to "survive for six years and stay no longer than ten."
2. Serve on the board of a major bank or of a major corporation. I had learned much as a director of Norwest banks (now Wells Fargo) in Sioux Falls, South Dakota, and Omaha, Nebraska, and wanted to learn more.
3. Serve in a U.S. cabinet or sub-cabinet role. A government agency would function far different from a university. If I survived the university presidency for ten years, I would only be fifty four and should find other interesting experiences.
4. Visit ten countries not previously visited. I had then seen only parts of Argentina, Mexico, Canada, and several countries in Western Europe.
5. Operate our own farm land, including my home farm, at least a few years. My parents' one hundred thirty acre farm had been in the family since 1871, farm technology had changed from my youth, and it would be fun to master some of that technology.

During the Kansas State presidency, I would have major board experiences. Elected to the board of the Federal Reserve Bank of Kansas City by member banks in the states that bank serves, Kansas, Nebraska, Wyoming, Colorado, New Mexico, and Oklahoma, I would learn much about this country's financial system. The System's role in managing the country's money supply, setting the discount rate (interest rate paid on overnight deposits by member banks), and supervising banks and bank holding companies, would make this one of the most broadening experiences one could ask for. It would also give me the base for continued attention to both the political causes and societal risks of burgeoning federal debt.

On the board of Kansas Power and Light Company, I would gain acquaintance with public utilities, generally gas, electricity, and water, and the regulatory role of state utility commissions.

My job as a land grant university president would take me to several of those ten countries implied in the fourth goal above. And, after the ten years became eleven, I would be inside the federal government, playing a variety of roles in the Ronald Reagan and George H.W. Bush administrations. As a part of those jobs, I would travel and work in more developing countries. When Bush failed in his effort for a second term, my job as a sub-cabinet officer, assistant secretary in USDA, would end and it was time to fulfill the fifth goal, operate our own farmland.

This book describes some of our experiences after the presidency. It will not read as a novel, with a plot for the reader to unravel. Nor, will it read as a textbook, neatly arranged by topic. Rather it is a sequential story.

Early chapters, for example, include international experiences one might not expect of one in either a university or government role. Most readers might have assumed that an academic, whether teacher or administrator, spends every day with students, books, and paper; that a Washington bureaucrat spends most days with regulations, members of Congress, and lobbyists; or that one eventually turned farmer would spend most days on the tractor or tending animals. Not so, at least in this case. In the early chapters, the reader will move from the campus to Argentina or the Philippines, or from the halls of a federal agency to the red soils of Sumatra. A similar change of scenery will appear in later chapters, during our time back on the farm.

As others read the memoir of my earlier years, *From Troublesome Creek*, they mentioned the life lessons that my early encounters had provided. Encounters described in this book also provide lessons, but more are lessons about societies, countries as a whole, or a unit, such as a federal agency or a Congressional committee. For example, the first chapter tells of repeated Argentine government overspending, each leading to hyper-inflation, a military coup and, though not described in the book, political recriminations. Other chapters tell how a federal agency can exploit the Civil Service system or a Senate committee can become a sports arena for embarrassing the opposite political party.

Encounters in Eastern Europe describe the absence of personal enterprise and responsibility after forty to seventy years under the Soviet Socialistic system. In this case, there are also several lessons related to subject matter disciplines. Faculty in engineering, chemistry, physics, veterinary medicine, business, or agriculture were adapting more quickly to private enterprise than were those in the social sciences. The first dealt with buildings to be built, chemical reactions to be catalyzed or inhibited, forces to be calculated, animals to be treated, or animals and crops to be tended. They faced the physical or biological problems that existed and addressed them. Those in what are called the social sciences, such as economics, sociology, or political science, were having more difficulty. Those latter faculty tend to focus on a society as a whole and how it is influenced by governmental policy or other factors. They can miss the innate features of individual people, the pride, motivation, competitiveness, or want of satisfactions that drive individuals.

For some of the social scientists, an over-riding concern was that abandoning the controlled society could or would result in "unfairness." The Soviet Union under Stalin, with Stalin and his mentor, Lenin, using what Marx had learned while studying economics in Paris, is an example. Argentina under Peron, Communist China under Mao, and Cuba under Castro also illustrate. Though their governments were predicated on a concept of "fairness," the individual citizen lost pride, motivation, competitiveness, satisfactions of "winning," and, especially, their freedom to be responsible for themselves.

Perhaps the most unexpected societal lesson for me was that much in Eastern Europe was tied to tradition, while in Southeast Asia the focus was consistently on the future. For example, on the front lobby walls of university buildings or research institutes in Southeast Asia, I would see goals and objectives, perhaps elements of a five-year plan. On the lobby walls of schools and research institutes in Eastern Europe would be portraits of their founders.

Encounters back in our home community have also provided some lessons in group behavior. When two or three took the lead on a needed project, others would commend and support, then grab the lead on the next needed project. That was consistent with what I had observed as I worked in other Midwestern States. Communities that advance have leaders and neighbors who support and congratulate others' efforts and successes.

CHAPTER I

FROM IOWA STATE TO ARGENTINA

"A young priest, an instructor at the Salesian Order's boarding school in rural Argentina, showed us the school's poultry operation. The hens were in buildings of mud bricks and with dirt floors and fenced "runs" under shade trees. More bricks were being made by the students, from soil, straw, and water mixed on site. The mix had been spread out about two inches thick, cut to size, and allowed to dry in the sun. He showed us three chick batteries, one with small chicks on a meal ration, and two small, non-electric incubators that held eggs for hatching. There were also about thirty rabbit hutches."

It was a quiet Saturday morning, late October of 1961, in my southeast corner office, main floor of Curtiss Hall, then yet Iowa State College. I was in my seventh year on Iowa State's Animal Science faculty, and was likely grading my students' Friday quiz papers. In burst Leslie Johnson, my always jovial animal science department head, "How would you like to go to Argentina with Dean Floyd Andre and me?"

I knew that Johnson, Andre, and several of my colleagues had been in Argentina earlier as part of an ICA-financed (International Cooperation Administration) project to consult on agricultural research and extension, most focused on livestock. After WWII, President Truman's "Point Four" program to help war-torn countries and some less-developed war allies had resulted in this new agency, ICA, and it had enlisted the help of universities. Iowa State had contracted to help modernize Argentina's agricultural sector. Johnson told me Argentina had a series of agricultural secondary schools across the country that needed a curriculum up-date and that Iowa State had also been asked to design a masters' degree curriculum in animal production at a federal experiment station in Argentina's Pampas region.

"But I don't even have a passport!" I responded.

Johnson knew the system, "You can get the application forms at the post office. Go down and pick up Form 57, Form 52, and a passport application."

Over the week-end I completed the application, read some project reports Johnson had given me, and on Sunday night Shirley and I were in the audience as Andre told a Presbyterian Church group about his previous year's visit to Argentina.

After completing my bachelor's degree at Iowa State nine years earlier, and then a masters' degree in animal nutrition, we had moved to Oklahoma A&M (now Oklahoma State University) to teach and work on a Ph.D. Two years later, we had returned to Iowa State for an opportunity I could not pass up, to teach and gradually take the lead in the animal science department's freshman courses. I would take more graduate courses and do more doctoral research in Iowa State's facilities, and transfer those credits back to A&M to complete the Ph.D. in 1957. A year later, Andre had asked me to move up one floor in Curtiss Hall and just down the hall from his office to head a curriculum called Farm Operation. With two young instructors and a secretary, I was now responsible for advising about six hundred students, most in a four-year program and the rest in a two-year certificate program or a winter quarter program. It was a three-quarter time responsibility; I continued to teach an animal science course each quarter.

Though I had never taught in a secondary school, I would feel comfortable in this secondary school advising role in Argentina. As I had recruited agriculture students at both Oklahoma State and Iowa State, I had worked rather closely with agriculture teachers, and had become rather well acquainted with secondary school curriculums. Within the university, I had chaired our animal science department's curriculum committee and was now chairing the college curriculum committee.

By coincidence, the final two weeks of the introductory course I was teaching that quarter would be on dairy. Dairy specialist Fred Foreman was scheduled to handle those lectures and, with questions I would draft for my portion, he would administer the final exam.

The Des Moines airport was yet to see jet planes. It was a DC6 to Dallas, night in Dallas and another DC6 to Panama City. From there I had my first jet experience; the Braniff 707 seemed to thrust straight up from the Panama City runway! After a short 3 a.m. stop in the high altitude, thin air of Lima, Peru, we watched the last of the Andes in Saturday's early dawn, made a short stop at Asuncion, Paraguay, and reached Buenos Aires late morning, ready for a hotel room and sleep.

The next three weeks would expose to me a "new world" and, at the same time, plant in me a desire for more experiences in international agricultural development. Most of those experiences would come decades later, on four continents, and would provide fascinating encounters that I could share with others, several in later chapters of this book.

Argentina after Peron

At this writing, February, 2015, Argentina is in the midst of its eighth economic crisis of the last hundred years. Most have resulted from government overspending, consequential inflation, and corruption, and several of those crises have resulted in a military coup. The country seems to alternate between overspending and military dictatorship. The military usually agrees rather quickly to an open election, a liberal leader is elected, and the cycle repeats.

My 1961 visit was after the presidency of Juan Peron, who had resigned during an Army coup six years earlier. He and his wife, Eva, had fostered unprecedented social programs, had spent far more than the country's productivity could finance, and the military had come to the country's economic rescue. Though there had been several subsequent leadership changes, inflation had remained rampant.

I would encounter the consequences of that inflation. The Argentine peso was losing value so rapidly that people were putting any free money into hard goods, such as equipment or autos, even extra refrigerators or stoves. Salaries were being steadily raised, sometimes monthly.

I would also encounter a country's agriculture system ready for big changes. And, I would encounter the frustration of knowing only the English language.

A map of South America with the two countries in which I worked outlined. Buenos Aires, shown as a dot at the mouth of the La Plata River is Argentina's capital city. Rosario, upstream on the La Plata and the second largest city, is also shown as a dot. Encounters in this chapter were from Buenos Aires to west and south of Rosario. Major sites of my later work in Bolivia are similarly marked.

The smell of an open grill was in the air as Andre, Johnson, and I walked into the small restaurant well after seven o'clock on a Saturday night, our first night in Buenos Aires. We had walked the four blocks from our hotel along dimly lit streets past leather goods and book stores, and often under weathered scaffolding. Construction projects had been interrupted several years earlier, after steel, lumber, and concrete prices had outrun contractors' bids. The contractors had simply stopped work.

The two-page grill menu showed almost exclusively beef entrees, from steak to mixa grilla (beef sausage, liver, and kidney), plus salads and wines. Following my senior partners' lead, I ordered biftec (steak), ensalada mixa (dinner salad), pan (bread) and casa vino (wine of the house). The casa vino was a dark red; the steak was lean, perhaps 3/8 inch thick, broiled over an open flame, and tender and flavorful. Argentina then had the highest per capita beef consumption in the world; beef processing also accounted for the leather goods shops we had passed.

Following are largely condensed notes from my travel log, beginning the following Monday:

"Monday, November 6. Andre, Johnson, and I walked five blocks to the CAFADE offices (the acronym for Spanish words I was yet to learn, and CAFADE the federal agency charged with modernizing Argentine agriculture and therefore managing U.S.-donated funds and the Iowa State contract). At eight o'clock stores were not yet open, but coffee bars were crowded. Volkswagen "beetles" were the most recognized autos on the major thoroughfare. Horse-drawn produce and beer wagons plugged the side streets.

CAFADE Director Roberto Petrone (who was also minister of agriculture and head of the Argentine grain exchange) and a Senor Bignoli, CAFADE's leader of "Operation Carne (meat)," the U.S.-financed meat animal project, outlined Argentina's needs and their expectations of Andre, Johnson, and me. Next we met with Roberto Arono, director of agricultural education in the Ministry of Agriculture and a Father Grehan, a Catholic priest who directed a series of Salesian secondary agricultural schools. Both the Salesian Order and the Ministry operated such schools across the country, and the Ministry also operated a home economics school for girls. We would be visiting selected schools.

An essential first day visit was to the U.S. Overseas Mission office, to check in with ICA staff who monitored the U.S. contracts in Argentina. They would handle any paper work associated with our presence.

We joined a former Iowa State colleague, forage specialist Jess Scholl, and his wife for lunch at the Boston Bank Building. Then on the Wisconsin faculty, Scholl was doing research on grasses and legumes for Operation Carne. Offices had closed at one o'clock for lunch and would remain closed until 4:30. In 1961, the siesta was still a tradition.

For me, it was time to study my Spanish dictionary; morning conversations, most through interpreters, had been frustrating for me. The dictionary also helped me read the descriptions and locations of six Salesian schools proposed for our visits. Some were three-year schools and others five-year, their specialties from wine to livestock, and their enrollments from seventy to one hundred eight six. Each operated some farmland, ranging from forty two to six thousand hectares (one hectare equals 2.47 acres). Later discussions would disclose that not all took students to our equivalent of twelve years' schooling; some only to ten or eleven.

We were expected to outline two curriculums, pre-university and terminal, each with admission criteria, courses (such as math, chemistry, economics, communications), agricultural course content, and work experiences. It would be up to the ministry and the Salesian order to decide how many schools should continue and whether a specific school should offer one or both curriculums. And, there was yet the issue of the desired masters' degree curriculum at the Pergamino experiment station. We had much work to do.

Though my 1961 visit was in the painfully high inflation aftermath of an economic crisis, never in my future global experiences would I see a country more "poised to pounce," to increase agricultural productivity and competitiveness in the global economy. And, I would see encouraging signs. I summarize this first global experience as three "encounters," estancias (ranches) in the vast and flat Pampas, the secondary boarding schools, and features of daily life, Argentine culture, food, drink, and traffic. I start with the latter.

Coke or Beer?

I had been told to not drink water from a tap or fountain, and in the hotel to drink only that from the pitcher provided in my room. But what would I have to drink at the office? Mid morning and at about 4:30 each afternoon, staff would bring each worker small cups of coffee, strong and thick with sugar. I rarely drank coffee, but consumed a lot of water. Eventually I found some Coke at a shop across the street from the CAFADE offices, but after the third bottle in one day I was high on the caffeine. My only option was beer, for lunch, mid- morning, and mid-afternoon, as well as at the hotel bar before going out to dinner.

In the country I would encounter more surprises. There was little traffic as we headed northwest out of Buenos Aires (B.A.) on a two-lane, paved road, up the La Plata River valley for orienting visits to a few estancias (ranches) and Rosario, the country's second largest city. Most on-coming vehicles were brightly painted livestock and produce trucks headed toward B.A. Produce trucks were a bit less bright in color and likely had the name on the side, but the livestock trucks were of brilliant green, red, and yellow, their color patterns and brilliance reflecting their owners' individuality and pride.

We followed a 1939 Chevrolet sedan, its driver eager to pass the truck ahead. The driver pulled far out, stretching his neck to check for on-coming traffic. Then it came to me; he and his steering wheel were on the right! Until 1939, Argentina traffic was of the British system, vehicles driven on the left side of the roads, and many cars on the road were yet of the 1930s.

Lunch was at a truck stop, the lot packed with more brightly painted trucks. Grass-fed cattle were headed to processing in B.A., and produce to wholesalers and open markets. Our menu: steak, salad, and bread. The truck stop's restroom merited a photo: a hole in the floor and with a foot tread on each side. It would be best not to slip.

By evening we were back in B.A. for a reception at the American embassy, a weekly event for visiting U.S. business people, consultants, and their Argentine government or business counterparts.

The next morning began a full day drive west from B.A. in a little French Citroen, built in Argentina. The Citroen was light weight; the seats, front and back, were only a thinly cushioned canvas slung from a pipe frame. Our driver and guide, Bravo, a young animal husbandry graduate (zootechnic in Argentina), told us the car was designed so that if one reached a creek or river with no bridge, the car could be disassembled and carried across in pieces, then reassembled. The doors lifted off their hinge. Only the motor would require two men to carry.

Our destination was a ministry boarding school near Belle Ville that we would visit the next morning; we would stop at the school at about 7 p.m. to assure the director we had arrived in the area, before driving on to Belle Ville and our hotel. Phone service was not dependable.

The hotel was two-story and our doors opened to a roofed walkway and courtyard, toilet at the far end of the walkway. Dinner was steak, salad, bread, and wine.

Breakfast, in a small room off the lobby, was *café de leche* or *te de leche* (a half cup of tea or coffee and the cup filled with boiled milk), plus a sweet pastry with *dulce de leche,* a spread comprised largely of caramelized milk. I found this to be standard breakfast fare and I soon learned to enjoy it. I could say the same for our steady lunch and dinner menus, steak, salad, and bread.

I then had time to walk the streets before we headed to the school and would describe Belle Ville as like "a small town on the U.S. great plains in the 1920s." There were dry goods, grocery, and meat shops, plus auto and bicycle sales and repair shops. Girls and boys were on their way to school, obviously wondering who this "Anglo" might be and why he is in town.

Up to this time, we had traveled on major highways, two-lane and paved. However, after our school visit, we would travel "cross-country" to a second ministry boarding school, near the village of Casilda. It was early afternoon and we were driving on mostly dirt roads, only a few sections graveled. Any road markers were faded or rusted, and nailed onto fence posts or telephone poles. We got lost a few times, apparently missed some of the signs, and had to ask directions to Casilda. We met a few Model A Fords (built from 1928 to 1931) and late '20s or early '30s Chevrolets. A light shower hit, and we noted farmers coming in from their fields astride their horse-drawn corn cultivators. It struck me as what I would have seen in Iowa after a June shower in the early 1930s.

We would arrive at the Casilda School an hour late, so our school tour and briefing had to be condensed. Fortunately, our late evening drive on to a hotel and dinner in Rosario would be on a paved and well-marked road.

Rosario is the country's second largest city, lies alongside the La Plata River, and is the business and cultural center of northwestern Argentina. November is spring in the southern hemisphere, so it was yet daylight at 9:30 and, after steak, salad, bread, and wine, Johnson and I took a long walk in a nearby city park. As in U.S. cities, the park was crowded with families, benches were well occupied, and people were feeding the pigeons.

On our Saturday drive back to B.A. we stopped mid-morning to see a swine operation with which Bravo was familiar. After a tour of the farm, the manager offered us a snack of beer, bread, and sausage. By then it was near noon; we were hungry and ate our fill. It was only after we were back in the car and on our way to B.A. that I learned the sausage was uncooked. Not understanding Spanish, I had missed that fact in the manager's invitation.

After this first week in Argentina, we, along with CAFADE and U.S. mission staff and other consultants and spouses, were invited to Minister Petron's home for a Sunday afternoon "Asada," an outdoor welcoming celebration and dinner. There were beer, small sausages, and tough, chewy rolls as appetizers, and, for me, stimulating conversation. The main entre, around which we gathered at five o'clock, was a split lamb carcass staked and roasting in front of a log fire. Salad, bread, vegetables, and, of course, wine accompanied the lamb. A real treat!

Grass and Cattle — or Corn?

The Argentine Pampas, the lowland plains that extend from the Andes foothills to the Atlantic Ocean, was in 1961 almost a sea of grass covered with cattle. Yes, there were occasional flocks of sheep, a rare swine operation, and some land was in small grain, wheat, barley, or oats.

To more fully acquaint Andre and Johnson and, especially, to give me, the new visitor, some understanding, several estancias were on each week's travel schedule. No small farms or "campos" were included, the choices likely reflecting our hosts' acquaintances and relationships, as well as type of units that hire the secondary school graduates.

My condensed notes from selected visits also tell a bit about the earlier settling of this open country by families from southern Europe, especially Spain and Italy.

"Mid-morning visit near Barado, Estancia Carendonga, an estancia of about a thousand hectares (HA). This was where Scholl had been researching the effects of fertilizers and lime on four species each of grasses and legumes. I noted a small flock of Correidale sheep and our host pointed across the pasture to a herd of about three hundred Angus cows. He was proud that one of his bulls had won his class at a recent Palermo show."

"Mid afternoon we were at nearby Estencia Huetel, four thousand HA and a real show place! Eight hundred HA were devoted to formal grounds surrounding the mansion, and included a lake and a chapel. This ranch had been in the family, the ancestors from Spain and Switzerland, since about 1880. The main enterprise was a flock of twelve thousand Columbia ewes, and shearing was underway by a hired crew, each shearer handling a ewe per minute."

"The next morning we were back on the road, forty km. to Estancia La Verde (The Green Ranch), with eight thousand cattle, and two hundred sheep on nine thousand hectares. The manager told us, with apparent pride, that it took three cattle, ten sheep, and one hundred kilos of bread per week to feed the ranch's one hundred ten workers and family members.

Grass finished cattle were sold for processing at a thousand pounds and two years of age. They would be lean, relative to U.S. feedlot cattle, and would have graded "low choice" in the U.S. grading system. That fit with the steak we had had daily for lunch and dinner. A sideline was show cattle, those cattle kept in an elevated barn that allowed a bit of breeze, and fed a cooked grain mix."

"Mid afternoon we were at a four hundred hectare estancia, Tres Margarita, where we saw two year-old steers on pasture and also fed oat silage. The silage had been chopped and piled on top of the ground just three weeks earlier and covered with soil."

"There was yet another ranch, Estancia Sante Juane, twenty five thousand HA and managed by Johnny and Nicolas Avellaneda, twenty six and twenty-year-old grandsons of the founder, a Senor Du Hau. The ranch exists as a corporation, with twenty one grandchildren as owners. On the estancia are seventy five families and bachelors, totaling more than five hundred people. Each of twenty three 100-cow dairy units is handled by one man who lives near that dairy. The cows receive no grain; they are maintained on grass pasture plus a grain-type sorghum that is grazed in late summer and a rye pasture grazed in the winter. Production averaged ten liters per day (less than three gallons).

The ranch also had twenty five hundred beef cows, with a ninety two per cent calf crop, and twenty three hundred sows, averaging six to seven pigs per litter and the pigs marketed at seven months of age.

Manure was piled high behind the dairy and swine buildings and we were told it had been accumulating for thirty years."

As we visited these vast, grass-covered estancias, I recalled an evening discussion three years earlier in a Storm Lake, Iowa, hotel after a small group led by Andre had visited the Allee farm near Newell, Iowa, recently gifted to Iowa State's Agricultural Foundation. Our focus was how the Allee farm, several hundred acres of high quality, nearly level land, all in grass, should be used by the university. (The foundation owned other farms, and any net income could help finance university programs.)

After an agronomist in the group suggested corn variety trials (Allee had been an early pioneer in developing inbred lines of corn), Johnson spoke up. Noting the acres of good pasture and the large cattle barn, "This would be an ideal place to demonstrate managing a herd of beef cows."

That drew a quick response from Extension Economist Herb Howell, "Cows, hell! You would help the Foundation's finances a lot more if you would plow up that good Clarion-Webster soil and put it to corn and beans!"

The Pampas was an enormous parallel, with potential to produce far more beef, pork, and milk per hectare if converted to grain production. Why was it all yet in grass? Was it family tradition? Was it that current operations were content with the current income? Or, could part of the reason be the government policy of high export tariffs on grain and meat? (To a U.S. reader in the early 2000s, export tariffs on agricultural commodities seem incomprehensible, but the high spending Argentine government apparently had seen the country's agricultural exports largely as a revenue source.)

It seemed to me the situation would soon change. Education, including the proposed masters' degree at Pergamino, would be among the drivers of that change. So, too, would be some of those twenty one grandchildren owners of Estancia Sante Juane or *their* heirs—and their counterparts for other estancias. Among them would be some who understand the global nature of the beef and grain market, the Pampas soil's potential productivity, and the gross revenue that land could generate by growing grain and marketing some of that grain through livestock.

Johnny Avellaneda had told us they had recently pulled some fences and were planting some corn. And, from my summary: "The next day, en route back to B.A. we saw our first upright silo and what I thought would likely become the country's first cattle feedlot as we know them in the U.S. It was a thirty six foot tall, sixteen foot diameter Harvestor silo, and from it ran about ten meters (eleven yards) of feed bunk with an auger down the middle. The Harvestor had been filled with a chopped grass/legume mix that was being fed to light weight yearlings. And, the manager planned to build a second Harvestor.

In nearby fields, grain sorghum and alfalfa was being irrigated, perhaps the first irrigation in Argentina of other than for vegetable and fruit crops. Perhaps we were seeing the first steps in Argentina's agricultural intensification.

P.S. In the year, 2000, Shirley and I would join a group largely of California Farm Bureau members to visit South American Agriculture. Our dinner host the first night in Buenos Aires, the current minister of Agriculture, described the Pampas, "You can put a plow in the ground at Buenos Aires and not lift it out of the ground until you get to the Andes foothills. It is one of the world's great expanses of crop production, corn, soybeans, wheat, and sunflowers." Before becoming minister, he and his family had developed a large custom farming operation on the Pampas, raising and marketing grain for the largely absentee owners of those vast estancias (including, no doubt, some of those twenty one grandchildren of Estancia Sante Juane, or their offspring). They handled about two hundred thousand hectares; investors providing the operating capital for equipment, crop inputs, and labor, and sharing in the profits.

The travel brochure had mentioned a Sunday "Asada," and I hoped it might be at one of those estancias I had visited four decades earlier. Did we get to a working estancia and a Sunday "Asada" in that 2000 visit? Yes, but not west of Buenos Aires. Our tour bus headed south and east, to an estancia on lower-quality, high-salt land not far from the coast. Grain production had forced the cow herds off that high quality Pampas land.

Schools and the Catholic Salesian Order

To give advice that would be applicable and useful, we needed to understand the Argentina education system, visit some of the schools, and talk to students and teachers. When Argentine students finished the equivalent of Grade Seven, they entered one of five secondary schools, pre-university, teacher preparatory, commercial, technical, or agriculture. Though Spanish was the country's language, there were four years of English in the secondary schools and some students also studied English in primary schools.

From my notes, here is what we found at the first Salesian boarding school, several miles from the town of Belle Ville: "An arched entry, grounds in natural state, no lawnmower evident. Director Mattioli greeted us, showed us a herd of Duroc swine, no evidence of cross-breeding. Cultivation underway in some irrigated vegetable and fruit plots near the river.

The school buildings needed both paint and up-to-date equipment, but the teachers were enthusiastic and eager for our thoughts. There were large diagrams and charts posted on the wall for teaching a crops course and a projector that accommodated three by four-inch glass slides was in use. The director was enthused about a new "2x2" slide projector that had just arrived and when I told him about an overhead projector I was using in my Iowa State animal nutrition course, he asked for details on both the projector and our method for making transparencies. He also asked for copies of recruitment letters we sent to high school students.

How about the students? I was surprised to learn that less than twenty per cent of the students, all boys, came from farms, and none from near the school. The rest came from cities, mostly Buenos Aires, Many were from what were described as "problem families" and enrolled here because "they like the open air and practical work." Only one or two of the students were sons of former students. The director and staff could give us no follow-up information on graduates; we were told only that "most went into the industry."

Considering the country's economic situation I was not shocked regarding the facilities, only disappointed that we did not see a focus on or knowledge of employment after graduation. Perhaps the school is filling a need in accommodating these mostly urban students from "problem families," and the faculty enthusiasm would be helpful. Perhaps some of these young men could catch some enthusiasm for agriculture.

Later, at a Ministry school, Casilda, Director Helander, an Engineer Agronomo graduate of the University of Buenos Aires and one-time forage research worker in Patagonia (southern Argentina), had been in the job seven years. In contrast to Mattioli, rather new at the Salesion Order Belle Ville School and eager for suggestions and change, Helander seemed more content, less willing to discuss school weaknesses and strengths.

In visiting with and about the students, there was little difference from those at Belle Ville. In a brief tour of facilities, we saw a fifty five horsepower Fahr diesel tractor, with a three-point implement hitch, electric starter, and lights, and a smaller, thirty horsepower tractor. Tillage and planting equipment was modest, nothing near new. Classrooms were clean but needed paint and new equipment.

A week later, we pulled into a Salesian agricultural school near Del Valle, and our appearance was a surprise to the staff. The school director, Father Pacioni, had expected us the next morning and was absent. A change in our schedule had not gotten through Argentina's undependable phone system.

In Pacioni's absence, a young priest, an instructor, showed us the school's poultry operation, hens in buildings of mud bricks and with dirt floors and fenced "runs" under shade trees. More bricks were being made by the students, from soil, straw, and water mixed on site. The mix had been spread out about two inches thick, cut to size, and allowed to dry in the sun. He showed us three chick batteries, one with small chicks on a meal ration, and two small, non-electric incubators that held eggs for hatching. There were also about thirty rabbit hutches.

By then it was time for the afternoon faculty and staff lunch and, over beer and what I call "marguerites," a caramelized milk and nut spread on soda crackers, several faculty described the school and its students. Twenty five per cent of the students were from within a hundred kilometers of the school, many the sons of ranch hands or estancia owners. The faculty consisted of fifteen priests who each taught about twenty four clock hours per week. It was emphasized that one does not have to be a priest to teach at the school, and the school would welcome an Iowa State agriculture graduate to its faculty.

Our host told us they helped their students' "moral formation on a religious basis," develop their practical and technical development so they can make a living, especially "awaken their abilities and vocational interests."

We then toured the school's pastures and crop plots. Faculty comments told us they were alert to good livestock and crop management, cross-breeding, equipment maintenance, and the technical phases of agriculture. We were impressed.

The next morning we were back at the school and the formal welcome that had been planned. All the students were in white clothes and applauding, and the school band played as we entered the grounds. All faculty were present, and there were photographs and introductions.

Rector Father Pacioni told us that each of his faculty had six or seven years of university work. We visited a fifth-year chemistry class, and talked with several of the students. Most were from rural provinces and expressed clear purposes, including farming, university, or work on estancias with livestock. All of the students had visited the research station at Pergamino, three said they received extension or research publications in their homes, and fourteen of their homes received farm magazines. All their parents had visited the school. Students and faculty were "on the ball."

Later that day we were at the Ministry's home economics post-secondary school near Bolivar, designed to prepare extension workers. It was not a secondary school. Instead, it provided one year of post-secondary training, and a second year was being planned. Home economics was not then offered in Argentina's universities and this was the only school in the country available for such training. The director had just finished her masters' degree at the Inter-American University at Tura Alba, Costa Rica.

Though I think of Home Economics as focused on food and family, including clothing, child development, and related disciplines, a woman veterinary graduate was teaching a livestock course that included milking cows, vaccinating, making cheese, gardening, and tending poultry. At the same time, we watched girls spinning yarn—using a mechanism that appeared more primitive than a spinning wheel—and cooking on an oil-fired stove in a large kitchen. I wondered if the curriculum might have compared to the Home Economics curriculum at Iowa State in the late 1800s.

At an eight o'clock dinner, students gathered around our table to ask about Home Economics in the U.S. Most of the young women were from small farms and small towns, felt their instruction was valuable, and were eager to learn and to become home economists. Surprising to us was that there were only fifteen students, though the facilities and the seven instructors could have handled forty to fifty. We were not able to learn the reason for the small enrollment and therefore questioned the rationale for the proposed second year.

Though all the Ministry schools we had visited needed attention, this one, as the country's single school for home economics and with students focused on this career, merited immediate attention.

What were my general conclusions from that Argentina experience and their impact on me? At a breakfast meeting soon after our return to Ames, Iowa's State 4-H leader C.J. Gauger asked me that question, then invited me to speak to the Ames Rotary Club. After sharing with the Club members what I had encountered and observed in Argentina, I closed with "things I am thankful for." Among them were:

1. The Roman Catholic Church. Not before had I seen such dedication to youth as I had seen by the Salesian Order and their boarding school faculty.
2. The U.S.' land grant universities. University faculty in Argentina needed to develop closer working relationships with their related industries.
3. Our U.S. financial system. I had seen the consequences of government over-spending, run-away inflation, and the consequences.

My encounters in Argentina had let me see more clearly my U.S. environment. Perhaps more important, in terms of my future years, these Argentina encounters and the undeveloped potential I saw in that country's agriculture, planted in me the desire to see more and do more in this international arena in the years ahead.

In my mailbox on our return to Ames was a letter from the dean of agriculture at Kansas State University inviting me to consider a position there as associate dean for instruction and student advising, and we would move to Kansas State the following June. K-State had long been helping build a land-grant type university in India and I would learn during my interview of negotiations for a similar effort in Nigeria. In accepting the associate dean job, I asked that I play some appropriate role in that Nigeria project.

In due time, I would work with several Nigerian students in K-State's college of agriculture, graduate students as well as undergraduates preparing for graduate school or planning to apply for admission to veterinary medicine. However, before the Nigeria's Ahmadu Bello University had reached the point where I might be useful in a short-term assignment, four years later, I was on my way to South Dakota State University to serve as dean.

Mexico, Maize, and Short-Straw Wheat

My next experience in another country's agriculture would come early in my South Dakota time, when leaders of that state's Wheat Growers Association urged that I accompany them to Obregon, Mexico, where our SDSU wheat geneticist, Darrel Wells, was speeding his genetic selection and variety development work by growing a second wheat crop each year.

This would also be my first exposure to one of the fifteen international agricultural research centers financed by the U.S., other countries, and private foundations. Well's work was at a branch location of one of those centers, CYMMIT, a wheat and maize (corn) research center near Mexico City where to-be Nobel Peace Prize laureate Norman Borlaug and his colleagues were developing the high production, short straw wheat varieties that would help feed millions around the world.

The branch unit that accommodated Well's and other U.S. scientists' work was in the productive, flat land near Mexico's western shore and the town of Obregon. Through the CYMMIT scientists, as well as those of Pioneer and other private company geneticists, who had research plots just down the road, I gained more awareness of both global food needs and the efforts, by both the public and the private sectors, to meet those needs. My interest in global agricultural development was further enhanced.

Most of our South Dakota State University years were state-focused, the students and the research and extension clientele that my College of Agriculture and Biological Science served. There did come along, though, another international experience. For reasons I never learned, I was one of fifty Americans invited by the then Federal Republic of Germany to help celebrate the twentieth anniversary of the Marshall Plan. My wife, Shirley, joined me, and the experience is briefly described in an earlier memoir, *From Troublesome Creek.*

After South Dakota State and a brief time as a vice chancellor at the University of Nebraska, I would be back on the Kansas State campus, this time as president.

CHAPTER II

KANSAS STATE IN AFRICA AND ASIA

"We visited two villages, where village elders were conducting "town hall" meetings on current issues. This is where Botswana's extension staff linked with their clientele. Extension staff presented education opportunities; concurrence given by village elders provided credibility for them to proceed with their work.

We also visited two farms, perhaps selected for being more progressive. In each case, the husband was away, tending the family's small cattle herd on open range. The wife and children tended the grain sorghum crop, the family's food staple, to be stored in large crockery vessels and a small, round metal bin."

By the time I returned as Kansas State president in 1975, some of the young Nigerians who had come from Ahmadu Bello University (ABU) to study, and that I had known during my associate dean years, were faculty and department heads in ABU's colleges of agriculture and veterinary medicine, the latter yet the only veterinary college in central Africa.

The year, 1977, would see the end of AID financing and K-State's nearly fifteen-year involvement, and Shirley and I would travel to Zaria, the site of ABU, in late May to represent K-State in celebrating ABU's achievements.

Our College of Agriculture director of international programs and long-time friend, Vernon Larson, (we had both joined K-State in 1962) had made our travel arrangements. He had told us we would be met at the Lagos airport by a representative of the International Institute for Tropical Agriculture, IITA, and that we would stay the first night at IITA's guest house in Lagos. We would then drive north perhaps one hundred kilometers to Kaduna for a day's visit to IITA's cassava and rice research before flying on north to Zaria and ABU.

We deplaned and followed returning Nigerians through the small and crowded airport terminal to await our baggage. In earlier foreign travels, we might look for our name on a hoisted sign held by our awaiting host or guide. That was not necessary here; whoever our host might be would easily spot us; we were the only whites in a sea of blacks. We had a rapid orientation to what it might feel like to be a minority.

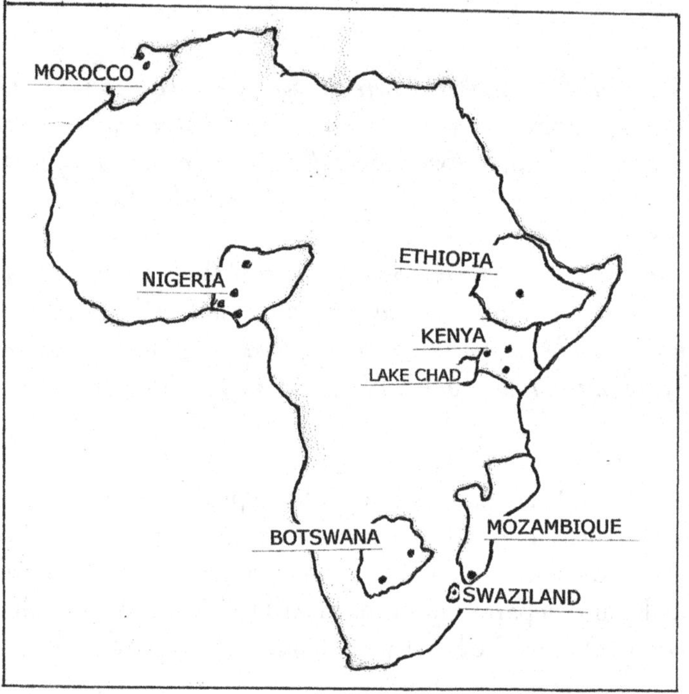

Among the more than fifty countries on the African Continent, my work would, in time, take me to seven. Our first trip included Nigeria, Kenya, and Botswana. Encounters described in later pages include Ethiopia, Mozambique, and Swaziland, as well as return visits to Kenya and Botswana. A week in Morocco for an AID staff conference also allowed visits with USDA/Foreign Agricultural Service wheat promotion staff in Casablanca and with University of Nebraska faculty at a development project in the semi-desert, encounters not included in the book.

Universities and Institutes

IITA was another of those fifteen international agricultural research centers mentioned earlier. At IITA, we saw first-hand the efforts that scientists, both native Africans and scientists from the U.S. or Europe, were devoting to increasing the production of that area's two major human foods, rice and cassava.

Corn is the traditional energy source for people in Central America and the northern part of South America and potatoes have long been the food staple in northern Europe and, in time, what became the United States. In the drier uplands of West Africa, however, it is a different root crop, cassava (known as tapioca on U.S. grocery shelves), around which most diets have been built. In the higher rainfall lowlands, it is rice.

Walking through greenhouses filled with genetic selections and crosses of rice or cassava, led by staff through batteries of field plots for fertilizer, pest control or other work underway, and visiting over lunch at the director's home, we learned the importance of these two crops.

We were most impressed by the number of young scientists and students from other western Africa colleges and research institutes, plus a few from Southeast Asia. They were learning not only current rice and cassava genetics and technology, but also how to do credible research—the number of plot replications, the value of detailed observations and notes, and the statistical techniques for determining the degree of confidence one should have in research results.

As Shirley and I waited at the Kaduna airport for our flight on north to Zaria and ABU, we would see another feature of Nigerian culture. Our IITA hostess told us she had come to the airport earlier that morning to be sure that our names were on the flight manifest. Further, she advised, "When your name is called, get on that plane! Do not hesitate or get pushed aside. Get on the plane!"

A twin engine plane, with a capacity of perhaps forty people, landed, a dozen people deplaned and walked through the fence gate toward the terminal. A gate-keeper then began calling names to board. Two nuns were among those waiting to board and we had visited briefly with them. Neither our names nor those of the nuns were among the first several announced. Our host called out, "How about the Ackers?" After two more names were called, our host called out again, "How about the Ackers?" We then heard the gate-keeper, "Acker and Acker." We rushed through the gate and up the steps.

As the plane departed, the two nuns were still behind the fence, and next plane to Zaria would be in two days. Perhaps they had failed to pay the local gate-keeper her expected bribe.

Back on campus a few weeks later, Veterinary Hygiene Department Head Embert Coles, who had spent considerable time at Ahmadu Bello, told me his experience at the Zaria airport for a flight back to Kansas. He was in the midst of a conversation with his ABU hosts when his name, "Coles," was called. Someone else yelled "Here!" ran up the plane steps, the steps were lifted, the door closed, and the plane departed. Coles had to wait two days for the next flight.

The progress at ABU had been tremendous and our Kansas State faculty deserved much credit. About seventy five K-State faculty, from veterinary medicine, agricultural economics, agricultural engineering, animal science, or soils had served, in most cases, two or more years on the ABU faculty. Perhaps another three dozen agriculture and veterinary faculty and persons from such as the K-State admissions or publications offices had been at ABU for short-term consultation and help.

Dr. Stanley Dennis of our veterinary college, who had served as Ahmadu Bello's Dean of Faculty and Head of Veterinary Pathology, was our last remaining Kansas State person at Ahmadu Bello, and was then serving as Assistant Dean for Graduate Affairs. He and his wife would depart for Manhattan July 1.

During that celebratory visit I sat with Dr. Dennis as we watched the veterinary dean and department heads, all but one department head a Nigerian, leading their "global faculty," eighty per cent Nigerians plus expatriates from several countries. A similar pattern had been achieved months earlier in the ABU College of Agriculture.

At Benin, to Listen and Encourage

By 1982, USAID was giving preference to university consortiums for development work. In response, Kansas State and its counterparts in Nebraska, Iowa, Missouri, and Oklahoma had formed the MidAmerica

International Agricultural Consortium, and had submitted a proposal to help develop Botswana's agricultural research and extension system. Faculty might come from any of the universities, but K-State was the lead institution and Agricultural Economist David Norman headed to Botswana in late summer to lead the effort.

About that time, by coincidence, Nigeria's University of Benin, perhaps three hundred kilometers east of Lagos, had asked for a visit from K-State administration to assess and advise on their agricultural research and education programs. I wanted to see the task that K-State was taking on in Botswana, and Nigeria was on the flight path, so I accepted the Benin invitation.

Shirley and I were met at the Lagos airport by a Dr. Esechie, a K-State graduate and University of Benin faculty member, and driven to Benin City for a three day visit. As with every other experience we have had in developing countries, the openness, graciousness, and hospitality of our University of Benin hosts seemed without limit. Though we saw needs with which universities such as K-State might help, we also saw highly able, well educated, and dedicated faculty. The government had committed additional resources and the university had a large tract of land for research. A faculty committee had developed a plan for strengthening forestry, fisheries, and agriculture curriculums by adding faculty and undergirding these curriculums with such disciplines as biochemistry and botany. I think the main contribution by our visit—and what they needed from K-State—was for us to listen to their plans and give them encouragement to move forward.

When I learned of a major palm oil research station near Benin City, our host arranged a visit for us. Research was focused on the qualities of the oil from diverse genetic selections.

The University of Benin graduate student assigned to drive us back to the Lagos airport apparently wanted to be sure we did not miss our plane. The speedometer fluctuated from one hundred twenty to one hundred fifty Km/hour (seventy to ninety mph) all the way. No amount of our protest could he hear or accept. And our nervousness was not abated by the dozens of wrecked and burned out vehicles that dotted the road right-of-way.

At the Lagos airport, ready to board our departing flight, whom should we encounter but Kansas State Sociology Professor Wayne Nafsinger. He had just arrived to do some contract research on Nigeria's rural population and would head to the bus depot for his country travel. Though the bus might be crowded and slow, we assured Nafsinger it might be a safer way to travel than in a graduate student-chauffeured sedan.

We stopped off for a week-end in Nairobi, Kenya, and a two-day safari at Governor's Camp, about a hundred miles outside Nairobi. As the twenty-passenger twin engine plane landed at the Governor's Camp airstrip, waiting to board were K-State Agronomy Professor Ernest Mader and his wife, Betty. Mader had just completed a several month assignment in East Africa and they had taken in the Governor's camp safari en route back to Manhattan.

Snapshots taken during morning, mid-day, or late afternoon rides on Kenya's Serengetti Plain led by our Governor's Camp guide. Clockwise from the upper left: Shirley at our week-end quarters, elephants, a wildebeast, and zebras.

Our several days in Botswana would provide a bonus. Several of my former South Dakota State faculty were also in Gaborone, the capital city in the southern part of the country. SDSU, under an AID contract, was working with the country's two-year agricultural college just down the road from the ministry's agricultural research center where some of our Kansas State faculty headquartered.

Botswana: Plow Twice

Every culture and every country has intelligent, ingenious, and productive people. A country's productivity or level of living may be handicapped by a country's government policy, limited natural resources, or technology, but every country's people should be recognized and respected for their human capacities. Our time with K-State faculty in Botswana would illustrate.

During a two-day trip with Kansas State's Jim Jorns, we visited several villages north of Gabarone, toward the Zimbabwe border. Jorns had spent the previous night in a village north of Gaborone, in a "motel" rhondoval, a separate dome-shaped "room" of packed earth construction.

We visited two villages, where village elders were conducting "town hall" meetings on current issues. This is where Botswana's extension staff linked with their clientele. Extension staff presented education opportunities; concurrence given by village elders provided credibility for them to proceed with their work.

We also visited two farms, perhaps selected for being more progressive. In each case, the husband was away, tending the family's small cattle herd on open range. The wife and children tended the grain sorghum crop, the family's food staple, to be stored in large crockery vessels and a small, round metal bin.

Farming tools consisted of an oxen drawn plow and a hoe. Sorghum seed saved from a year earlier was sown by hand on the ground, and plowed in. This seemed to me far too crude; seeds would be at varying depths, but here I learned a lesson. Our hostess explained that rainfall was both low and highly variable, and variable seed depth was drought insurance. If it rained soon after planting, those seeds in shallow soil would germinate and flourish. With little or delayed rain, those deeper seeds would germinate and provide at least sufficient yield to get the family through the year.

A few watermelon seeds were also scattered at planting time. Our hostess explained that the watermelons provided both water and nourishment when she and her children were hoeing out weeds among the sorghum plants.

Homes in a typical village in northern Botswana, thatch-covered, adobe rhondovals.

A common scene in rural Botswana, sorghum seed being plowed in, with seeds buried at varied depths as the soil is turned.

Our staff and their counterpart Botswana scientists tried a variety of cultural practices, in comparison with traditional methods, and the most significant sorghum yield increases came by *plowing twice*, before and after the seed was sown. The first plowing loosened the soil, which allowed, with the second plowing, better seed/soil contact. More intimately surrounded by soil, seeds gained both moisture and nutrients. More seeds germinated and survived.

College Degrees from Four Acres

Rather early in our time back at Kansas State, we had signed a contract with AID to provide technical assistance to two Philippine universities and the country's Department of Agriculture, and we soon had faculty at Central Luzon State University (CLSU) north of Manila, and in the Ministry. En route home from our twenty fifth wedding anniversary trip to New Zealand and Australia in 1977, Shirley and I spent several days in the Philippines. We wanted to see the living and working conditions of our staff and meet Philippine officials and our faculties' counterparts.

The morning after a Sunday night welcoming dinner with Department officials we were flown by Department helicopter from Manila to the Central Luzon State University campus. From the helicopter, we watched mature rice being cut and threshed by hand, the heavy stalks beat on the ground to shatter out the grains. In the total distance north from Manila we saw only two small threshing machines in operation and five or six tractors, the latter being used for tillage. A good many water buffalo were being used to "cultivate" the flooded plots prior to planting another crop of rice. At any given time in that tropical climate, one would see rice paddies at all stages of production.

On the Central Luzon State University campus with University President Ferdinand Campos and our Kansas State project leader, Peairs Wilson. I had succeeded Wilson as associate dean at Kansas State in 1962. He had later gone to the University of Hawaii as dean and, following his retirement from that university, we hired him to run our Philippine project.

Perhaps the most productive tract of land we saw—and that I had seen in my professional life—had been at the four hectare home farm of two CLSU graduates. Their father was our host. Shirley and I stood among tomato and pepper plants and other vegetables on a wide rice paddy "dike" and watched scores of tilapia in the flooded paddy. Above one corner of the pool, propped up by bamboo poles, was a wire cage of perhaps fifty laying hens. Above the opposite corner was a similar cage of what I would call broilers. At another location on the dike were two sows and their litters of pigs.

Nutrients from the poultry and swine droppings fertilized the rice and likely helped nourish the tilapia. Some of the feed for the pigs and poultry was raised elsewhere on the property, and supplemented by household waste and vegetative trimmings.

That four hectare farm near CLSU had put two children through college and two more would soon be on the way.

We would later see such nutrient cycling on the University of the Philippines swine research farm supervised by my one-time Iowa State graduate student, Dr. Jose Eusebio. That farm's cycling scheme used pond algae as part of the swine diet, and fermentation of swine waste produced the gas that ran the farm laboratory's refrigerator.

Dr. Jose Eusebio, right, and his wife and family. Eusebio had been my masters' degree student at Iowa State. Several years later, after I had left for Kansas State, he had returned to Iowa State for his doctorate.

The Philippines; to Go Amuck!

Though our international work focused on food and agriculture, we also broadened our understanding of societies and cultures. An example is an hour-long visit with U.S. ambassador to the Philippines, William Sullivan.

I asked Sullivan what he considered the main features of the Philippine society and culture. He told me 1) Philippine people are family oriented and this extends beyond the "biological family." They depend on each other, help each other, stay close to each other, and this provides, in addition to the biological family, a "community family." 2) The Philippino is tolerant of adversity. He illustrated: In the intense traffic, though he might sit in a traffic jam for an hour or two, one rarely loses his temper. A Philippine farmer accepts total crop devastation with somewhat a "resigned" attitude, feeling that it is perhaps "God's will.

Things will be better next year." Their tolerance apparently surpasses what many of us can understand and continues until a limit is reached; then they "go amuck," with complete anger and public demonstration. He told us the phrase, "going amuck," spilled into the American vocabulary by our Philippine experience in WW II. 3) Going for the big gamble rather than deliberate and stepwise movement toward an economic or social goal, whether within an individual's business or on the national scene. His illustration was a Philippine decision about a year earlier to hold government-owned sugar off the market while the price continued to rise, with an expectation of "making a big killing." He said he had made a personal call on the president, pleading with him to feed some of their large volume of sugar into the world market, reasoning that if the world price went too high, increased global production would be attracted and the world price would fall devastatingly. That devastating price drop had occurred.

It seemed to me that the second feature Sullivan described, accepting "God's will," can make difficult the acceptance of new technology. There has to be some level of dissatisfaction with the present status, or at least an aspiration to make things better, if a person is to be receptive to new technology. Especially in the Philippine society, according to Sullivan's observations, raising the level of Philippine dissatisfaction with the present state of affairs would be necessary for rapid agricultural development.

To better understand the development potential of Philippine agriculture and more of the country's higher education system we would take a later flight to Las Banos, home of the University of the Philippines, and beyond Las Banos to larger ranching, livestock, and poultry operations in a southern peninsula of Luzon. Our hosts ranged from a small farmer with a six thousand-bird broiler house to one with eight such broiler houses plus six caged layer units, each with about six thousand birds. Even in the larger operation, all bird care was by hand, with no mechanized feed distribution or egg gathering.

As in our visits to other countries, hospitality was so generous as to be almost embarrassing. Invited for afternoon "tea and coffee" at the latter operation, the table was loaded with more than thirty plates of twelve different food items, including candied fruit, nut bread, yeast bread, pineapple cake, cold bacon, and Canadian bacon.

While in the Philippines, we spent a half day at the International Rice Research Institute (IRRI), one of fifteen international institutes the U.S. helps finance. The institute's job is to develop higher yielding and pest resistant varieties, as well as better production practices. It also trains research and extension education workers from rice growing countries. I would see, both in my later Southeast Asia travel for AID and our leisure travel in the early 2000s to Viet Nam, some of the rice varieties that IRRI had developed.

Spelled out on the wall facing us as we entered the rice institute's lobby were its mission and goals, the expected impact of the staff's work. We would see much the same in Philippine universities, either in building lobbies or in a conference room for staff and visitors. Those forward-looking messages were a feature of not only the Philippine culture, but the culture of most of Southeast Asia. We would later see the same type of forward-looking statements at research facilities in Indonesia, universities in Taipei, and a steel plant on the south coast of Taiwan.

A Surprise in Swaziland

It was the fall of 1984 and I was in Swaziland, a tiny country almost surrounded by northeastern South Africa. Midway in my Kansas State presidency, President Ronald Reagan had appointed me to a five-member Board for International Food and Agriculture Development, the board established to advise AID on its development work. As part of that responsibility, I would review in Swaziland an AID-financed project handled by two U.S. universities, Pennsylvania State University and Tennessee State University, and designed to strengthen the country's agricultural research and extension programs.

AID's mission director had met me at the country's major airport, a few kilometers southeast of the capital city, Mbabane, Monday afternoon, after the longest travel time and miles of my career. It had been a three-day trip, including a thirteen-hour flight from London to Johannesburg, South Africa, then only forty five minutes to Swaziland's Manzini airport. He then dropped me at Hotel Ezulwini Sun Cabana, in a rural setting several kilometers short of the capital city of Mbabane. It was what appeared to be a combination motel and casino, one of several that cater to nearby South Africans, whose country did not welcome casinos.

This was spring in the southern hemisphere, cropland had been freshly tilled and was ready for planting, largely maize. I was impressed by the terraces, strip cropping, and planting on the contour, even on land of less than three per cent slope. I was told the country's king, yet in his early twenties, emphasized conservation farming.

The schedule for my first morning in Swaziland was an AID-financed grain storage project in the northwest part of the country and the visit would include a surprising encounter. I had been alerted that the project manager was on home leave, and that a young woman, a Peace Corps volunteer serving as the manager's assistant, would give us the project details. That arrangement was not uncommon. Numbers of Peace Corps volunteers assigned to a country sometimes exceeded the number of host situations and AID projects could use some help.

As we drove onto the site, I first sighted two Butler bins, made at Columbus, Nebraska, and we stopped at a small trailer house where the Peace Corps worker lived. As we each introduced ourselves, the young woman's response to me was not what I had expected, "I understand you recently bought a farm!"

The previous April, at an auction in the tiny Brayton, Iowa, town hall, Shirley and I had been the successful bidder on several hundred acres of hills and Troublesome Creek bottom land that joined our home farm. How would a Peace Corps volunteer, isolated in the Swaziland highlands that had taken me three days to reach, know that a Kansan among her Tuesday morning visitors had purchased an Iowa farm? And, why would she know that?

Volunteer Maggie Smith was quick to explain. She had served several years as an Iowa State University Extension specialist stationed at the Council Bluffs area office and had worked closely with members of the Southwest Iowa Hay Growers' Association. A leader in that group had been Steve Olsen, to whom we had rented that newly acquired farm.

Smith then told me why she was in Swaziland. Though she had enjoyed her work in southwest Iowa, her long term goal had been to work internationally. Each position for which she had applied, however, had required previous international experience and she had had none. Eventually she decided she would get that experience, had resigned her position and joined the Peace Corps.

Cattle, the Family's Bank Account

Swaziland is about the size of New Jersey, population about six hundred thousand, altitude ranging from mountains to low plateau. About sixty five per cent of the country's land and people are in what is called the "Swazi Nation," controlled by one hundred seventy tribal chiefs. Average homestead for these people is 1.4 hectares (about three acres) and the major crop is maize (corn).

A typical family owns about fifteen cattle, the cattle herded by a family member as they graze on open and unfenced tribal land. The family will also have two or three small pens of chickens. The cattle are the family's assets and major source of cash income. The maize, eggs, poultry meat, and vegetables provide the family's basic food needs. Maize storage is generally a twenty-bushel metal canister setting on four posts, with metal rat guards around each post. (Shirley and I had seen the same in rural Kenya and Botswana.)

Most of the Swazi Nation men work away from the homestead, perhaps on pineapple, cotton, or timber plantations or dairies established on the country's deeded land, about thirty five per cent of the country, or in manufacturing or brewing industries.

With the man of the farm working away from home, it is often a child, perhaps twelve to fourteen years, herding the cattle. Children herding cattle instead of being in school was an emerging social issue in the country.

I wondered," Will this issue of getting children into school instead of herding the family cattle be the wedge that will eventually bring fencing, some form of grazing land ownership or assignment, and, in turn, an incentive to manage the grass for higher productivity?"

A cattle pen at the edge of a small Swazi village. The pen was rarely used; a family's herd would be on the open range, tended by either the father or a young son.

In briefings before flying to Swaziland I was told that there were no Mbabane social activities on the week-ends; every government official or business person returns to their homestead, and my experience would confirm that. I would spend considerable time with Penn State and Tennessee State staff and their Swazi counterparts in the Ministry of Peasant Affairs and Agriculture in the capital city, Mbabane. I did not talk to a single Swazi extension agent, research scientist, or bureau administrator at the Ministry that did not have a Swazi Nation homestead to which he returned on week-ends. The same was apparently true for business people in Mbabane or other towns; there were no Friday afternoon meetings because everyone was catching a bus to their homestead.

Soybeans for the Swazi Diet

The Penn State and Tennessee State faculty and their Swazi counterparts were focused on increasing the protein level of family diets by supplementing the maize diet with soybean-based foods. Their work, therefore, included both growing and storing soybeans as well home preparation of soybean-containing foods. They were comparing soybean varieties for both climate tolerance and, in the food dishes prepared, acceptable color or texture. Thirty years earlier, a similar effort to raise soybeans had been short-lived. Soybean varieties then used had thrived, but the color, texture, and other features of the soybean-based foods were not in keeping with what the people would accept.

The Penn State-Tennessee State team was also helping Ministry staff develop training programs for extension workers and had created an office that would publish fact sheets, bulletins, and other materials for these extension workers and their clientele.

I should tell the reader that there was a specific reason for the Penn State-Tennessee State partnership and for my being asked to review its work. For agricultural development work, AID and its predecessor agency had contracted largely with those universities established under the Land Grant Act of 1862, such as Iowa State or Kansas State. Later legislation, in 1890, under the "separate but equal" philosophy that then prevailed, provided for a second land grant university for the black population in southern states. In time, Congress had specified that AID find ways to involve those 1890 land grant universities and this had been one of the early efforts. The larger and more experienced Pennsylvania State University had been partnered with the less experienced 1890 land grant, Tennessee State.

The two-university partnership was working well, and I would report to BIFAD and AID leadership that it could be a model for other such partnerships.

There would be another outcome of my Swaziland travel. Though our U.S. universities were playing a valuable role in development, I had observed that when faculty returned to their home campus, they often received little recognition and reward for having interrupted their campus life and career and, most important, their student body had gained too little from the faculties' experiences. I had become convinced that every university should establish and articulate a global posture, especially in its undergraduate curriculum. During my long return flight, I drafted mission, goal, and strategy statements for any university's global involvement, and that topic would become a chapter in my later book, *Can State Universities be Managed?* published by the American Council on Education in 2006.

Under the Street Lamps in Beijing

I was invited to be part of a Kansas trade delegation led by Kansas Governor John Carlin in 1979, and to see elements of China in the first decade after elevation of Den Xiaoping to Party leadership. First, some recent history: In 1958 China's Communist Chairman Mao announced the "Great Leap Forward," intended to double the country's production, with renewed collectivization of farms and businesses, production quotas, and government allocations. Collectivization of private farms, taking the land away from land-owners and giving it to the masses either in small tracts or as collectives, had been the framework of Mao's rise to power in the late 1920s.

Production had not leaped forward, however, and the Chinese economy had stagnated. Reports may have shown farms and factories meeting production goals, but that had not happened. There was no incentive to produce.

Mao, however, had blamed the failure of his Great Leap Forward on "infiltration of bourgeois elements" and announced in 1966 a "Cultural Revolution," designed to rid the Chinese society of those bourgeois elements, any form of capitalist or intellectual activity, and any person rising above the masses. He would return China to a strict Maoist orthodoxy of everyone being equal. Many national and provincial leaders were sacked, some imprisoned. University faculty were displaced, some imprisoned, and many sent "to the countryside" to labor. Research programs were decimated. During the Revolution's time, from 1966 to 1976, China's development as an economic power and, especially, its ability to produce enough food for its people, suffered a tremendous setback. It was only after a change of Chinese leadership in the mid 1970s that some private initiative could again appear.

Looking back from the time of this writing, September, 2014, China was in 1979 still in the "dark ages" of its post-Cultural Revolution. I share some impressions of those "dark ages," starting with the evening our Kansas trade delegation landed at the Beijing airport.

"Upon deplaning at the Beijing airport we were led to a terminal reception room to be formally welcomed by our hosts. The room's walls were lined with overstuffed couches and chairs behind coffee tables, crocheted doilies on the arms and backs of the couches and chairs.

Bottles of orange drink awaited us on the coffee tables. (We would be in such a setting many time in the ten days ahead.)

The ride from the airport to downtown Beijing, about fifteen miles, was on a two-lane, concrete road lined with trees and rather dim street lamps. Under many of the lamps were clusters of people, boys playing card, girls visiting, women crocheting or knitting, and families visiting. Some were seated on the concrete roadway, not on the shoulder. Cars circumvented them; if two cars were to meet, one simply delayed to avoid the people. I could see no lights in the houses; under the street lights was the place to gather.

We passed many one-story structures, the businesses facing the street and the homes in the back, surrounding a courtyard. We saw no buildings more than two stories high until we reached central Beijing and Peking Hotel. The halls, lobbies, dining room, and individual rooms of the hotel, built during the time of Soviet "assistance," seemed cavernous, disproportionally large in relation to the furniture, carpet runners, or the people.

In central Beijing, the east-west street in front of our Peking Hotel was extremely wide, perhaps one hundred fifty feet, full of bicyclists, often moving in ten to fifteen-wide rows. There were a few government cars. No private cars were allowed in all of China.

As we rode in government cars to visit the agriculture ministry, I saw Beijing as a city of government offices and office workers, a few department stores, clothing stores, and shops for personal items that people needed."

In 1979 the only vehicles on Beijing streets were bicycles, government autos, and a few city buses.

"Ministry offices were in a one-story brick structure that surrounded a courtyard, bare land or un-mowed grass. Meeting rooms matched the airport reception room, overstuffed chairs and couches lining the room, doilies on the arms and backs."

P.S. In my memoir of our Kansas State years, *Two at a Time,* is a section, Mopeds and Doilies, in which I said that in 1979, these were the two Chinese franchises I would like to have. Doilies were ever present and I could see that demand for mopeds would explode. The doilies were also evident in 1985 and there were a few more mopeds. However, by the time of my visits back to China in 1998 and 2001, streets and roadways would be packed with mopeds, but I would find not a single doily on commune or government furniture.

To Help My Country

In a Beijing reception for members of Kansas Governor John Carlin's trade mission in August of 1979, I fell into a conversation with a junior minister of finance. He had earned a doctorate in finance at Columbia University and had been on the Columbia faculty several years. I asked, "Why did you return to China?"

His response was matter-of-fact, "To help my country."

I followed up with several questions regarding democracy vs. communism, and how, with a degree in finance from a capitalist country, his talents could be helpful.

His response to that was uninhibited, in essence, "Communism will adapt to best serve our country's needs."

At a later dinner hosted by the chairman of the China Council for Promotion of International Trade the deputy Council director for American and Oceanic affairs described to me "efforts at economic development to raise the level of living for the people." He said there would be significant changes in the Chinese culture and the way of doing business, and that "the proof of the pudding is in the eating." He followed up, said that if a philosophy or policy did not bring about an improvement in the level of living, then the philosophy should be changed.

We talked about incentives. Though he did not mention "cultural revolution" per se, he said the efforts to distribute property of the wealthy had gone too far. Those with large holdings had been reimbursed at the rate of five per cent per year for ten years, a fifty per cent payment for the property confiscated.

He also said that former holders of wealth were now receiving relatively high pay for their continued and present management of the property and that the pay would likely go higher.

He also predicted that prohibition of private automobile ownership would be relaxed

P.S. As I would see in a 1985 visit with Kansas legislative leaders, in 1998 as an Iowa State University visiting lecturer, and in 2001 as a reviewer for a United Nations project—and as my wife, Shirley, would see in 1998 after her 1980 visit as part of a People-to-People program—Chinese communism would rapidly adapt.

A People's Commune; From Tractors to Lorries

We later headed to the country in that 1979 visit, to visit a large commune, driving south from Beijing's "city center." We passed community toilets, generally brick or plastered structures, along Beijing's streets. A common sight was the human waste being pumped out of the structure's underground holding tank into a small tank on the back of a truck. Or, in some cases, the waste was dipped from the underground tank by means of a bucket on a long pole and poured into a small tank on a cart being pulled by two or three horses. The destination for much of the waste, of course, was to nearby farmland, to fertilize crops.

Beijing seemed to exist on a flat, endless plain. Beyond the outskirts we passed over a few flowing streams, most generally twenty feet wide and flowing well. The stream banks were diked, and on each dike were one to three rows of trees, all neatly trimmed from the time of planting. The trees gave a neat, stately appearance to the countryside.

Nanyuan People's Commune had been established in 1958, perhaps as part of the "Great Leap Forward," by the merger of five agricultural cooperatives. It included more than twenty one hundred hectares (about five thousand acres), more than ten thousand households, and forty one thousand people. It was organized into sixteen production brigades and one hundred twenty six production teams. Though some wheat and rice were produced, the major products were vegetables for the Beijing metropolitan area.

All the commune land was irrigated, from both wells and the river. Though harvesting of the wheat and rice, as well as plowing, was mechanized, most of the work with vegetables was by hand.

The commune had had one lorry (truck) when it had been established, but its lorry fleet had grown to one hundred thirty. Most product delivery in those early years would have been by hand, bicycle, or tractor-powered cart. The tractor was likely similar to the two-wheeled garden tractor common in the U.S. in the 1950s, hooked to a cart and guided by the worker sitting on the front of the cart. We had seen many of these tractor-cart delivery vehicles on our drive from the city.

A typical means of moving farm produce in 1979, a rather powerful two-wheel "tractor" connected to a two-wheel cart, the driver sitting on the front of the cart to guide the tractor.

The commune was not limited to food production. It also included nine small factories producing goods for commune members and the surplus sold elsewhere. Such was common in several communes visited; one manufactured and sold two-wheeled trailers.

Six years of primary school was available to all commune children and those who passed an exam could continue to five years of middle school, all on the commune. The average worker wage was four hundred Yuan per year, equivalent to about three hundred seventy five U.S. dollars. Housing, children's education, and family medical care were provided by the commune.

How about a private home? We visited a two-family, two-home compound, each home a three-room structure, two bedrooms plus a center room that served as the kitchen. In each of the two bedrooms was a large, solid-base bed with six to eight comforters stacked at one end. In the kitchen area was a three-foot square concrete stove, about two feet high and with an eighteen inch lid in the center. The kitchen area was largely open to the south and a courtyard, the latter bright with flowers. Off to the side of the courtyard was an enclosed toilet for the two families. The home we visited accommodated nine people, including six children and a grandmother.

Chopsticks and a Challenge

At a Saturday evening banquet at Beijing's International Club hosted by the chairman of the China Council for Promotion of International Trade, I would watch Kansas Governor Carlin, a conservative dairy farmer from the hills west of Salina, being repeatedly challenged by our host to down a jigger of 110-proof sorghum alcohol in one gulp.

We had been welcomed in the large reception room, similarly lined with overstuffed couches and chairs, and given orange soda. After ten minutes of visiting, we were led to the dining room and twelve-person round tables. We were served eight courses. Each of the courses, except for the last three, what one might call desserts, were brought on dishes or platters, each placed on the table's super-size rotating "lazy susan." With chopsticks, our table hosts would serve their nearby guests items from each dish or platter. And, though we could ask for silverware, chopsticks were at each of our place settings. The courses were:

1. Cold appetizers, including peanuts in brine, fried fish, cold duck and chicken, kidney, and hard boiled eggs.
2. Fish stomach with shrimp and vegetable balls.
3. Wheat noodles, heavily spiced.
4. Grass carp.
5. Mushrooms in a sauce plus a small slice of squash.
6. An almond flavor soybean curd (yogurt) containing fruit cocktail.
7. Ice cream, with a light orange and lemon flavor, plus a cookie.
8. Fresh peaches and sliced watermelon.

Beer, a sweet grape wine, and Mao-t'ai, the 110-proof sorghum liquor, were served with the meal. (The name, Mao-t'ai, is of the river near which the sorghum is grown and the product fermented and distilled.)

Though several of our hosts avoided the alcohol and drank only orange soda during the meal, the chairman drank heavily. He appeared especially encouraged by the Mao-t'ai and at the end of the meal raised his small Mao-t'ai glass to the total group and exclaimed, "Gambay!" (Bottoms up!) Some of our hosts did so with evident reluctance and I noted the vice-chairman handed his glass to the chairman.

It was then that Governor Carlin faced one of the uncomfortable decision points of political leadership and of being an official guest in a foreign country, to accept the challenge or risk offending the host.

Though I failed to count the successive challenges, I am sure that Carlin had an uncomfortable night.

P.S. An eventual bonus from that trade promotion trip to China was a son-in-law. A few months after our return, out family encountered on a Topeka, Kansas, street one of the governor's traveling aides, Terry Nygaard, then with the Kansas Board of Agriculture. I introduced him to our daughter, Diane, and he is the father of our 30-year-old grandsons.

In time I would become part an integral part of our country's major international development agency, the U. S. Agency for International Development. Some of my encounters in more developing countries and also in the Washington bureaucracy are described in the next chapter.

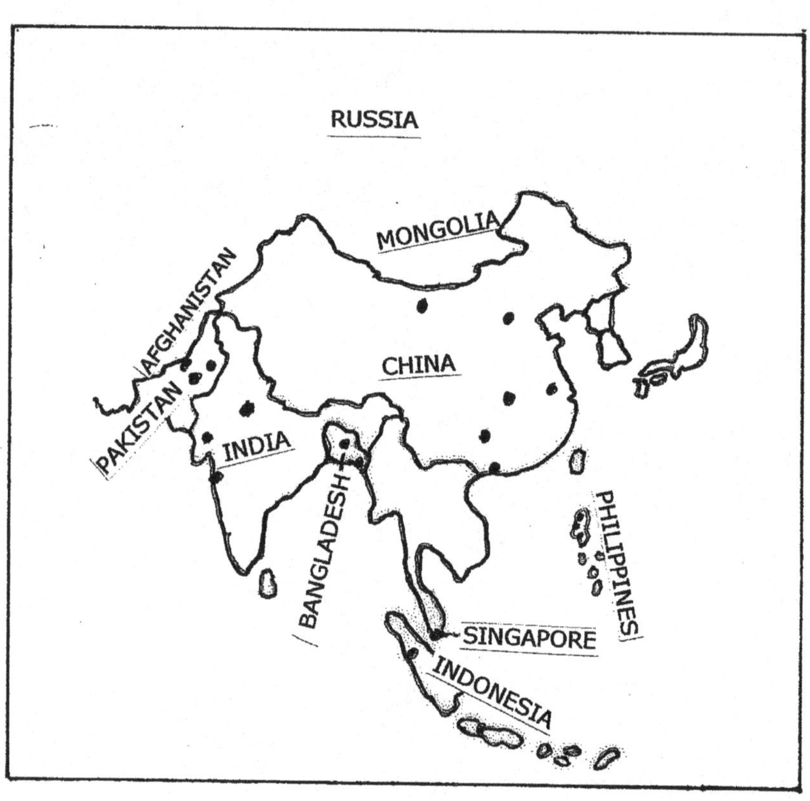

A map of South East Asia, the dots marking major locations visited in Pakistan, India, Bangladesh, China, Indonesia, and the Philippines.

Chapter III

To the Washington Bureaucracy

"It was my second week in Washington that I encountered Secretary Lyng just outside USDA's second-floor dining room, and he recalled our earlier visit, "Welcome to Washington," he said with a smile, 'I'm sure you know that you have joined (in AID) the most bureaucratic agency in Washington.'"

Ten years in the Kansas State presidency had been my self-imposed limit, and at the end of ten I told the Board of Regents I would resign at the end of eleven; they should have time to choose a successor. In the middle of that eleventh academic year, January of 1986, Kansas Senator Bob Dole publicly suggested that I should be considered for the Number two spot, Deputy Secretary, in the U.S. Department of Agriculture (USDA). Both Secretary Jack Block and his deputy had resigned and Dick Lyng of California, who had served as deputy secretary early in the Reagan administration, had been nominated for the secretary position but had not yet been confirmed by the Senate. The deputy spot would also be a presidential appointment with Senate confirmation.

I was also contacted by Peter McPherson, Administrator of the Agency for International Development (AID), about a role in that agency. I knew McPherson, having served since the early 1980s on the agency's advisory Board for International Food and Agricultural Development (BIFAD). Several vacant posts in that agency, some also presidential appointments, could be both challenging and rewarding.

A Political Appointment?

In executive branch departments, the top three position levels, secretary, deputy secretary, and under or assistant secretary (and their counterparts in the independent agencies, such as AID,) are political appointments. After the president nominates, the appropriate Senate committee then considers the nominee. Committee staff members gather information and then meet with the nominee to delve into issues of concern. Next is a Senate committee hearing on the nomination and, in time, a committee vote on recommending the nominee to the full Senate. These processes can happen quickly or take months, and inter-party "games" or, sometimes, senators' concerns on a specific issue, can delay or de-rail a nomination.

As a university president, I had tried to remain apolitical; I needed to work well with members of both political parties. Though a registered Republican, I did not work on campaigns and my donations to Ronald Reagan's campaigns had been modest. That may be a limiting factor in being considered for a presidential appointment.

In a late February trip to Washington, I interviewed with two staff in the White House personnel office, one responsible for AID positions and the other for USDA positions. Their job was to determine if the person's philosophies meshed with those of the president, probe for any affiliations or past statements that might later be embarrassing to the president, and ask about support to political campaigns. Early in each visit, the staff member turned to a computer screen to read the record of my contributions to Reagan or the National Republican committee.

I also visited that day with Lyng, who, awaiting confirmation by the Senate, was using an office in the Old Executive Office building. Senator Dole, as majority leader of the Senate and a key member of the Senate agriculture committee, had played a leading role in Lyng's nomination.

It was a generous and helpful visit. First, I was impressed by Lyng and his manner; he was low key, sincere, and obviously well acquainted with the department and current issues. He would be the type with whom I would enjoy working. I told him I was interested in both USDA and AID and he described the role he expected the deputy secretary to play, coordinating many internal department matters, but travel at least a day a week. He did not downplay the cost of living in

Washington, said one would be lucky to break even financially. Nor did he downplay the time and risks in achieving Senate confirmation.

There were also non-political administrative positions in either agency. Appointment to such could be by an Interagency Personnel Agreement (IPA), with which I would stay on the University payroll, with uninterrupted health insurance and retirement benefits. The university would be reimbursed for all costs, plus a modest overhead fee. Appointment could be consummated in short order, with approval only by the agency head and our board of regents. The White House personnel office would not be involved.

Most university presidents who leave their position prior to retirement age and return to faculty status are given six months or a year sabbatical leave at full pay before going back to the classroom or their research area. An IPA, even if I returned later to the campus, would avoid that cost to Kansas State's budget.

The Senate confirmed Lyng in early March and I called his office to offer congratulations. He returned my call within the hour. He had just returned from a session on the hill with several senators, said he had found his "popularity had peaked two or three days ago." I told him I was even more interested in the deputy position than before I met with him, but that I also knew others were being considered and that he should have his personal choice as deputy.

Word from several friends in D.C. and elsewhere indicated that USDA's assistant secretary for conservation, Peter Myers of Missouri, with whom Lyng had worked during his time as deputy secretary, was Lyng's preference. I also learned that North Carolina Senator Jesse Helms was pushing one of his constituents for the deputy position. Lyng did not need a battle with or between two influential Republican senators, Dole and Helms, and I was not about to be a part of such. I called Dole to express thanks for his interest and support and that I would next call Secretary Lyng to withdraw my interest. I would plan to go to AID.

I had also kept in contact with Kansas' junior Senator, Nancy Kassebaum. As a member of the Senate Foreign Relations committee, she was close to the needs of AID and had high respect for its administrator, Peter McPherson. Though she emphasized the agency had large internal management and leadership needs where I could be of help, she cautioned me about its many bureaucratic traditions. I had encountered both in Kansas State's AID relationships and my BIFAD work. That did not deter me, however. I was enthusiastic about the national value of our foreign assistance work in agriculture and related areas, and every large entity has bureaucratic problems.

An IPA was soon worked out with Administrator McPherson for me to head AID's food and agriculture programs.

Early fall of 1986, Shirley was riding the D.C. area Metro three days a week to her work in the White House Volunteer Office. I read the morning paper en route by Metro to my AID office. Her destination was the ground floor of the Old Executive Office Building, the ornate structure just west of the White House. My destination was first across the Potomac in Arlington, Virginia, and later in the State Department Building, two blocks north of the Lincoln Memorial.

We were living in a rented three bedroom colonial, a fifteen minute walk from the end of the Metro Orange Line, in Vienna, Virginia.

Shirley would develop her calligraphy skills, addressing President and Mrs. Reagan's congratulatory notes and Christmas cards. Some days she would be on the White House call-in phones, hearing citizen concerns for relay to the appropriate agencies, or would be helping as needed in one of the White House offices. On the days the President received a foreign head of state, she and her fellow volunteers might be on the White House lawn as part of the welcoming group. And, at Easter, she would be on the lawn helping with the Easter Egg hunt.

Three days a week Shirley reported to the White House Volunteer office in the Old Executive Office Building just west of the White House. This day she was helping in one of the White House offices.

My job was administering and coordinating the agency's food and agriculture programs in and for developing countries. My staff were on three continents, in three Washington-based regional bureaus, and some down the hall from my office.

Though my work involved considerable travel to those three continents, I soon found that, as in the University, a major responsibility was "selling the program." In this case, my targets were members of Congress and their staff as well as politically active interest groups. Environmental groups feared our programs were damaging the developing countries' natural resources and agricultural groups feared our programs were building competition for U.S. exports.

The programs I led had many connections to USDA. My agriculture and human nutrition specialists depended on and worked closely with USDA's Agricultural Research Service, country mission staff or Washington bureau staff sometimes contracted with USDA units for their specialists to lead individual projects, and every food aid allocation involved both agencies. AID staff would assess recipient country needs, both type and amount of food; USDA would find the product, either commodity surpluses purchased and in storage or contracted from a commodity processor, and arrange its transportation to the country.

Consequently, it was not uncommon for me to be in USDA's corridors, especially in my first weeks as I worked to establish relationships.

The Most Bureaucratic Agency

It was my second week in Washington that I encountered Secretary Lyng just outside USDA's second-floor dining room, and he recalled our earlier visit, "Welcome to Washington," he said with a smile, "I'm sure you know that you have joined the most bureaucratic agency in Washington."

Lyng got no argument from me. I had known it was bureaucratic, but I had had no idea of the extent.

In our Kansas State work with AID, contract negotiations had seemed endless. We could never determine, for example, which Agency signature meant "approval" so that we could begin recruiting or reassigning faculty to meet a project starting date.

Now, working on the inside, I saw and experienced far more bureaucracy. And, it did not take long to recognize the two major causes, the first being agency structure. In addition to the three regional bureaus, Africa, Latin America, and Asia/Near East, each fully staffed with subject matter, contract, finance, and personnel offices, there were three other same-level bureaus, Science/Technology, Food Aid, and Policy. There were also Agency-wide contract, finance, and personnel offices.

If the agriculture officer in the Agency's Indonesia mission, working with his Indonesia counterpart, designed a five-year project to encourage vegetable crop production, within the budget already allocated to Indonesia, he or she needed far more than the mission director's approval. The project details and budget also had to go to the Asia/Near East Bureau in Washington for approval by three different parties and to the Policy bureau to insure that it was "within policy." Only after the project was approved by all could a contract be negotiated with a university or USDA to provide the expertise. And, that negotiated contract faced similar steps.

The second reason was the agency's general lack of a domestic, private sector constituency to keep it on track and make it responsive. USDA, in contrast, had thousands of domestic constituents, from farmers to food processors to timber owners, and dozens of politically strong organizations, from the American Farm Bureau Federation to the Association of Conservation Districts. Should USDA err in or delay an important program, the Secretary's office would soon have phone calls and visits from major and politically strong organizations. Domestic constituents do keep an agency on track.

A few members of Congress, especially those who controlled Agency appropriations, seemed to fill that "constituency void." Also, any senator could place a "hold" on any AID project. For example, a U.S. senator from a northwestern state placed a hold on a forestry project in a South Asia country demanding that the seedling stock come from one of his constituents. Unfortunately, the seedling species that constituent could provide was not adapted to the target region.

Constant staff rotation also added to seemingly bureaucratic inertia. Generally half of the people in an approval chain were Foreign Service officers, usually with successive three-year assignments in a mission, then Washington, then a different mission. New arrivals needed time to get oriented to their post.

A consequence, unfortunately common among the agency's dedicated and quality staff, was, "We can't change the system; so why hurry and why worry?"

I offer another observation, as a newcomer to an eastern, metropolitan environment, a not uncommon lack of what I call "sense of place." While growing up in the Midwest, we knew where we were in relation to New York City or Minneapolis, to California or Texas. And we knew the direction to go to get to either. We had an early and rather well-developed "sense of place," not only within the United States, but also within our state or county.

I asked one of our secretaries on a Monday morning if she enjoyed the week-end.

"Oh, yes," she said, "We visited my sister in Fredericksburg."

I asked, "Which Fredericksburg, the one in Virginia or in Pennsylvania?"

She looked at me with questioning surprise, so I followed up, "Did you go north or south?"

This time her response was even more surprising, "I don't know, but we took I-95."

I then knew; she had gone south to Fredericksburg, Virginia.

She was a capable young woman and was doing excellent work, but her responses revealed that her "sense of place," relative to Washington, was only via a numbered highway.

We would find other limited perceptions or "senses of place" among Washington, D.C. area natives, or those who had moved to D.C. from Boston, New York City, or other countries. They would often confuse Iowa with Ohio, less often with Idaho. Whereas my grade school classmates could have pinpointed Massachusetts, Oregon, or Alabama on a map, some with whom I worked appeared to perceive Iowa or Kansas as only "somewhere out there toward California."

Forty Apple Trees

My staff urged that I soon travel to one of the Agency-financed overseas projects to see and understand the work of our country mission staff and contractors, the conditions under with they operate, and the relationships with host country officials. A scheduled review of a soils project on Indonesia's island of Sumatra provided an early opportunity.

Indonesia is a densely populated collection of more than thirteen thousand islands lying south of Singapore and the Philippines and had been under some form of Dutch control from the 1602 establishment of the Dutch East India Company, except for World War II Japanese occupation, until independence in 1949. The most densely populated island was Java and, from the 1920s, both the Dutch and the Indonesian government had worked to disperse the population by moving families from Java to the more sparsely populated Sumatra. Unfortunately, most Sumatra soils were of low quality, and to make them more productive was a major effort of AID's Indonesia mission. I accompanied a team of USDA and AID soil scientists named to assess the mission's progress.

On a Thursday, after a gamma globulin booster shot for travel in the tropics, a weekly meeting with senior agriculture and human nutrition officers in the regional bureaus, and hearing a review team report on a sheep and goat project in Africa, I had grabbed my bag and headed to Dulles Airport for a six o'clock flight. I changed planes at Los Angeles, Honolulu, and Singapore, and, having crossed the International Date Line, arrived at a Jakarta hotel at six o'clock Saturday evening (without my bag). After checking in at our hotel, I had only a beer with our review team and went to bed.

Sunday morning my bag had not yet arrived, so I purchased a set of underwear at a shop off the hotel lobby and we headed back to Jakarta's open air terminal and a two-hour flight to Padang, capital of West Sumatra Province and on Sumatra's south coast. We were met by our soils project staff with two Land Rovers and we headed inland toward Sijunjung Regency (district) over winding mountain roads. We stopped on the way for sandwiches, cookies, and orange drink from an ice chest in the rear of the Land Rover.

An accompanying photo tells the story of Sijunjung's soils, the land cleared of timber and the soil low in organic matter. Though there is high rainfall and much vegetation, the high temperature rapidly breaks down the organic matter and the soil lacks "tilth," a structure that allows rainfall to penetrate, soil micro-organisms to flourish, and oxygen and nutrients to reach plant roots. Erosion is a serious problem, even on mild slopes.

We visited research plots focused on soybean varieties that might be adapted, simple terraces to prevent erosion, and "alley-cropping," soybeans or other crops grown between rows of shrubs or trees, the latter providing some shade to temper the heat.

Upper photo: Soybean variety trials in the foreground and roadway, homes and land to be cleared in the background. Lower photo: Alley cropping demonstration, tilled land between densely planted young trees. The trees will protect vegetable or other crops from intense heat from the sun and from wind. Note also the motor bike, primary transportation for research and extension staff.

Students out for recess ran across the road to see what we were doing at some soybean research plots.

We also visited several farms, the first considered by West Sumatra and soils staff to be a model farmer, one who implemented about every practice their research efforts had yielded. Our host was especially proud of what he had done to make his four-hectare farm on sloping ground productive. Considering the low organic matter, former timber-covered soil that his family had been assigned, I understood his pride.

He was raising soybeans, as well as corn, between rows of shrubs. Most impressive to me was his apple orchard. Though in a high rainfall area, the rainfall is seasonal and, being near the equator, there is high evapotranspiration, moisture loss from the leaf surfaces. To insure that each tree received and held its share of rainfall on the sloping land, he had moved the soil surrounding each tree with his hoe so that each tree was in the center of a square "dish."

Apples were his cash crop; the corn, beans, grass, and a generous vegetable garden gave adequate nutrition to his family. His two heifers' diet included native grasses supplemented by the corn and beans as well as trimmings from the shrubs. And, when the heifers calved, the family would also have milk.

Foreign Aid: Good or Bad?

One of the first major issues I encountered was concern by members of the American Soybean Association (headed, coincidentally, by one who had been a fellow Nebraska vice chancellor) and other U.S. commodity groups that AID's agricultural programs would increase competition for their export market. That concern was also being echoed by some members of Congress.

Some Kansas agricultural leaders had quietly questioned Kansas State's work with colleges of agriculture in India, Africa, and the Philippines. They worried that we were helping build competition for their wheat or other exports. For that reason, when invited to speak at a Farm Bureau, Conservation District, or other agriculture event in Kansas, I would address the issue directly. I would include data showing that U.S agricultural exports to South Korea and Taiwan after World War II and the Korean conflict had dramatically increased after U.S. agricultural scientists had helped those countries develop their agriculture.

The data were convincing. I just needed to explain that in less developed countries, when one increases food availability and consumption, people are more productive, both physically and mentally. And, if people are more productive, their incomes increase and they buy more food and, usually, more nutritious food.

When incomes had gone up in South Korea and Taiwan, the result of U.S. and other countries' help in developing their agriculture, food consumption patterns shifted from a traditional rice diet toward wheat products, and then toward more animal products.

GDP (Gross Domestic Product) increased in those countries at the rate of six to ten per cent per year. Yet, no matter how hard our visiting U.S. scientists and extension personnel worked, agricultural production in those countries rarely increased more than three per cent per year. Traditions, farmer caution in accepting technology, and infrastructure limitations (supply and distribution of fertilizer, irrigation systems, or movement of product) constrained technology adoption. With more consumer income and food demand than production increases could accommodate, those countries looked elsewhere for animal products or for corn, wheat, and soybean meal to feed their poultry and livestock.

And, the U.S. had generous supplies of corn, wheat, and soybean meal for export.

Now, as AID's director of Food and Agriculture, I was the point man to hear those concerns. More than once, I was asked to brief House and Senate Agriculture committee staff on our programs. To build political support or prevent erosion of support for AID's programs, I needed to "sell the program." This was not unlike my role as a South Dakota State dean and director, Nebraska vice chancellor, or Kansas State president.

I share here a summary of my testimony in early February, 1987, to the Senate Agriculture Committee's subcommittee on Agricultural Research, Conservation, Forestry and General Legislation. U.S. agricultural exports had steadily declined from 1980, commodity prices had weakened, farmland values had dropped sharply, and farm foreclosures were not uncommon. Farm leaders and members of Congress were looking for a culprit, and AID's agricultural program was a candidate.

Here is a summary of the four-page presentation I made to the committee. Point 1 was background; Points 2, 3, and 4 were the main message.

1. Several factors contributed to U.S. decline in agricultural exports in the early 1980s.
    a. High value of the U.S. dollar had put U.S. grain prices above world levels.
    b. Reduced economic growth globally.
    c. Heavy debt load of low and middle income countries.
    d. Increased production elsewhere, especially in Australia, Argentina, and China.
    e. High farm subsidies encouraged more production in the European Economic Community.
    f. Added import duties and other constraints in some importing countries.
2. From 1974 to 1985 the *increase* in U.S. agricultural exports to developing countries were larger, both percentage wise and in total dollars, than the increase in exports to developed countries. To developed countries the figures were thirty one per cent and

$4.3 Billion; to developing countries seventy per cent and $5.2 Billion.

3. From 1971-73, while our U.S. scientists were still helping South Korea's agriculture, the U.S. commercial agricultural exports to that country averaged $197 Million. From 1980 to 1983, the average was $1.7 Billion.
4. Five principles apply
   a. Poor people do not buy much.
   b. GDP (Gross Domestic Product) grows most rapidly when the sector that employs the most people strengthens. In developing countries, that is agriculture.
   c. Improved nutrition improves productivity.
   d. As income goes up, diets both improve and diversify.
   e. As countries develop, they increase both imports and exports. Exports of what they efficiently produce help finance their imports.

I would highlight those five principles in every presentation to interest and commodity groups, as well as in sessions our AID information staff would arrange with editorial boards of major newspapers. There was some positive effect; in time, I would hear an officer of the American Soybean Association include in his testimony to a foreign aid subcommittee of Congress that increasing the income in developing countries was a key to the U.S. exporting more soybean meal to those countries.

Would You Like to See?

At the same time that U.S. agricultural groups were pointing fingers at AID's agriculture programs, those programs were also being criticized by some in the environmental community. They worried that intensive agriculture put developing countries' natural resources, their soil, water, or native plant species, at risk. The expressions were common enough that I decided I needed to spend some time with Washington-based leaders of these groups, to "seek their input" on AID's programs. As the new leader of agriculture programs, I would have no reason to be defensive of existing programs, and these Washington people would be more likely be candid in their comments.

My assistant, Foreign Service Office John Swallow, and I made a list of the environmental groups that had criticized or shown interest, such as the Natural Resources Defense Council, National Wildlife Federation, or Society of American Foresters. After individual visits to several of their offices, we invited key people from fifteen such groups to a meeting "to hear all their concerns about AID's agricultural projects."

I took along my three regional bureau agriculture leaders and our Agency-wide natural resources leader, emphasizing to them that our job in the meeting was to listen. No matter the complaint, we would make no defense of any project. We would listen.

That would be difficult for these career staff, to not rise to defend, but I insisted. I wanted the environmental groups to know they were being listened to.

We also chose a meeting place outside of AID, a conference room at one of the forestry association offices. People with concerns will be more open in neutral territory.

We listened for nearly an hour, to mostly general statements: "Intensive cropping in Central America is ruining the soil." "Herbicides and fertilizer are killing wildlife." "Machines are replacing workers in high population countries." "Fragile grassland in Africa is being converted to crops."

When we asked for elaboration, so we could better understand the speaker's concern, little was offered. But, we continued to listen.

As the complaints seemed to be winding down, one of the group spoke up, "I guess I really don't know much about your projects." A couple others chimed in, "We would like to know more than we now know."

I asked, "Who in the room has visited some of our projects in Africa, Central America, or Southeast Asia?" Not a single hand was raised.

I followed up, "Would you like to?"

From several, "Well - - yes - - ."

"You are invited," I said, "You tell us what you want to see and where, and we will make the arrangements."

As the session with environmental groups had progressed, from one topic to another and in time, to the need to actually visit some projects, one or two of the participants had emerged as leaders. In this case, the most vocal was a Bob Blake. I do not now recall the organization where he was employed, but it was clear he was respected by others and that he had an effective voice on Capitol Hill. A month or so later, in an appropriation committee hearings, I would listen as Blake urged that AID's 103 account (agriculture, rural development, and nutrition) be increased by fifty million dollars in the next fiscal year.

Those two issues, export competition and risk to the environment, became rather high priority for my time. In weeks ahead I would be in such places as Indianapolis, Austin, Oklahoma City, Cheyenne, Omaha, Des Moines, or Minneapolis with any assembly of agriculture or environmental leaders where I might receive, or seek, an invitation. Drafting a mission statement for the food and agriculture programs, one that might "capture the imagination of Congress and that the public could not deny," was also a part of the effort.

A Large Mission in a Few Words

On a cold mid-December day I was in Room C of the Pan American Health Organization (PAHO) offices, just a few blocks from the State Department, chairing a fifteen-member group that would draft a mission statement for the AID's world-wide agricultural programs. The group included key Washington staff of major agriculture, commodity, environment, and natural resources organizations, plus my lead agriculture officers in our three regional bureaus and the agency's lead natural resources person. I was determined that when we left the room we would have hammered out a statement that was brief, credible, and clear.

For more than a month, my assistant, Swallow, my three bureau colleagues, and I had been seeking input from these organization people, including the open meeting earlier described, plus mission staff around the world. All parties needed to feel ownership of any mission statement developed.

Overseas travel by several of us had delayed this effort and I had been sidelined a few days after a late November Saturday morning racquetball game had put me into surgery. My opponent had moved in front of me as I scrambled for the ball. I vaulted over his shoulder and the point of my left shoulder hit the floor. I had torn my shoulder ligaments and my upper arm was hanging down about six inches. At the hospital emergency room I asked the surgeon for advice. He said I had two choices, "Surgery, or let it hang there the rest of your life." I scheduled surgery.

Back to the mission statement: Anyone who has been through such an exercise knows that to get every participant's idea or priority inserted can easily result in a long treatise with little communication value. We worked to keep the discussion focused.

By noon we had agreed that the statement had to cover soil, water, and perhaps native flora and fauna; that was the environmentalists' concern. It had to cover peoples' diets or human nutrition, a major need in target countries. It also had to cover increased food production; food aid was being sent to most countries and that should sometime end. And, though food may be available in a country or an area, the families had to have sustainable income to buy the food. We kept reminding ourselves that for effective communication, the statement had to be succinct.

The day proved to be one of the most rewarding of my time in the agency. Every person in the room did their part, and by four o'clock we had on a blackboard that the mission of the Agency's agriculture, rural development, and nutrition program in target countries was to "increase the income and expand the availability and consumption of food, while maintaining and enhancing the natural resource base."

When I reported the outcome to McPherson, he added four words, "of the poor majority," after the word, income.

That mission statement was spread widely through the Agency's bureaus and to missions world-wide, repeated or reinforced in regional conferences, and was a helpful staff guide. Whether it "captured the imagination of Congress," I cannot testify, but if repeated enough, it should help the public or the involved organizations understand the program's purpose and focus.

A Beer for My Time

It was March, 1988, and at the end of the day I had walked the several blocks from my office in the State Department building to the

International Club on Eighteenth Street to join former Minnesota Governor and former USDA Secretary Orville Freeman for a beer. He had a favor to ask.

Freeman was a man I had long admired. He had been secretary the entire eight years of the Kennedy/Johnson administration and was a strong supporter of food aid. My admiration had formed one evening in the fall of 1962 or '63 in the Salina, Kansas, municipal auditorium. I was then associate dean of agriculture at Kansas State, wanted to see and hear the secretary, and had invited several department heads to go with me. The auditorium was packed, mostly with farmers from across the state disturbed about some changes in USDA's wheat program.

Freeman spoke about twenty minutes, emphasizing his department's efforts to increase exports, the importance of U.S. food aid, including Kansas wheat, to developing countries, and President Kennedy's dedication to farm prosperity.

The audience had been told they could ask any question they wanted, three by five-inch cards had been distributed for written questions, and the cards were collected at the end of his talk. Aides, mostly staff from the USDA agencies' state offices in Salina, had gathered quite a stack of cards. Freeman was handed a card; he read the question and gave an answer. The question may have related to wheat exports, details of the feed grain program, why some USDA production projections had missed the mark, or whatever.

The packed auditorium got warm. After handling the questions from a few cards, Freeman took off his suit coat, quoting his dad, "You can't get much work done with your coat on." He continued with the questions for at least ninety minutes. No topic of USDA responsibility seemed to be missed. Freeman's knowledge and his ability to answer each question, often with program details, were impressive. Only once during in those ninety minutes did audience reaction signal that he had erred on a detail.

I had met Freeman a few times during the intervening years. After his service as secretary, he had remained in Washington as a lawyer/lobbyist and consultant, then as executive officer for one or two agricultural organizations.

Now, to the favor: He had invited several leaders of the U.S. House and Senate and their key staff to meet with former USDA secretaries, the latter to present a "united front" endorsement and support for increased food aid appropriations.

Freeman knew well that to influence a member of Congress, one does not invite them to hear a speech on the issue for which you seek support. Rather, one invites them to *speak* on the issue. Members enjoy speaking, and will likely say positive things on the issue they have been invited to address.

In this case, Freeman had asked Senator Bob Dole, then Senate majority leader, and two other senators to each say a few words to this distinguished audience of former secretaries about the importance of food aid. The former secretaries would applaud, several would extend a compliment, and each senator would leave the event having convinced himself or herself of the wisdom of more federal money for food aid.

Freeman had a role for me, and he was candid. He had heard my presentation on the win/win of food aid and agriculture development for both the target countries and U.S. agricultural exports, and said it would be good for the former secretaries and other attendees to also hear my story.

Most important, however, was that because senators' schedules were tight and unpredictable, he was asking me to be the initial speaker *only if* no senator had arrived at the program starting time. And, if I *were* speaking, he wanted me to *be willing to wrap it up* as soon as a senator walked in, so the senator could be introduced.

Freeman's plan made sense and, having known all the former secretaries who would be there, I would enjoy participating. Cliff Hardin had been the University of Nebraska chancellor during my time in three neighboring state universities, Earl Butz had been dean at Purdue my early years as dean at South Dakota State, and both Bob Bergland and Jack Block had been guest lecturers at Kansas State during my presidency. Further, the first senator would likely be late enough that I could give my whole twenty-minute speech, reinforce with data what these secretaries already knew.

On the appointed date and hour all the former secretaries were in place, most having arrived early for reminiscences and perhaps friendly debate on current issues. As expected, no senators had yet arrived, so Freeman simply welcomed the group and introduced me for an up-date on current food aid and overseas agricultural development projects. It was near the end of my twenty-minute presentation when Senate

Majority Leader Bob Dole appeared in the doorway. In one sentence, I "wrapped it up," took a chair, and, along with the former secretaries, listened to Dole's strong and reasoned support for more U.S. food aid.

How Orville Freeman Became Secretary

Back to our conversation at the International Club: With Freeman's request agreed to and the beer unfinished, I asked Freeman what led to his becoming secretary and he told me the story. He had been one of the youngest governors in Minnesota history when elected in the late 1950s, and was seeking re-election in 1960, the year John Kennedy was the Democratic nominee for president. Freeman had endorsed Kennedy early in the Democratic primary and he admitted that to endorse a Catholic in Lutheran Minnesota while running for re-election himself might not have been wise.

Kennedy was elected, but Freeman lost.

When such a high-profile supporter loses re-election or retires, it is common that the new or re-elected president will offer him or her a cabinet post, ambassadorship, or other good job. Freeman expected that he would get such a call, and passed the word to Kennedy's staff that he would be interested in about any cabinet post except secretary of agriculture. The farm economy was not in good shape and, as a farm state governor, he had experienced enough pressure from farm leadership.

Freeman told me that he had then watched successive cabinet announcements being made by Kennedy, and had received no call. Eventually, the only cabinet post left was agriculture. He passed another word to Kennedy staff; he would be interested in the agriculture post. Another week went by.

Freeman and his wife were at a Minnesota National Guard Christmas party in mid-December when he got the call: Could he fly to Washington the next day to meet with the president-elect?

A Kennedy staff member met Freeman's National Guard jet, and he was whisked to Kennedy's home in Georgetown. The house was crowded. Kennedy took him by the arm, "Let's go someplace where we can visit privately," and led him into the bathroom.

Freeman continued the story, "I sat on the edge of the bathtub, Kennedy sat on the 'throne,' and he told me he would like for me to be the secretary of agriculture."

I wanted to learn more, "What instructions or priorities did Kennedy lay out for you?"

He said Kennedy had just one stipulation: "I've had so much pressure to name a southerner as secretary, you need to pick a southerner as your Number Two.

Freeman then followed up. A few days later, back in Minnesota, he got a call from former President Harry Truman, and it went like this, "Congratulations on Kennedy choosing you for secretary of agriculture. I understand you want a southerner as your deputy. I would sure like for you to consider my good friend, Charlie Murphy from down in North Carolina." Murphy had been an administrative assistant and special counsel to Truman during his presidency and likely had been one of those southerners urged on Kennedy for the secretary post.

Freeman said he responded, "Mr. President, if that is what you would like, I will ask Mr. Murphy."

Freeman would serve two presidents in those eight years, Kennedy and, after Kennedy's death, Lyndon Johnson. Murphy would serve as Freeman's Under Secretary, then the title of USDA's Number Two post, Freeman's first four years.

During the balance of my time in Washington, I would see Secretary Freeman on several occasions, and Shirley and I were among guests at a Sunday afternoon reception he and his wife, Jean, hosted in their Arlington condominium that overlooked the Pentagon. Our last visit was when he stopped by my new office in April of 1992, to offer congratulations on my moving into the USDA assistant secretary post.

Secretary Freeman and his wife moved back to Minneapolis in the late 1990s, his health failed, and he passed away in early 2003.

Before the Sunday Night Movie

Monday and Thursday evenings during the summers of my youth, we headed to a local village, Lorah or Wiota, for free movies. We sat on planks over concrete blocks in the town park and the projector started when the sun dropped below the west horizon. Now, on a Sunday evening nearly five decades later, Shirley and I were in a tiny village near the city of Anand, Kaira District, State of Gujarat, on the west edge of India. There would be a free movie in the town park that evening, but our focus was on what was happening at a milk receiving station before the movie would begin.

We had learned of the Kaira District Cooperative Milk Producers' Union, credited with not only achieving an extraordinary increase in milk production and consumption in the Anand area, but demonstrating for the rest of India that it could be done. We wanted to see for ourselves what had brought about such a dramatic increase in milk production in a nation of a billion people, of which nearly two thirds were small farmers.

This was near the end of a multi-purpose trip with my traveling partners, Bob Scherer, CEO of the National Cooperative Business Association (NCBA) and fellow Iowan Dean Kleckner, President of the American Farm Bureau Federation (AFBF). We were functioning as a program review team, in essence, for both AID and USDA. Our first stop had been Indonesia's island of Java, where Kleckner and I were the formal review team for an AID-financed cooperative development project being carried out by NCBA. Two days later we were at USDA's Market Development Office in Singapore, where a Foreign Agricultural Service staff member introduced us to importers of soybeans, corn, and processed food products from the U.S.

A bonus in that city-state was a morning at what was called Singapore's "high tech park," about three hundred hectares devoted to intensive agricultural production, such as vegetable and flower greenhouses and intensive pork and egg production units. In the egg unit's packing room, we watched an eighteen-inch wide windrow of eggs flow on a wide belt into equipment that would electronically check the eggs for quality, then place the eggs, each stamped with a "hi-tech" logo, into ten-egg plastic containers, most for local retailers, but some for export to Australia. With so many people on so little land, production systems had to be intensive.

From Singapore, Kleckner had returned to the U.S. to handle his AFBF duties. Scherer and I had flown on to Delhi where I was scheduled to speak at the International Cooperative Convention. Our wives had left Washington to meet us in Delhi.

After the convention and a day trip to the Taj Mahal at Agra, the four of us had flown to Ahmadabad, a major city south of Hyderabad, and had gone by car to Anand.

Credit for much of the success of the Kaira District Milk Producers' Union had been attributed to a Dr. Vegrghese Kurien, who, by coincidence, was at that time headed to Washington and Des Moines to receive the World Food Prize for his efforts. We only regretted that our visit to his home base was at a time of his absence.

We stood that Sunday evening near the entrance to the Kairi Cooperative milk receiving station, watching men and women get in line to deliver their day's milk production from their cow or water buffalo. Most carried a covered metal pail; others had metal or crockery containers balanced on their heads. At the milk receiving window, their container was emptied into a weigh vessel, and they moved on toward a short line at a second window. In the meantime, a small milk sample had been taken from the weigh vessel for an instrument that, by what is called electrophoresis, measured the percent of fat and non-fat solids in the milk. Less than two minutes later, the value of each person's milk having been calculated, each received at the second window a slip of paper showing milk weight and composition, and their payment in cash or paper money.

Then they would enjoy the movie.

Family members in line at Kairi Dairy Cooperative receiving station to have their day's milk production weighed and sampled, and for payment.

Each had not only watched their milk being weighed, each had likely glanced at the scale as their neighbor's milk was being weighed. And, likely, each had paid some notice to the number of coins counted out to their neighbor at the second window.

Kurien and his colleagues, in developing this cooperative and its system at the local level, had harnessed the motivational value of immediate feedback. Each person knew their day's milk production and composition, and each left the station with coins to spend. There was also competition, each saw how his or her milk and payment compared with their neighbor's or friend's.

Could there have been more effective motivation to increase production?

We would spend part of the next day in the city of Anand at Amul Dairy, the cooperative's major milk processing plant, which received and handled the milk from hundreds of those small village stations. We would see in-line pasteurizing equipment, vats of cheese in the making, and a line of milk tank cars ready to leave the plant for distant cities.

By the year 2000, we would later learn, more than ten million dairy producers in more than a thousand small dairy cooperatives across India were supplying almost five million tons of milk annually to the country's cities and towns. Milk as we saw being delivered in small pails and crockery that Sunday evening in a small village was reaching nearly a quarter billion people.

Cooking Oil for the Refugees

Draped over my study door is what appears to be an eight-foot sash. Instead, it is a series of four-by-five-inch carpets, practices by a fourteen-year-old Afghanistan boy in a refugee camp just outside Peshawar, Pakistan. I purchased the item in a camp store at the end of my visit in August of 1988. This was near the end of the Soviet invasion of and war with Afghanistan, which lasted from December of 1979 to February of 1989. Our purpose at Pashawar was to understand the dire circumstances of several hundred thousand Afghanistan refugees that had sought refuge in neighboring Pakistan, especially to see the distribution of cooking oil and rice provided by the U.S.

We had entered a tent city on the edge of Peshawar and less than thirty kilometers from the Afghanistan border. It was a camp that held at least ten thousand refugees from war-torn Afghanistan. Steve Abrams of AID's congressional relations office had arranged to take four key staff members of the House agriculture and appropriations committees on a tour of food aid projects in South Asia countries, to see for themselves how food aid funds were being used. Because food aid is part of the "farm bill," reauthorized about every five years, the House agriculture committee had to be "on board" for continued support of food aid funding. Because appropriation bills originate in the House, the appropriations committee also had to be "on board." As leader of AID's food and agriculture programs, it was important that I be a part of this traveling group, to answer any questions. Being rather new to my job, I would also learn.

I first saw a long line of people, each carrying a small pail, pan, or crockery and patiently shuffling forward for their turn. A block ahead, at the far end of the line, a young woman with a long-handled dipper was giving each person their ration of cooking oil. At the end of a second line, small bags of rice were being handed to each.

Availability of vegetable oil for cooking is basic in South Asia and much of Africa. In the U.S. and Western Europe, countries with higher consumption of animal products, lard or butter has been the traditional lubricant and heat transfer agent for cooking. In South Asia and much of Africa, with rice, beans, nuts, cassava, and other vegetable products as the food staples, palm oil, peanut oil, or olive oil is the lubricant and heat transfer agent; a family does not feel they can get along, cannot begin to prepare a meal, without cooking oil.

This was part of a three-country South Asia schedule, and Pakistan was our first country. With AID's Pakistan mission director, we had visited ministry staff in Islamabad, Pakistan's capital city, to understand how our food aid fit into the country's priorities and concerns, and also to get their perspective on the Afghanistan refugee issue.

But there were issues for these refugees beyond food. What of the future of these families? Some had been in this and other camps four or five years as fighting had continued. Could they expect to eventually return to their homeland? Would there be jobs? Would the adults have lost their skills? More important, what about the children? Would there be an education void? Would they ever get trained for an occupation?

Who would do the training in these camps? An estimated hundred thousand Afghan refugees were being accommodated in Pakistan, a high proportion in the Peshawar area.

Fortunately, other countries had stepped forward. Some had sent teachers, and larger tents in this "tent city" held classes, from primary on up. The Dutch had established several vocational schools for young people. And, because carpets are a major product of South Asia, carpet weaving was a favored training program. We took the time to walk through the carpet weaving facilities and I was impressed.

Most important to our mission, we saw the necessity for cooking oil, a place for more U.S. peanut oil and soybean oil.

Life on the Dike

Bangladesh, one of the world's most densely populated countries and perhaps the one most prone to flooding, was next on our travel schedule. Also one of the poorer countries of the world, Bangladesh lacked infrastructure, roads, bridges, electricity distribution, and, at that time, dependable communication systems.

Our target projects in Bangladesh were those financed in part by U.S. Food Aid. In this and many other countries, U.S. food aid serves several purposes. The food commodities may be distributed as payment to local residents for their work, such as installing a needed sewer system or planting trees. In the case of Bangladesh, one of the major needs was for graded up roads, above the flood plain, so farmers and others could get their goods to market.

We traveled from the capital city, Dhaka, in the middle of the country, to Chittagong on the southeastern coast. Along the way, we visited a rural electrification project being handled through a contract with the National Association of Rural Electric Cooperatives. However, it was flood season and the Bramaputra and Ganges Rivers that flow into the country from neighboring (almost surrounding) India, kept our traveling party largely on the dikes.

Pictures are worth a thousand words, and the accompanying photos perhaps best show and describe our Bangladesh experience.

Rural life in much of Bangladesh is truly "life on a dike." Clockwise from the upper left: our group walking toward a rural village, a close-up of the pedestrian bridge ahead, a load of cotton atop the family houseboat and on the way to market.

A farmstead along side the river in its normal "flood stage." Note the stacks of harvested forage and also the recently harvested water vegetation drying on a rack above the river's edge.

Waiting to load a ferry at Dakha. Most of the public transportation and shipment of produce or product in Bangladesh was by ferry. Railways existed along the eastern and western borders, but there was only one rail line in the country's interior. And, there was only one highway bridge across the Jamuna River, which bisects northern Bangladesh.

CHAPTER IV

FOOD FOR WORK; SCIENCE FOR THE FUTURE

"We were standing on a hillside just south of Guatemala City's airport, among rows of make-shift homes that were not connected to any form of sewer or water supply. Another of the "food for work" projects, teams of community residents were digging the trenches for and installing sewer pipe. Residents worked in morning and afternoon teams, six hours each, and each team received three pounds of rice, two and a half pounds of corn, and two pounds of beans per cubic meter of earth moved."

Though AID's role in assessing each country's need for food aid was handled in a separate agency bureau, some of its *use* in the target countries was an integral part of the total food and agriculture development efforts. It was therefore important that I understand our food aid strategies in the two major recipient regions, Africa and Central America. My encounters would include intense pressure for more food aid, repeated demonstrations of win/win consequences of food aid, and research institutes that provide both genetics and technology for developing countries.

Friday Night at the Zebu Club

It was a Friday night in March, 1987, and the Zebu Club on the ILCA (International Livestock Center for Africa) campus on the outskirts of Addis Ababa, Ethiopia, was packed. A three-piece combo, comprised of an AID worker, an NCR (National Cash Register) salesman and an Irishman, was loud. From time to time, the combo interrupted their dance music to lead group singing. The bar stools and card tables were occupied, mostly with staff from ILCA, U.S. and other embassies, PVOs (private voluntary organizations), and other expatriates, media and business people plying their trade in what some would call the desolation of East Africa.

Outside were tennis and squash courts and a swimming pool, well used by families during the week and week-end.

It was the end of my first two days of a planned sixteen on the ground in Africa. I would become acquainted with 1) the four international agricultural research centers on the continent, 2) AID's East Africa office in Nairobi, Kenya, and 3) Food aid programs in Ethiopia, Kenya, Mozambique, and Zambia. Washington staff had briefed me and I had read documents and reports, but I would learn most on site.

After an overnight flight to Heathrow airport west of London, then another overnight flight to Addis Ababa, I had arrived in the capital of what is considered the poorest country in the world. Riding from the airport through a dry and treeless landscape, we had passed men, women, and young boys with packets of firewood, mostly sticks one to three inches in diameter, strapped to their back. Firewood is valuable and scarce; they must have walked miles to sell what they carried in the capital city.

After dropping my bag in my hotel room, I had looked out the window at rusted metal roofs and dirt paths, the latter connecting the open-air homes and businesses. Under one of those metal roofs was an apparent tailor, his back against a fence and one foot working the pedal of an old Singer sewing machine. I had no time to observe more; ILCA's acting director general and I were off to the ILCA campus.

With two of his ILCA staff, I watched a slide show of their grass variety and grazing intensity research, work underway at the station and also on land in Nigeria, Mali, Kenya, and elsewhere. I wondered, "Of how much value is this work?" Little African land is fenced and most cattle owners are nomadic. Grazing land is held "in common" by tribes or communities and there are too many cattle or goats for the grazing land that exists. With no fences, there is no incentive to seed more adapted species or to control invasive species. There is also no incentive to "leave half the grass" as Kansas Flint Hills cattlemen do. (The half left ungrazed captures sun, oxygen, and water to manufacture more vegetation.) In Africa's open pastoral system, when one's cattle have grazed down the grass, they just move on.

What impact could ILCA have? Staff told me they direct their attention to those "settled" farmers, most with one or two cows or a couple goats, and to training livestock research and extension workers from north central African countries. I wondered aloud, "Is there opportunity for a tribe or community to form a grazing cooperative or joint venture among cattle owners, build fences, establish more adapted species, and perhaps try rotation grazing systems now being encouraged in the U.S?" Staff response was cautious, "So many traditions." They also reminded me, "These people have no bank account; a man's herd is his estate." It is no matter to them that too many cattle damage the grass and land.

My late afternoon was spent at the official residence of the U.S. Charge' de Affairs (ambassador role but lesser title). The U.S. had broken relations with Ethiopia's Marxist government in 1977, but when Ethiopia's mass starvation was exposed to the world in 1984, the U.S. had joined other countries' efforts and agreed to provide one third of the food aid, at least through 1987. I learned there was a big debate underway between AID staff in Ethiopia who had calculated the need vs. Washington AID staff. In-country staff saw starving people; Washington wanted to pressure the Marxist government to incentivize food production. The charge' warned me about what I would encounter the next day, frustrations of in-country AID Food for Peace (food aid) workers, "urging" by a United Nations representative in his office, "pleadings" by other country PVO representatives at a luncheon and, late afternoon, an "expression of hope" by the Chief Commissioner of the Ethiopian Relief and Rehabilitation Commission that the U.S. "would come through."

I felt more pressure that next day than I would receive from university deans and department heads at Kansas State's budget allocation time. And, it was more frustrating. In the university, I made allocation decisions. Here, I was but a listening representative of the U.S., not the decider. An inter-agency committee in Washington, with representatives from State, USDA, Treasury, and AID, made the food allocation decisions.

That evening I enjoyed a true Ethiopian dinner at Hotel Afrique with AID and ILCA staff plus, especially, Pat Green Nuwanyakpa, at one time my Kansas State assistant director of affirmative action and now personnel director for a PVO, World Vision. The dinner and the following visit to the Zebu Club would wipe away my day's frustration. Pat is a Topeka native, had married a Liberian then completing his Ph.D. in Animal Science at Kansas State. He had taken a two-year assignment with ILCA and was in Cameroon seeking a license to become a consultant and a representative for foreign firms wanting to do business in that country.

The hotel restaurant had mostly small, curtained areas for couples or small groups, but we had a small room with a bar, couches, and a cluster of low wicker tables and chairs. First came beer and several wines, the latter made from honey and rather bitter. Then were brought three round wicker trays, perhaps thirty inches in diameter, each with two layers of enjera, a thin pastry baked on a flat stone or grill. Enjera is made from a sour dough, the main ingredient being flour from tef, a grass-like grain.

Successive dishes of hot food soon followed, and included cooked greens, curry chicken with hard-boiled eggs, beef ribs, curry fish, curry beef, and a dish that included small pieces of enjera in a sauce. The contents were poured onto the enjera. One person in the party did not eat animal products, so one tray of enjera was devoted only to the greens, creamed corn, carrots, and a spicy bean dish.

No silverware was provided. One would tear off a piece of enjera and, holding it between the thumb and fingers, scoop up a small portion of food, and put it in one's mouth. Custom includes feeding each other, once as a courtesy and up to three times depending on regard for the other person. Before the server removed the trays, she insisted on one round of being "the feeder." The meal's climax was two legs of lamb, the meat having been cut into hanging ringlets for braising, and delivered with sharp knives for each person. We then moved on to the ILCA campus and the Zebu Club.

Conversation at the Zebu Club was easy and a good time was evident. AID mission staff told me that such social closeness of expatriates in what are called hardship posts makes life more enjoyable. Families are happier than when living in Washington.

The optimism of ILCA's grassland researchers, the intense feelings of the food aid personnel, the dining experience, and the "good time" feeling at the Zebu Club told me why these people, especially AID and PVO staff, may spend a major part of their lives in Africa.

Saturday morning I flew on to Nairobi, Kenya, from Addis Ababa; I was eager to revisit a few familiar Nairobi shops and Kenya's railway and national museums before my Monday visits to the city's several international agricultural research centers and AID's east Africa offices. En route from Nigeria to Botswana a few years earlier, Shirley and I had spent an enjoyable week-end in Nairobi.

This time, Shirley and her sister, Jeannie, would arrive about the same time I would arrive, after having visited relatives in Germany. While I worked in Nairobi, they would be at Governor's Camp in the Sarengeti, watching gazelles, giraffe, lions, wildebeest and other species. Later, as I would head to the rural areas to check out several Food for Work projects, there would likely be space for Shirley and Jeannie in the AID van.

Science in Central Africa

Kenya had long been a stable country and Nairobi was considered the business and cultural center of eastern Africa, so it was logical that several international agricultural research centers serving the eastern African area be located there. Nairobi was started about 1898 as a railroad training camp halfway between Lake Victoria and the Indian Ocean port city of Mombasa. It's National Leaky Museum suggests a deeper history. The museum's full display of early man and predecessor species tell why anthropologists believe the roots of the human species are not far from Nairobi.

ILRAD (International Laboratory for Research on Animal Diseases) was focusing its seventeen million dollar annual budget on the two diseases most limiting to African livestock, East Coast Fever, transmitted by ticks, and trypanosomiasis, a parasitic disease similar to sleeping sickness in humans. I was impressed; there might not have been at the time a U.S. veterinary college as equipped to work on those two diseases. Some U.S. colleges had sent staff to conduct research that required such facilities or talent. The Lab operates free of any individual government constraint on hiring, so could hire the best from anywhere in the world, most on two-year renewable contracts.

Having just visited ILCA, I was pleased to confirm cooperation between the two centers; ILCA identified herds and animals across

Africa that were tolerant or resistant to trypanosomiasis, while ILRAD was developing selection programs, embryo transfer, and other devices to increase the population of those disease tolerant or resistant cattle. All of this recognized the higher risk of disease spread that resulted from African traditions, the lack of fencing and nomadic herding of cattle on tribal or government land.

ICRAF, the International Council for Research in Agroforestry, had been established in Nairobi because trees are a part of the farming system on eighty per cent of the farms in the East African highlands, one thousand to twenty five hundred foot elevation. Trees not only produce essential firewood, individual species provide fodder for livestock, fruit, shade for a tea crop, "living fences," and, in the case of leguminous trees, soil nitrogen for adjacent crops. As with most other international centers, much of the work involved hosting young scientists or extension workers from other countries seeking experience in research techniques. ICRAF was also sending some of its staff to those countries to give advice and counsel on their developing research and education programs.

The hosting of young scientists was especially evident at my next stop, ICIPE, the International Center for Insect Physiology Experimentation. Headed by a Kenyan, and located at that time on the biological sciences campus of the University of Nairobi, ICIPE provided a place for Ph.D. entomology students from African universities to do their thesis research.

I was impressed by the extent to which U.S. agriculture could benefit from these or other centers, especially in the research techniques and the disease resistant or insect resistant genetic material that may be found. I was reminded that virtually all of the drought resistant features of grain sorghum then grown on the U.S. high plains had come from sorghum lines in East Africa or South Asia.

At AID's Regional office, staff briefed me on some applied research projects, including the use of remote sensing for mapping soils and for predicting shortages in food production and supply. That was a familiar subject; we had obtained federal funds to establish a remote sensing research institute at South Dakota State during my time there. Reflections off the soil surface, grazing land, or a growing crop differ in texture, color, and temperature in accord with soil type or vigor and growth stage of the vegetation. Reflection data recorded by a color camera, infra-red camera, or other device in a plane or satellite, correlated to the known soil type or measured production of a crop, yield computer programs that can be later used to remotely map soils or assess crop condition.

More timely, perhaps, had been their briefings on the dangers our PVOs were encountering in moving food aid to starving people in southern Sudan; either the Sudanese government or rebel forces had been commandeering some of the food and the trucks.

Back from their safari, Shirley and Jeannie joined me and my AID Nairobi host, Bob Armstrong, as we head north through Kenya's tea-growing country to visit Edgerton College, an agricultural school branch of the University of Nairobi. AID was making a major investment in that school's development, the work being done through a contract with the University of Illinois.

The following day we drove further northwest to Marigat and a "Food for Work" project of the World Food Program, a United Nations organization. As in many eastern African countries, firewood availability is a limiting factor in food preparation. At nineteen small nurseries, tree seedlings were produced from seed and made available for transplanting on small farms and homesteads as eventual sources of firewood. Food provided by donor countries is the payment incentive to the local workers who plant the seeds, care for the nursery, and transplant the seedlings.

In Kenya I saw first-hand some of the critical steps in central Africa's eventual movement to commercial, productive agriculture. From what we saw, increases in food and fiber volume and quality would not only elevate the nutrition of local people, but would help ramp up the economic engine of several central African countries—and perhaps make unnecessary those "food for work" projects.

I would expect to see some of those economic engines running strong in my lifetime.

Not every country which the U.S. tries to help has a democratic form of government. My next stop was Mozambique, a small country in southeastern Africa with a communistic government, that form of government perhaps a result of the country's prolonged rebellion from being a Portugese colony.

What the Portugese Left

My local AID host, Jim Maher, and I were driving down the main street of Maputo, Mozambique's capital city of more than a million people, and the street was virtually empty. We saw no parked cars and only one or two moving cars per block in city center. Shop windows were virtually empty, and sidewalk cafes had only a few people at tables. There appeared nothing on the tables, not even salt and pepper shakers, and no waiters were in evidence.

Maher, who had met my plane, said the country "just isn't working." We turned down a side street to the waterfront and bare shipping docks, then past a row of cranes, all dead still and rusting.

Maher followed up, "When the Portugese left in 1975, after several hundred years of rule, there were essentially no native blacks with any skills. Even the cab drivers had been Portugese." After the fierce fighting by Mozambique natives for independence, Portugese administrators, shop owners, and equipment operators apparently had just picked up their administrative manuals or tool boxes and took their experience and skills back to Portugal.

We had stopped briefly to drop my bags at an AID office, in the beautiful embassy and high-end residential section of Maputo overlooking the beach. Both the AID building and a former residence across the street, to which the U.S. embassy would move, were being renovated, with walls and fences heavily reinforced with concrete and steel. The surroundings, especially the sandy beach that seemed to extend forever, told me again why some of my AID colleagues prefer postings away from Washington.

Our first visit was with Commerce Minister Aranda da Silva, a white Portugese in his early thirties. Though the Mozambique government was avowed communistic and displayed the red star, da Silva started by telling us their current policy was to not give donated food free to those who could buy it. He emphasized that many of the government policies had to change; those of the previous ten years "have not been working." The large state farms lacked management capacity. Mozambique, in his opinion, had to move to small, farmer-operated units. "We strongly support the private sector," he said, "the government is prepared to make more changes and those changes must happen or the country will die."

"This from a communist government official?" I thought. Then I reminded myself that he was in his early thirties; like the young economists I would later meet in Bulgaria and Poland, his mind was yet open to options. His statement also echoed that of the junior minister with whom I had visited in Beijing eight years earlier, "Communism will adapt to best serve our country's needs."

Da Silva followed up with some illustrations, of both policy changes that had been made and reactions to those changes. The government had recently decontrolled vegetable prices and prices had sky-rocketed, but production had increased. The vegetable prices were such that government employees and other lower income people could hardly afford them.

The farmers were happy with the higher prices, but had become frustrated that the government no longer set the price; they had to *negotiate* prices. For generations, the Portugese-controlled government and the succeeding communist officials had set the price. One farmer had burst out at a protest meeting, "What kind of government are you if you don't set the price?" He and his neighbors felt the government was shirking its duty. After centuries of colonial control and a decade of central government control, Mozambique farmers' adjustment to free enterprise decision-making and the concept of "supply and demand" was difficult.

There were other problems. There was continued fighting, pro-communist vs. anti-communist groups, as well as territory control squabbles in the countryside, and farm operations were neither safe nor secure. Production was down and the country needed food aid, largely but not exclusively from the U.S. Also, with the continued fighting, there was difficulty in getting the food aid to people who needed it.

Tuesday was a government holiday and offices were closed, so Da Silva, Maher, and I spent the morning with a former Catholic priest, married and defrocked, who was leading a group of small agricultural cooperatives in the Maputo area, mostly women members who produced vegetables, fruit, and pigs. We drove to the two-hectare plot operated by a forty six-member cooperative, forty four women and two men. Banana and mango trees were heavy with fruit and newly transplanted tomatoes, onions, and greens were doing well.

Members lived on nearby farms and grew their own produce; the cooperative was a central point to learn about adapted varieties, irrigation, record keeping, and when to harvest. For both cooperative and individual farm produce, it was also the central point for dispatching trucks or carts to the market. A social hall and nursery school across the street were also part of the cooperative.

It was hot, ninety five degrees or higher, so we eventually retreated to the mission director's home for dinner and a long evening of conversation regarding both the frustrations and satisfactions of work in such a country.

The next day I would learn the reality of distributing food aid in a war-torn country. CARE contracted with AID and the Mozambique government to unload the food aid from the ships at the government-owned docks and to move the food-laden trucks to rural areas, often with military escorts in convoys. Even some farm tractors were used to pull four-wheel trailers with bags of grain and other commodities to the smaller villages. Though Maputo was peaceful, that was not the case in the surrounding country-side. CARE's Mozambique head, Glen Porter, told me that he had hardly a truck without bullet holes, or a driver without scars. Fortunately, though they had lost some trucks, there had been few driver deaths.

I had planned to see more food aid programs in a visit to Zambia, but learned the Zambia Food for Peace officer has been called to Gabarone, Botswana, to help revise that country's food aid strategy and so I would fly there. Though I regretted missing Zambia, I was glad for the change; in Botswana I would get involved in discussing the many issues that affect a country's food aid strategy. I would also get an up-date from the Kansas State faculty who had hosted Shirley and me several years earlier when its Botswana project was just getting underway.

Later that year I would visit food aid programs in five Central and South American countries. I was fortunate that Shirley could sometimes travel with me (at our personal expense, of course) and she was always welcomed by our country hosts. We hold enduring respect and appreciation for the hospitality afforded us in every country we have visited, whether there on behalf of a university, federal agency, the World Bank, or some United Nations unit. We often felt a tinge of embarrassment, that we were being received and hosted far more generously by people with limited resources than we in the U.S. generally treat our visitors.

For the next several encounters, our younger daughter, LuAnn, had also joined us. I would learn more about how U.S. Food Aid is administered, especially where some of the food is "monetized," a portion sold on the local market to provide money for needed infrastructure.

A map of Central American countries between Mexico and Panama. Locations of Guatemala City, capital of Guatemala, and Tegulcigalpa, the capital of Honduras, are marked.

Sewer and Water First

We were standing on a steep hillside in Guatemala City, just south of the airport, among rows of make-shift homes that were not connected to any form of sewer or water supply. It was in what was called the

Kingston district of Guatemala City. Another of the "food for work" projects, teams of community residents were digging the trenches for and installing sewer pipe. Residents worked in morning and afternoon teams, six hours each, and each team received three pounds of rice, two and a half pounds of corn, and two pounds of beans per cubic meter of earth moved.

After a regional AID staff conference in Jamaica earlier in the week on food aid philosophy and logistics, and a side visit to some production projects in that island country handled by U.S. PVOs, we had flown to Guatemala to see what really happens.

This sewer pipe project, chosen by the community as their highest need, was managed by a U.S.-based PVO, CARE. A portion of the country's food allotment had been sold to finance purchase of the sewer pipe, the city engineering office had designed the project and written the specifications, and a CARE engineer was supervising the pipe installation.

Local residents digging trenches for installation of sewer lines in the Kingston District of Guatemala City, each worker team paid with rice, corn, and beans from the U.S. food aid program.

As soon as this project was finished, these same residents would be digging trenches and installing water lines to serve their homes, that is, if the food aid continued.

We then moved to another "food for work" CARE project, building a retaining wall in an even more needy part of the city. It was on a steep hillside with no platted streets, an area occupied by what were, in reality, squatters, migrants from the country looking for jobs in the city. Homes had been built of everything from rusted tin to scrap lumber or concrete blocks, and seemed to be stacked on each other along the hillside. Only a narrow path wound down the hill between the rows of houses. The retaining wall would help hold the "homes" in place.

Working our way through a community of make-shift homes put together by Guatemalans seeking employment and a better life in Guatemala City.

Another bonus of our international work was the chance to see some of the world's sights for which we otherwise would not have had the opportunity. AID and CARE workers had the week-end off, so on Sunday, Shirley, LuAnn, and I took a one-hour flight via Aereoquetzal Airlines to Santa Elena in northeastern Guatemala, then thirty minutes by taxi to Tikal National Park. We hired a young American student for a four-hour guided tour of Mayan ruins, the ceremonial, athletic, educational, business, and residential structures of the Mayan civilization that existed from about 400 B.C. to 700 A.D. That civilization had dissipated in time, and the structures abandoned. They were re-discovered in the 1800s, fully overgrown by jungle and, in 1956, University of Pennsylvania scientists had begun removing jungle overgrowth, excavating, and restoring some of the structures.

The central temple, one of many Mayan structures in Guatemala's Tikal National Park

Holding the Fruit Fly in Guatemala

The Fruit Fly has been described as the world agriculture's most damaging and costly pest. It thrives in a wide variety of climates and can infest deciduous, semitropical, and tropical fruits, as well as some vegetables, and most every country with temperate to tropical climate has battled the pest. The most damaging among the many species and genera seems to be the Mediterranean fruit fly (med fly). Hawaii, and nearly all southern U.S. states, from California to Florida, have had intermittent infestations.

The U.S., Mexico, and Guatemala had long ago mounted an effort to establish a firm barrier to remove the pest to, and establish a firm barrier at, the southern Guatemala border, and both AID and USDA were involved. This was a chance for me to see the effort first hand.

We had driven about twenty kilometers south of Guatemala City to the "Moscamed" facility, there to be met by Pat Gomes, Assistant Area Director for USDA's Animal and Plant Inspection Service. Efforts to date had driven the major infestation southward, moving the effective "fly-free" line to central Guatemala, and the continuing effort was a two-stage process further south and east. The first stage, on the southeast side of that line, was to aerial spray a hundred-meter-wide strip with malathion and a corn-molasses protein hydrolysate bait. The fly is attracted to the sprayed area and dies after its mouth part touches the large spray droplet. (To limit spray drift and avoid collateral risks or damage, the spray is under zero pressure, resulting in large droplets. Lakes, streams, fish ponds, bee yards, and sugar cane plantations were excluded from the spray pattern.)

Some flies will survive the spraying, so a second step is necessary. That step is to release from airplanes large numbers of sterile flies, the flies made sterile by radiation. This gives high odds that any matings will result in zero offspring.

How do they produce sterile flies? Flies lay eggs on a vertical cloth screen, the eggs drop off the screen into a water pan, then are placed in a wet, chopped cocoanut medium for their seven-day metamorphosis. After metamorphosis, the pupa were dried in a tumbler and placed in plastic bags for radiation.

No system is without problems. In this case, though the efforts to date had been effective and, of course, appreciated by fruit growers in Guatemala, Mexico, and the U.S., some Guatemala coffee growers had expressed fear the control efforts were lowering coffee yields. More significant, perhaps, was that AID, which provided some of the Moscamed project funds, was under U.S. court order to do a complete environmental assessment of control measures within the Guatemala environment before the next fiscal year's funds for the project could be spent. U.S. environmental groups had sued AID for using pesticides in developing countries in a manner different from U.S. guidelines.

USDA staff felt the spraying procedure to be appropriate, safe, and in accord with its guidelines. And, USDA's expenditures were *not* affected by the court order. Consequently, AID and USDA were, at the time of our visit, working to use the limited USDA money to fund the work.

This was a typical example of the complexities of work in developing countries, with good intent and needed efforts by conscientious and responsive U.S. staff, but subject to constraints by interest groups far from the scene.

A Curriculum of Work and Study

More than thirty years earlier, while I was advising freshmen and teaching animal husbandry courses at Iowa State, my department head, Leslie Johnson, had told me about Zamarano, a widely respected Guatemalan school with a reputation for turning out students both educated and trained. Its curriculum was a combination of work and study. Our time in Guatemala was a chance to see the school and how it functioned.

Zamarano had been established in good quality farm land about forty kilometers east of Guatemala City by the U.S.-based United Fruit Company, at the urging of one of the Company's staff. He had seen the need for trained workers and managers in the area where United Fruit sourced much of its product, and had become the first director of the school.

The school was based on a strict work/study program of thirty three months, with forty two curriculum segments. On a typical day students were in the mess hall by soon after five a.m., then cleaned their dormitories and were in the field or in class with their instructors by 6:15. Those on the morning work shift quit work at 10:30, showered, ate lunch, and went to four hours of class beginning at 11:30 or 12. The afternoon work shift had classes in the morning.

The mess hall opened at five o'clock for dinner and students studied until eight o'clock, unless they had permission to study later. Classes were five days per week, but field work continued on Saturday.

Central and South American students and those for whom they work, including some I had talked to in Argentina twenty five years earlier, had claimed that these students learned as much or more in the thirty three months as those who had completed the five-year "engineer agronomo" degree at a Latin American university.

A year or so before our visit, Zamorano had initiated a fourth year of study, allowing specialization in animal science, agronomy, or agricultural economics, and leading to a bachelor's degree. However, enrollment in that fourth year is limited to Zamorano certificate holders with several years of experience.

Some Zamorano graduates had chosen to not wait for that fourth Zamorano year. At the time of our visit, about twenty five graduates were at Kansas State, completing B.S. degree requirements there.

Zamorano Director Salmo also told us he was interested in establishing a grain and seed processing center on his campus, in cooperation with and with help from Kansas State's Grain Science department and Mississippi State's Seed Science center.

In the next country we would visit, Honduras, we would see the value of small business loans funded by AID.

Shoes for Hondura's Soccer Team

We were in a shoe-maker's shop, a three-sided, tin-roofed shed of native lumber added to a family home. It was along the roadside on a hill overlooking the western edge of Honduras' capital city, Tegucigalpa. The shoe-maker and his family, including a son-in-law, told us they made five to six pairs of shoes every two to three days and sold them to a retailer in the city. He had borrowed two hundred limpala (about one hundred dollars) for two months to get started, had paid it back and borrowed again. Over time, he had borrowed and paid off four successive loans, each to expand his volume. He had established a good credit rating, and his fifth loan had been increased to seven hundred limpala (about three hundred fifty dollars).

AID had directly funded a cooperative lending bank established by a Honduran PVO and called by the acronym, AITEC. Earlier in the day we had visited the main office of AITEC, and its bank manager had taken us to see some of their Tegucigalpa borrowers. (I should add here that some such banks are funded directly with cash by AID, others are funded with the cash received from selling a portion of the food aid.

Each country's circumstances are different—need for food vs. need for small business loans, availability of locally-produced food, amount of food aid that can be provided, and AID's budget.)

Our first visit had been in a city center open market, a woman tending her stall filled with tomatoes, lettuce, cabbage, carrots, and other attractive, well-displayed produce. When we asked, through an interpreter, how her business was doing, she smiled, then stretched to reach behind the top display box of lettuce, and pulled out her passbook. She opened it to show us on one page the amounts of successive loans and on the opposite page, for each of the loans, her re-payment dates and amounts. The cooperative bank loan had allowed her to open and expand her market stall.

We would also visit a second shoe maker, in the heart of the central city, streets crowded with non-school-attending children, trucks, and carts. At the back of this narrow "assembly plant", an open-sided, covered deck built over a ravine, eight boys, ranging in age from twelve to eighteen, worked at small tables and sewing machine. They were putting together both work shoes and cleated soccer shoes, the latter with the Flamingo label. The shop owner was proud of his product and his workers, and claimed his Flamingo soccer shoes were used by the country's top soccer teams.

We could not resist asking why some of the younger boys in the photo were not in school. The owner had a ready answer; he told us that school was not top priority in some of the more impoverished families. Families needed the boys' income to survive and it was "better to provide work for the boys than to let them get into trouble on the streets."

I examined several pairs of shoes, saw why he was proud of his crew's work, and paid 35 limpala ($17.50) for a pair of work shoes. Nearly ten years later, after four years back on the farm, I was still wearing them.

Another local PVO, Honduran Institute for Development (HID), also received some AID funding, and a day later we visited two of HID's borrowers. The first was a strawberry cooperative of about fourteen growers, high on the mountain north of Tegulcigalpa where rainfall and humidity are higher. Each grower also raised strawberries on the cooperative's land. As I had seen in Mozambique earlier in the year, the cooperative served as a center for both learning production techniques and help in marketing. Growers could exchange experiences and, as a group, seek help from ministry scientists or extension staff on strawberry varieties or disease and pest control.

Late that day, about six o'clock, we stopped at a new, small bakery on the south edge of the city. The operator, a woman in her early forties, had worked in a bakery, then started one in her home. About three months before our visit, she had borrowed enough money to rent a shop and to purchase a large, used oven, a mixer, and a used display case. She was happy and proud, told us she sold all that she could make. Her major products, in volume, were rolls and cookies, but her specialty was a small pastry filled with just a touch of pineapple. It had been a long day, visiting a number of projects in the country, and dinner would be late; we purchased and enjoyed three whole-wheat rolls to "tide us over" until dinner.

We were convinced: Food Aid is a win:win; it provides food for people who desperately need it and it provides a market for U.S. food commodities, commodities often in surplus.

Food for Work can also be described as a triple win, food for needy people, high priority societal needs such as the work on the sewer and water project in Guatemala City, and a market for surplus U.S. commodities. A fourth "win" is also usually evident, satisfactions and self-esteem from productive work.

At this writing, March, 2015, I ask, "Would not Food for Work be a worthy concept within the U.S.?" Cities, schools, libraries, and universities can use people's skills and labor, much of our country's infrastructure needs repair and maintenance, and, most important, productive work yields satisfaction and self-esteem for the worker.

Personal connections are another bonus of professional travel, or to gain an up-date about a person from an earlier work setting. Such occurred at a cocktail-buffet in the home of the AID's Honduran development officer Richard Peters and his wife our second evening in the country. Their home was high on a mountainside, providing a panorama of Tegulcigalpa at night. Mrs. Peters, a native of Los Banos, Philippines, had been, from the third grade through the university, a classmate of my long-ago Iowa State graduate student, Pepe Eusebio. Another guest, the FAO (Food and Agriculture Organization of the United Nations) director for Honduras was an Argentine foreign service officer, a professional colleague of several with whom I had worked in that country twenty six years earlier.

Innovators and Early Adopters

Two of my Iowa State colleagues in the late 1950s and early '60s, Rural Sociologists Joe Bohlen and George Beal, had made their professional reputations as researchers and presenters across Iowa and other Midwestern states, categorizing farmers and community leaders according to their speed in adopting new technology or ideas. By means of interviews and other techniques they had characterized farmers and leaders into five categories, from innovators and early adopters to those who resisted any new technology. This day I would visit two Honduran farmers, one who might be described as an innovator as defined by Bohlen and Beal. However, the settings and the technology levels would be on a different level from those of the Iowa farmers Bohlen and Beal had interviewed.

We had left the main highway to bounce and twist what seemed like five miles on a rough, eroded, and rocky road. We had passed a number of women and children carrying water from community wells, two schools, a community clothes washing tank, and farm homes of wood or adobe, most without doors or windows.

Our first destination farm was on a mountainside of at least a twenty per cent slope, and about an acre in size. The house was about twelve by twenty feet, made of adobe blocks and covered with plaster. There were no evident doors or windows in the openings and the roof was thatch. In a small pen of barbed wire and intertwined sticks, about five feet from the house, were a mother goat and her kid. We were told the family had lost another mother goat and two kids because "the feed was too hot." Apparently the farmer had let some wet grass or other vegetable material ferment before feeding; at least he thought that was the cause of death. In an adjacent pen were two twenty-pound pigs, two hens, two geese, and two small turkeys.

Two small patches just beyond the house were planted "largely" to corn or sorghum, but the leaves were curled and yellow. The husband and wife both expressed pride, however, that the corn had been planted "on the contour," that a few small trees through the field tempered the heat of the sun, that they had inter-planted beans to provide nitrogen, and that their crop, though apparently drying up, was better than that of some of their neighbors.

Though without the benefit of good soil, these latter features prompted my AID guide's judgment that would this farmer could be a Bohlen and Beal early adopter.

The second farm, a few kilometers away, was a virtual oasis. This farmer had dammed a small, spring-fed stream and had installed plastic pipe over rocks and the soil surface to irrigate his crops, corn, onions, cucumbers, beans, bananas, tomatoes, and a few fruit trees.

As we had approached this second farm I had first noted a young boy moving across the road on a home-made, wooden scooter. The wooden wheels had a layer of rubber from an old tire casing nailed to their perimeter. At the front of the house, on a cement slab, was a home-made corn sheller, a thirty-inch, solid, wooden wheel, set vertically within a wooden frame, and turned by a crank. Into one surface of the wheel had been driven fencing staples, with their heads extending out about a quarter of an inch. Facing this staple-covered surface was a solid wooden plate with an angled groove to accommodate an ear of corn. At the top of the groove was a funnel, fashioned from a tin can.

Our young host demonstrated the family's corn sheller. He got the wheel to spinning, dropped an ear of corn into the funnel and the kernels would fly. To complete the job, most ears would have to go down the funnel two or three times. A box or cloth over the mechanism may have helped, but it worked and saved the hands.

This latter farmer was an obvious innovator, both innately and with help from a nearby Vermont Partners farm and training program which we had visited earlier in the day. Vermont Partners is a PVO of Vermont citizens paired with Honduras, parallel to Kansas' Paraguay Partners, and both a part of the "Partners of the Americas" program. Apparently the Vermont legislature had appropriated a modest amount of money for the effort, but most of the money for the program and training center/model farm had been provided by AID. Fifteen farmers had gathered at the center/model farm for training the day of our visit. The model farm house had been converted to dormitories, with bunks and inch-thick mattresses. Two women were in the kitchen preparing food for the noon lunch, one cleaning vegetables at a work bench, the other boiling potatoes on an earthen stove in the kitchen corner.

That earthen stove was, itself, an innovation, requiring half the fuel wood of the area's common stoves. Because fuel wood was increasingly scarce, promoting such earthen stoves had been an early center project. The basic stove building material, clay, varied in quality, so at each home location they would experiment by mixing different proportions of clay, sand, and water, make each mix into a ball, and let the ball dry fourteen days. The ball that did not crack was the mix they would then use to make the stove.

The stove, about two feet high and with walls ten inches thick, would be built in a kitchen corner. A square can would comprise the firebox, with the front open, and the baked sand-clay-water mix was extended across the top. In the case of the stove we saw, a twenty four-inch diameter metal plate had been built into the top, so that heat transfer was more efficient. A four-inch chimney of asbestos or concrete pipe extended from the back of the firebox up through the roof.

Innovation knows no geographic, societal, or ethnic boundaries. Innovators and early adopters have been evident in every society and every ethnicity that I have encountered.

Chapter V

An Agency in Trouble

"I found that I had a car and a driver, though the Metro or a cab could take me any place I needed to go, and more cheaply. As a university president with more than two thousand staff and with state-wide travel, I had not had an assigned car and driver. Our equipment inventory position was vacant, so I cancelled the car lease and my driver became inventory manager."

At the close of the Reagan administration, I had had enough of the Washington bureaucracy and we had moved back to Manhattan and Kansas State University to renew our academic life. We purchased and Shirley renovated a single-story home west of the campus and I was back at my specialty, teaching the introductory animal science course.

It was also a time of decompression, from a thirty seven year continuum of administration, dealing with personnel and budgets; travel; persuading regents, legislators, or deans; and capped by the stimulating activity of Washington.

Though I still considered teaching a class of freshman and working with individual students the most important job in a university, for me it was entirely different the second time around. It was like driving a beautiful route the tenth time; it might still be beautiful, but one looks for that new view.

Fortunately, I had retained a one-quarter time appointment with AID. My Kansas State appointment was three-quarter time for the academic year, but the AID work was year-long, mostly continued education of agricultural leaders and Congressional staff on the win/win consequences for U.S. agriculture of our international development work. I was in Washington a few days every month, and had some international travel. Our summer headquarters would be our Iowa farm.

Back on campus in September, the spark of academia had not fully returned, so in a short visit at a Washington meeting with long time friend, new USDA Secretary Clayton Yeutter, I told him, "If you need help in some problem area, give me a call."

Within days came a call from Dick Crowder, USDA Under Secretary for International and Commodity Programs. An agency reporting through him, the Office of International Cooperation and Development (OICD), needed a new administrator.

Don't Touch It!

Among USDA's forty plus agencies, OICD was among the smallest, about one hundred sixty staff and all headquartered in Washington. It had three responsibilities, (1) represent the Secretary in dealing with a long list of international organizations, from FAO (Food and Agriculture Organization of the United Nations) to the Organization of American States, (2) serve as a USDA contracting office to arrange and supervise specialists for work in developing countries, financed largely by AID but also by the World Bank, regional development banks, and the U.S. State Department, and (3) Manage international research and other foreign linkages funded by Congress and that did not fit in other USDA agencies.

On my next AID trip to Washington I visited with Crowder. The job would fit my background and interests and, from what Crowder told me about the agency, over budget for the current fiscal year, a history of little financial control, and many bills to AID that were unpaid, the job would be a challenge. After my visit with Crowder, I went directly to a hall-way phone booth. Since the major contractor for the agency's services was AID, I wanted the "low-down" from one of my AID friends. "Should I take the job? Tell me the problems in OICD as you see it."

I got an earful, frustrations from several years. The most serious statement, "We had a recent project that would require ten million dollars in order to do it right, but we only had five million budgeted. I told my staff to go ahead and contract with OICD for the ten million dollar program. OICD will never bill us." He added, "If I were you, I would not touch that job with a ten-foot pole."

However, he was not me; I seemed to enjoy challenges and had had a year-long rest from administration. I was also reminded that, though OICD may have problems, it likely had many good and sincere staff. With good staff, an organization's problems can be cured. In addition, Shirley had had so much fun working in the White House volunteer office, I knew she would be more than willing to head back to D.C.

However, this would be a political appointment and I had not been a strong contributor or worker in Republican politics. I doubted that I would get clearance by the White House, so declined the position. At the same time, I owed Crowder my analysis of OICD, and sent him a two-page letter outlining what I believed a new administrator would need to do. The response to my letter: "If you will take the job, I guarantee we will get it cleared in the White House."

With that, I could not say "No."

The call came about a month later, a Friday afternoon, from Sally Buikema, appointments aide to Secretary Yeutter, "The White House has just approved your appointment as administrator of International Cooperation and Development, effective immediately.

Fortunately, Shirley and I had a flight to Washington scheduled the next morning. We had planned to rent a car for a ride in the Virginia country side and spend some time with friends. She would fly home on Monday and I had a three-day AID commitment in Washington and Chicago.

"I can be in the office Monday morning," I responded.

I had alerted my Animal Science Department Head, Jack Riley, to both the possibility and the uncertainty of my returning to D.C. We had an investment club meeting that night and Riley and his wife were members, but Shirley and I stayed only long enough to tell Riley about the phone call and to resign from the club; we had more packing to do than for a week-end.

In D.C. at noon on Saturday, rather than renting a car for a week-end drive in the Virginia countryside, we looked at apartments and rented a sixth-floor, two-bedroom, sixth floor unit across George Washington Parkway from what is now Ronald Reagan airport. Sunday we measured the apartment floor space and laid out newspaper sheets to determine what furniture it could hold. We would sell our newly remodeled Manhattan house and take the rest of our furnishings to the farm. We also borrowed some bedding from former Ames neighbors, Dick and Carolyn Irby, and slept on the apartment floor.

Shirley flew home Monday morning to list our house with a realtor and make plans for moving. I rode the Metro to my new office on K-Street, OICD's temporary location while part of USDA's South building was being re-modeled. I met the key staff, called a furniture rental company to have a couch, chair, and TV delivered to our new apartment (charged to my credit card), and headed to the airport with AID staff for a flight to Chicago.

As with AID, I would find in my new agency, OICD, a high quality staff dedicated to the agency's several roles. However, it soon became apparent that, in addition to being in financial difficulty, the agency had too many organization units, too many layers of management, and too many people for the jobs to be done.

In AID, I had to work with the structure that existed. But in OICD, I was the administrator; I might encounter some Civil Service constraints but, in time, I could change the structure.

Is He Still Alive?

That question was from an FBI interviewer my second week at OICD. For the presidential appointment, I had completed an extensive form for FBI clearance, and the White House had obviously approved the appointment, but the agency was now following up with a personal interview.

That form had included personal information, the address of each of the thirteen places we had lived, title and salary for every job held, and names of three people who had known me the longest. I had listed Creighton Sindt, home area farmer and friend of forty years, my Wiota school superintendent, Joe O'Connor, and farm neighbor Russell Jordan. I had led a horse on the hay-fork for Jordan the summer after my seventh grade.

This young man, apparently a fresh college graduate in his first FBI job, was charged with determining if my oral answers were the same as I had provided on the form. He also had a few other questions.

"Is Shirley your wife?"

"Yes."

"Is she the only wife you have had?"

"Yes."

"And you are fifty nine?" he asked with apparent wonder. Perhaps I was the first senior appointee he had been tasked to handle; most had likely been White House and cabinet department aides just a few years out of college and who had earned their appointments by campaign leg work.

"Who were your parents? When were they born?" The form had shown birth dates, 1895 and 1896. A puzzled look came over his face, he looked up from the form, and exclaimed, "I've never known anyone whose parents were born in the last century!"

He scanned further down the form, "You've known this Mr. O'Connor for fifty four years? And he was superintendent when you were in the first grade?"

I nodded.

"Is he still alive?" he asked, with evident disbelief.

On my next week-end visit to the farm, I enjoyed sharing this encounter with O'Connor, then only seventy seven.

Correspondence Control

An un-written rule regarding bureaucracies: It takes only forty people in an organization to create enough work to keep all forty busy and with no product coming out. My new agency's correspondence control operation seemed to illustrate.

In my first weeks in OICD, I had few outgoing letters to sign. I was not surprised. Though the administrator signs most letters that leave a federal agency, OICD had few domestic constituents and few members of Congress had any issue with the agency. Our major clientele were other USDA agencies, AID, and development banks. However, we had a correspondence control officer, a pleasant woman located across the reception area from my office, and she appeared to be busy. I assumed she had more duties than handling the correspondence, probably helped other secretaries and staff. The letters she brought in for my signature were often clipped to a thick file and I would leaf through the file to the originating correspondence, to be certain the response prepared for my signature did the job.

I had also noticed, as I visited my two program assistant administrators and heads of their six divisions, that the secretary in each office was often entering information in a "correspondence log book." I had also picked up considerable frustration from staff on the numbers of times they had had to re-do response letters.

In my third week, I asked my correspondence control officer, Jean, about her work. "Oh, I am so busy, I can't really get it all done!" she said.

"What other tasks do you handle?" I asked.

"It is all on the correspondence," she explained, "I have to check every letter and a good many come up here with typos or poor sentence structure, I have to send them back to be re-done." She handed me a couple that she had marked up with corrections.

Now, I feel rather comfortable when it comes to spelling and grammar, and the original responses looked good to me. But Jean had found a way to make her job important. "Jean, how many letters have you handled so far this month?" I asked.

"A lot," she responded, and held up her thick log book, showing me several pages with February dates.

"But, Jean," I said, "I have not signed many. How many went into the out-going mail box?"

"I'd have to check that," she said, "I record every one that comes in, as well as when I send it down to an assistant administrator, when it comes back up, and when I send it back for correction."

"Jean, please add up the number of letters that went in the mail during February."

The next morning she came in with the answer, thirty-five. I could not restrain my response, "Jean, you could have typed or re-typed these thirty-five yourself, in one week."

That afternoon I convened a meeting of those two assistant administrators, their six division directors, and their secretaries, plus Jean and my secretary, "We have what appears to be a self-made problem, and a lot of frustration, all related to the correspondence log books and repeated redrafting of letters."

I saw a good bit of head nodding and heard from several, "We sure do."

"I propose a solution," I said, "Unit secretaries: Tie a string around your correspondence log books, put them in the bottom drawer of your desk and leave them there."

This brought immediate protests, "How will we know where the letters are? What if we lose one?"

"You are all responsible people. And, there is another part of my proposal: A response letter sent forward by any staff member should have attached to it the floppy disk from the drafter's personal computer. Any line officer that feels need to revise a response letter will do it themselves. They will not send it back to the drafter. That includes me."

I then saw questioning facial expressions and from several, "Can we do that?"

"Are you willing to try?" I asked. To that question, there was considerable head-nodding and some emerging smiles.

I then turned to Jean, "Jean I would like for you to take the head secretary position now vacant in our information office." Though Jean smiled, I could tell she was worried, "Would some correspondence get lost or would a typo get through?"

Over-Structured, Over-Staffed, and Overdrawn

My new agency had long handled agricultural development projects for AID and other entities and the result in many countries had eventually been more U.S. exports to those countries. Under Division Director Arlene Mitchell, it had a good reputation with U.S. universities and other USDA agencies with which it had contracted for staff. The research division, headed by Val Mezainis, had established dozens of U.S. agricultural scientist linkages in Central and Eastern Europe well before "The Wall" would come down. However, the agency had serious problems with its major contractor, AID, in addition to being "over-structured, over-staffed, and overdrawn."

Of the agency's six operating divisions, three reported to each of two assistant administrators. A third assistant administrator, John Miranda, was responsible for budget, finance, and a two-person personnel office. A three-person information and congressional liaison office was headed by David Winkelman. My deputy administrator, Steve Abrams, was a former AID colleague with whom I had worked closely two years earlier. I also found I had an assistant, Verle Lanier, on loan from the Foreign Agricultural Service, and he proved to be especially helpful in my adapting to the routines and traditions of USDA.

Civil Service's employee classification system has a built-in incentive for agencies to over-structure and over-staff. The more employees in a unit or the more units one supervises, the higher the Civil Service rank and salary justified for the unit head. With only about one hundred sixty staff, but organized into six divisions reporting through two assistant administrators, OICD had used that incentive to the limit.

I also found that I had a car and a driver, though the Metro or a cab could take me any place I needed to go, and more cheaply. As a university president with more than two thousand staff and with state-wide travel, I had not had an assigned car and driver. Only on a few occasions, when I needed to go long distances for night speeches had my office arranged a student to drive for me. Our equipment inventory position was vacant, so I cancelled the car lease and my driver became inventory manager.

Eliminating the driver and correspondence control positions had made little impact, however, on what I had learned was a nearly million dollar deficit for the balance of the fiscal year. I therefore called together all the staff, from assistant administrator to the lowest rank clerk and even part-time student workers, and put the Agency's financial data on two large easel tablets for all to see. The data included appropriated and contract income, plus budgeted personnel, travel, and supplies expenditures for the balance of the year. We had two meetings, one at ten o'clock and one at two, so offices could remain staffed and to accommodate scheduled commitments. I wanted all to see the data. For those on overseas travel, we faxed a summary to each.

If one has to make personnel cuts, they will be better accepted if every person in the organization has the facts. If a position is cut, all would know it is was because of financial reality, not because of the person's performance.

My message was that the agency was over-staffed and over-structured, we would terminate all temporary positions at the end of the month, hire no one, and down-size our structure to fewer operating units. I assured all that we would follow Civil Service regulations in any position eliminations.

One could almost see a sense of relief. All knew the budget problem was bad, but they did not know how bad and did not know when "the shoe would drop," when some action would be taken. Now, they knew.

The most rapid way to both save money and simplify the structure would be to eliminate high-level and high-pay positions. But Civil Service gives priority to rank and years of service. If I eliminated the two assistant administrator positions, both at the GS-15 (Government Service) level, each of those persons could "bounce" a person one or two steps lower, a division director at the GS-14 or 13 level. One whose position was eliminated had several months to decide which of several positions he or she wanted to go to, or if they wanted to take early retirement. If a GS-15 chose a GS-14 director spot, the GS-14 could bounce a GS-13 person. And the GS-14 had several months in which to decide. My personnel office charted the consequences of that strategy and we quickly deduced it would take at least eighteen months to achieve the monthly expenditure level we needed for the balance of the *current* fiscal year. To simply eliminate top administrative positions was a non-starter.

The only solution was to out-place some people to other agencies and highlight early retirement incentives. Abrams and I made a list of the positions the agency did not need, a total of twenty two, and asked our personnel staff to prepare a complete file on each person. Depending on salary level of those we could outplace, quickly moving twelve to eighteen of those people to open positions in other agencies should let us get through the fiscal year.

At the same time, I needed to down-size the structure. After several discussions with key staff, I eliminated the two program assistant administrator positions and collapsed the six divisions into four, with their directors reporting to me.

The author and USDA Secretary Clayton Yeutter, a Nebraska native. We had been acquainted since college and FarmHouse Fraternity days, Yeutter at Nebraska and the author at Iowa State.

Secretary Yeutter gave our effort a boost. At his next staff meeting of under and assistant secretaries and agency administrators he announced that Abrams or I would be making an appointment with each of them and their personnel officer, carrying with us files for staff that might fit in their agencies. He asked each agency to be helpful. The important issue was to accommodate individual people with appropriate positions, and avoid terminating employment.

In less than three weeks, we out-placed fifteen, some of higher ranks and some clerical staff. One was not Civil Service, but a political appointee who had worked on the president's campaign and for whom we found an open staff spot in another agency.

Most difficult, of course, was out-placing the two GS-15 assistant administrators, high rank and high salary. Any open positions at that rank in another agency would likely have unique qualifications. One of the two was eligible for retirement, so I reminded him of that option and that, if outplacement was not successful and he did not choose to retire, I would simply leave him at his current desk, with "assigned duties." Though a capable person, that would be my only option, and he knew there were not many agency duties to be assigned.

The advantage in the second case was that he had a Ph.D. in an agricultural discipline, so there might be a science coordinating spot in USDA's Agricultural Research Service (ARS), the Cooperative State Research Service, which handled USDA funds to state experiment stations, or a senior scientist position at an ARS lab, either at nearby Beltsville or another research laboratory across the country.

The assistant secretary for science and education, responsible for ARS and CSRS, was out of town, so I had lunch with his deputy. He knew this assistant administrator well, it appeared they were good friends, and I was confident he would suggest several spots in CSRS or ARS. I was wrong. After a lengthy visit, the response was clear, "He is my friend, but he is your problem." It took a bit of help from Yeutter, but in a few days the man was transferred to that office's budget and office.

By out-placing fifteen staff, we had saved enough money to finish the fiscal year in the black, plus enough to put a personal computer on the desk of any remaining staff that did not have one.

The Calf Crop in the Upper Amazon

With two USDA colleagues, Ed Stubbs from USDA's Animal and Plant Inspection Service, Richard Rortvedt, one of my OICD division heads, and I were now spending a week in Bolivia. There were two reasons, 1) Bolivian president Pas Samoro had asked Secretary Yeutter for help with Bolivian agriculture and 2) U.S. Ambassador to Bolivia Robert Gelbard has asked Under Secretary Crowder to approve use of food aid sales money to finance demonstration programs for Bolivian wheat and soybean producers. Crowder was concerned that U.S. wheat and soybean associations would not look with favor on that kind of help to Bolivians.

My readers know, from their own experience or from earlier chapters, that a more productive agriculture is the "starter engine" for economic growth in developing countries. We also know economic growth brings increased demand for meat, and that grain imports, often from the U.S., are needed to feed the livestock and poultry. Secretary Yeutter knew that; early in his career he had directed a Chilean agricultural development project for the University of Nebraska. However, some second and third level people in USDA and some U.S. commodity leaders did not yet know that.

We were to assess Bolivia's agriculture situation, and the likely consequences of using the food aid currency as Gelbard had asked.

About the same time, President Bush had announced an "Andean Initiative," U.S. economic help to four Andean countries needing to improve their economies. The White House had tasked the State Department, AID, and the U.S. Trade Representative's office, as well as USDA, to take the lead for that "initiative." Yeutter, who had been U.S. trade representative under President Reagan, suggested the several purposes be combined, so we were joined by a State Department representative. Bolivia would be the first country visited.

We were headed south over north central Bolivia, the upper basin of the Amazon River, strapped into bucket seats along the wall of an ancient U.S. military cargo plane commissioned to the U.S. Drug Enforcement Administration (DEA). I unstrapped and stretched up to a small window; I wanted to see the Savannah below, open grassland with only scattered patches of trees and brush. First I noted some smoke, then several fires and fire scars on the open range. Being early spring, September in the southern hemisphere, ranchers were burning to control brush, as do Kansas Flint Hills ranchers.

The DEA pilot had warned us to stay strapped in, but we had seen a bit of the landscape in our commercial flight from LaPaz to the frontier town of Trinidad two days earlier and wanted to see more. Over the old engines' roar, the three of us could not hear the pilot's yell to get back in our seats. He pushed a button and the rear cargo door began to lower. We dropped to our seats and grabbed the straps!

Why the DEA plane? We had spent the day in northeastern Bolivia's town of Trinidad listening to ranchers, a veterinarian, managers of meat, fish, and Brazil nut processing plants, and other community leaders tell us their needs. Trinidad had all the features of a frontier town, a short main street and only a few paved streets. It was about twenty blocks square, and located in largely timber and grass country that straddled an upper Amazon tributary. It was also, by the way, the largest town and the capital of Bolivia's state of Beni.

This is the tropics; Aftosa (food and mouth disease) and brucellosis are common. The veterinarian told us cow herds average a forty two per cent calf crop. Most land is overgrazed. The area needs government disease testing programs and extension education. Money is short and ranchers need grain, high protein concentrates, and Vitamin A to supplement the grass in the dry season. The community needs good roads to LaPaz, other market centers, and distant export points. The area's good soil and high annual rainfall suggest high production potential, but that potential is not well used.

After a full day of listening, we had retreated to our modest hotel and its open roof-top lounge for a beer and to enjoy the view. Beyond the small residential area was open grazing land and semi tropic timber. We soon fell into a conversation with several DEA folks, part of our U.S. help to the Bolivian government with their drug interdiction efforts.

At an embassy briefing our first work day in country, we had learned that not only were AID projects focused on identifying crops that might replace coca, U.S. funding for Bolivia's military or other needs was dependent on Bolivia's aggressiveness in stopping coca production and export of its finished product. These DEA people were there to both help and monitor the effort.

From Trinidad, our USDA team's next planned stop was Santa Cruz, further up the Amazon basin to the southeast. Our scheduled commercial flights, via LaPaz, would have taken us a full day and into the night. The DEA pilot was flying at eleven o'clock the next morning to Santa Cruz and we were welcome to ride along. His opening of the cargo door had been a sufficient reminder; we were still strapped in our seats as we descended into Santa Cruz early afternoon.

I had to wonder if the odds for DEA success would be high. Bolivia is the poorest country in the hemisphere, and coca is a native plant that flourishes in its climate. The refined product is small volume, so cheaply and easily transported, and pushers in developed countries are ready buyers. Most significant, campesinos (small farmers in Bolivian highlands, most with only a few hectares) appear to have no alternative crop that competes in market value.

On a Sunday drive through the country we stopped to check out one of several campesino's front yards that we had noted, the ground of each blanketed with coca leaves drying in the sun. Our host was rather proud of his crop, told us it was high quality and would bring a good price. Though interdiction is government policy, our host was not afraid, embarrassed, or reticent as he welcomed us to his yard.

Wheat and Soybeans, a Two-Crop Rotation

Santa Cruz and surrounding area reminded me, in many respects, of Garden City and southwestern Kansas. Economic vitality was evident. The airport terminal was new and attractive. The road into town was four-lane and lined with thriving businesses, including six farm equipment dealerships. Most of Santa Cruz' hundred thousand people lived in neat homes on tree-lined, paved streets. The major differences: a more dense population, the area has a longer growing season, allowing two crops a year, and high rainfall precludes need for irrigation.

We checked in at an inviting Spanish motif motel, one with attractive surroundings, trees and shrubs, green grass, and a pool in a central courtyard. We were soon in a taxi, headed to the offices of the local horticulture association, an organization of about five thousand small producers, most with one to two hectares of fruit or vegetable production.

What did the leaders of this group tell us they needed? A good research and extension system, credit to expand a local processing and packaging facility, plus insect and pest control so they could export their fruits and vegetables to the U.S. and Europe.

Only three hundred miles from population centers in Argentina and Brazil to the south and east, there was also market potential. The bottleneck for that was the road; it was not hard surfaced and traffic crossed the major river on the railroad bridge, alternating direction and when the train was not on the bridge.

There was also some wheat production in the Santa Cruz area, and interest in more. Low-quality timber, mostly small trees and shrubs, was being cleared. Leaders told us they needed a second crop, to rotate with the wheat, and soybeans appeared promising. A two-crop rotation should help break any wheat disease cycle, and soybeans would leave some nitrogen in the soil for the following wheat crop.

We were doing double duty in this visit to Santa Cruz, assessing both broader country needs under the Bush Andean Initiative and the appropriateness of using the food aid money for a wheat and soybean demonstration project. Considering the future benefit to Bolivia's economy, and that increased income creates more demand for animal products, it seemed clear to me that fostering a wheat-soybean rotation would be a worthy use of that money.

Dinner in Bolivia was social time, and in Santa Cruz it would be another late night. We gathered about eight at what appeared to be the city's premier dinner club, guests of Santa Cruz leadership, and were escorted into a VIP lounge for drinks and conversation. Dinner was served in an adjacent dining room at ten o'clock, and it was a several-course event. We finished dessert after midnight and coffee was yet to be served.

The best part of that long evening for me had been my dinner conversation with Bill McKinney, a former World Bank staff member, graduate of the University of Oklahoma, and a cattle rancher. He invited me to join him the next morning for a flight to his ranch.

Coca Leaves for the Ranch Hands

McKinney picked me up at 8:30 in his pick-up, drove to an older airport near town and his single engine Cessna 180. His son, Billy, a 1987 Oklahoma State graduate, soon arrived and I helped him and his father load fence wire; bags of flour, macaroni, spaghetti, potatoes, and onions; and a small bag of coca leaves into the plane. The cargo weight was carefully tallied, just below eight hundred eighty pounds.

Billy told me the coca leaves were legal, explaining that for centuries the native Indian population had chewed coca leaves as U.S. baseball players chew tobacco. It is considered their birthright. The alkaloid helps them endure cold or heat, as well as pain, so they can work longer days.

Bill and I took off into a strong north wind and followed an Amazon tributary flowing north toward the main river. I noted below the exposed red soil of the roads and paths across almost bare grazing land. It was still early spring and there was little grass growth. We were soon over heavy timber, but some timber had been recently cleared and darker soils exposed. Trees and brush had been scraped into windrows, leaving tilled strips about two hundred feet wide. We were then again over timber, this time dense hardwoods among patches of lower bushes, spring blossoms of what appeared to be redbuds, plus shrubs with large, bright yellow blossoms.

About 11:30 we set down on a grass strip at Bill's twenty-five-hundred-hectare ranch. A few pigs scattered away from a fence on the right. On the left was a brick-making yard, a short windmill, its wheel spinning in a strong wind, a metal-roofed, one story house, and several thatch-roof outbuildings.

Five men, perhaps seventeen to forty years of age, appeared at the side of the plane, followed by two women. One carried a pitcher of orangeade and two large metal cups, and had a three-year-old girl clutching her skirt. The men unloaded the cargo, gave Bill letters and packages to mail back in Santa Cruz, plus messages to workers at our next stop, Bill's "feedlot." They also put in the back of the plane a bag of cheese made from surplus milk at the ranch, that to be taken back to Santa Cruz.

Bags of flour, potatoes, and other provisions unloaded from McKinney's plane for his ranch hands and families.

We wasted no time, took off again, and circled the ranch. Bill pointed out stretches of open grazing land amid the forest, new calves and their mothers in one pasture, yearling steers and young replacement heifers in two others. We then turned east; it would be about two hundred kilometers to Bill's feedlot, adjacent to the Trinidad/Santa Cruz dirt "highway."

As our Cessna settled to a stop at the feedlot, four men appeared to greet us. I noted a fairly new brick, metal-roofed house (the bricks made on site), a stucco-covered cement house, and thatch-roofed outbuildings. The brick home, with the living/dining/kitchen area open to the north and with only a screen enclosure, was Bill's and Billy's "home away from home."

It was well after lunchtime and, unfortunately, Bill's crew could not be notified that we were coming. Their radio and those of neighbors had been confiscated either by the government or DEA a few days earlier because of evidence that area people were warning drug traffickers of DEA surveillance. The foreman's wife rushed over to the brick house and quickly rustled up a lunch of a hearty chicken soup, rice, Harvard beats, potatoes, and about a four-ounce steak.

Bill and I then walked the land while three of his hands lassoed and dressed out an eight hundred pound, two-year-old heifer. Bill showed me the feeding and working corrals and also a field of Taiwan forage, a sugar-cane type perennial forage propagated by cuttings and chopped every thirty days. We watched three of his workers unload by hand from a two-wheeled cart some of that coarsely chopped forage for the cattle.

This was not the type feedlot of western Kansas, Nebraska, or Iowa; it produced only lean, grass-finished beef. Nor was McKinney's ranch we had visited earlier comparable to those of the Nebraska Sand Hills (Ten Ways to Sit on a Horse in *From Troublesome Creek,* iUniverse, 2013).

By the time we returned to the ranch headquarters, the heifer had been hoisted to a tree branch by means of a light block and tackle, dressed, the carcass split and ready to be cut into quarters. The empty forage cart floor was covered with palm leaves, and the four quarters laid in and hauled to the plane. The meat was placed on a canvas in the back of the plane and tied in, and we headed to Santa Cruz.

Scenes at McKinney cattle feeding unit. Upper left, his feedlot cattle; lower left, harvested forage being gathered and hauled to the feedlot; and at the right, the young heifer being dressed. Some of that beef, and perhaps the bag of cheese from our first stop, would be barter for the wire and provisions we had hauled from Santa Cruz.

Our next visit was at Cochabamba, a major city in the arid foothills west of Santa Cruz. The AID mission economist, now part of our team, was a native of the area, had a family friend in the poultry business, and arranged for the two of us to spend an afternoon with him. That visit yielded a fascinating story, potential for the animal industry in a low-income country.

Bolivian Broilers; U.S. Genetics and Grain

In the mid 1950s, Bolivia's per capita poultry consumption had been near zero. Forty years later, at the time of our visit, it was nine pounds, and our host was producing and processing four of those pounds.

He told us he had dropped out of school, spent years hauling sand and gravel and, in the mid 1950s, a neighbor had suggested the broiler business as a sideline. He raised a hundred broilers, but was having difficulty selling them. In that low-income country, beans, tortillas, and other corn-based foods were the normal fare. Broiler meat was expensive and therefore, to many, an unknown.

He said his wife came up with an idea; she had prepared some chicken-based meals, photographed the dishes, and a few newspapers published the photos. They soon sold a hundred broilers, raised and sold another batch, and kept growing.

He was now hatching ninety thousand chicks per week in his Cochabamba hatchery, the eggs coming from his own farms. Newly-hatched chicks were moved in a converted school bus to any one of twenty eight small farms that he owned, plus a few other farms where chicks were fed for him on a contract basis. For their fifty-five-day growing and finishing period, the birds were fed a mixed ration from his mill.

Most of the grain in the ration was raised in Bolivia; the balance, including some soybean meal and all the feed additives, were imported, most from the U.S. Adjacent to the mill were four 40,000-bushel Butler bins (made in Columbus, NE) that held the corn and soybean meal. His breeding stock, both male and female, came from U.S. broiler genetic companies and a U.S. broiler consultant spent two or three days with the company every quarter. Two hundred fifty people were employed at the mill and nearby bird processing plant, a total of two thousand by his company.

Yes, agriculture is the starter engine for economic development in a low-income country. Our host, at least for broiler production, had paved the way for other Bolivians. This was also more evidence that Ambassador Gelbard's request regarding use of food aid money made sense.

Nine Million in Accounts Receivable

Back in Washington, I still had the problem that my friend in AID had warned me about, unpaid bills for several years' projects. By March, Miranda and his staff had found and presented to AID sufficient documentation on past contracts, work done overseas by OICD-arranged scientists and for which the bills had not been submitted to AID, or had been submitted and not paid. If Miranda's documentation to date prompted AID payment, it would reduce our agency's ledger in the federal book-keeping system from a deficit of about nine million dollars to about four million.

On board when I arrived, Miranda had already established the magnitude of the problem and was tracking down documentation. My arrival had only given him support, determination, and confidence that whatever he found would bring action and collection.

There was never any suggestion or clue that someone had walked away with any part of the nine million dollars. The work had been done. Scientists and practitioners had been hired and paid by OICD, or they had been borrowed from a university or other agencies and those entities reimbursed by OICD.

In some cases, the reason for non-payment may have been AID's bureaucracy, the number of sign-offs required, and staff turn-over, or that OICD had not followed up. In other cases, OICD had apparently failed to itemize costs, prepare a bill, and send it to AID.

Most significant, apparently no one in the agency, or elsewhere, had paid serious attention to accounts receivable. The federal financial apparatus, whether in USDA, Treasury, or perhaps even OMB (Office of Management and Budget), had just kept showing a larger and larger deficit in the OICD account. Apparently, no one had yelled "STOP. COLLECT THE MONEY from AID."

On second thought, perhaps someone had called attention. However, political appointees at all levels tend to focus first on serving their missions and clientele, as well as the wishes of Congress. To stop further expenditures in OICD would have meant stopping a program, either the very popular Cochran fellowship program, named for Mississippi's Senior Senator Thad Cochran, the Caribbean Initiative of President George H.W. Bush, or some of the quiet effort of State Department-financed and OICD-arranged senior scientists establishing relationships in Eastern European countries. To stop any of that work could expose to Congress and the public an embarrassing state of affairs.

The problem had accumulated over several administrations and, no matter where one might point a finger for blame, most of the "splatter," embarrassing publicity from stopping a program would be on a current administration.

I would be gone before the deficit got to zero, but movement toward that point would be well on the way.

The Files Will be on the Curb

A long-term contract for the placement and handling of AID-financed foreign students attending U.S. universities, most seeking graduate degrees, would expire on June 30, and not be renewed. Instead, AID had opened the bidding to several university consortiums, the administrative function to be at one of the campuses. Kansas State was part of one such consortium, mostly then Big 8 universities.

Under the contract OICD would receive the files for recommended applicants from AID missions, mesh each applicant's needs and qualifications with universities and curriculums, and then handle associated administrative functions. That would include visas, travel arrangements to the U.S., orientation in Washington, and travel to their destination university. It also included monitoring and follow-up with international student offices on the campuses where those students were enrolled.

Frank Pfender, who had taken over handling the contract after OICD's performance had been judged sub-par by AID, had briefed me on the issue one of my first days. Consortium bids had been received by AID early in the year, but AID had not yet identified the successful bidder. That needed to happen soon so the transition from our agency to that consortium could be planned and some applicants or university-accepted foreign students would not get stranded. Pfender kept me posted, and by the first of March the winning consortium was not yet identified. Nor by the first of April.

I was not surprised, based on my three years in AID's slow decision-making processes. I also knew that, though Pfender was in almost daily contact with his AID counterparts, his phoned entreaties to AID program staff would not speed the process. There had to be threats.

April 1, I told Pfender to remind AID that the contract called for continued payment to our agency after June 30 if there was still work to be done on the students' behalf. In early May, I instructed Pfender to tell his AID counterpart that if the new contractor was not identified and in place in time for orderly transition at the close of business June 30, all the contract and student files would be placed on the curb in front of our building.

The message came back, "You can't be serious."

My response: "Dead serious; test me."

AID soon identified the successful bidder and negotiated contract details. By mid-June the transition was underway and by June 30 there remained only a few details regarding individual students.

Thanksgiving Week in Rome

Among international organizations with which OICD represented the secretary, the Food and Agriculture Organization of the United Nations (FAO), headquartered in Rome, was the most encompassing in programs. FAO's annual meeting was always scheduled in late November and, consequently, I would spend Thanksgiving week in Rome.

OICD colleague Wayne Denney and I had arrived at the Rome airport from an overnight flight from Washington and were met by Gerald Monroe, State Department's ambassador to the several United Nations' food-related organizations headquartered in Rome, and Dawson Ahalt, USDA's attaché to those organizations. The State Department has seniority in all U.N. relationships.

The U.N. and its component organizations got their start at the end of WW II, and the U.S. had played a dominant role, both in organizing and hosting its headquarters in New York City. Rome had been selected for most of those U.N. units related to food and agriculture, such as FAO and The World Food Program (WFP).

Congress and successive administrations had not been pleased with many of the U.N. and component unit policies, or with some of the leaders chosen. The U.S. relationship with FAO Director General Eduardo Saouma, former Minister of Agriculture in Lebanon, had been especially tense. Further, State and USDA had not seen "eye to eye" with each other on many FAO issues.

To reduce the stress, Secretary of State George Schultz and Yeutter had chosen two new people to be the Washington links to FAO. Schultz chose a relatively new assistant secretary of State, Jane Becker, to replace

John Bolton as their senior delegate to this annual FAO meeting and I would be the senior USDA member and delegation head. We would also be new personalities for dealing with Saouma.

Becker and I chose to ignore previous agency disagreements. We met several times to mesh our priorities in FAO dealings, the top priority being to hold FAO's expenditure increases to inflation and to finance any new programs by closing other programs.

To give the reader a glimpse of what one experiences in a meeting with persons representing one hundred fifty eight countries discussing global programs those countries help finance (the U.S. being a major contributor), I provide some excerpts from a November 19-30, 1990, log and report.

"Ahalt delivered Denney and me to a small hotel, S. Anselmo, in a residential area on one of Rome's seven hills and a twelve-minute walk to FAO. After a shower and nap, Denney and I walked down the hill and across a busy thoroughfare for a salad of soft cheese and tomato wedges, plus a main course of spaghetti and meat sauce, white wine, and a bottle of water.

Later, about five o'clock, our delegation, including Becker, Ahalt, and several other Washington-based and Rome-based staff, gathered in Monroe's apartment to be briefed on the FAO meeting agenda, discuss positions held by other countries, and enjoy a buffet. Monroe's apartment was across the street from the left side of Rome's famous Spanish Steps, in Rome's historic and higher-priced shopping area.

Monday, November 19. Across the hotel courtyard at eight to te' latte (a pot of hot tea and pitcher of hot milk), hard roll, croissant, butter, cherry preserves and peach marmalade, in a small breakfast room off the lobby. We joined FAO delegates from Sweden, France, and Germany, found a copy of the English language Herald Tribune.

We walked down winding streets, through a gasoline station and past a grocery, several bars, a bank, and furniture store, to FAO headquarters. FAO occupies a structure built by Mussolini in the 1930s for Italy's Colonial Department, which managed the Italian colonies in Africa. It is a few blocks south of the Coliseum and is flanked by large Roman baths and other ancient structures.

I picked up my name tag, signed a credentials card certifying that I was the U.S. delegation head, checked out a key to a small locker and met delegates from China, Philippines, United Kingdom, Canada,

South Korea, Malaysia, and Colombia. I then found our United States delegate sign at the front table, left, in the large Council Room. Venezuela's chair was on my right. I was told that for each meeting, a country name is drawn for the front left chair and the arrangement is alphabetical from that point. I wondered if the drawing was truly by chance; perhaps Souma also wants a better relationship with the U.S.

The opening session, chaired by Belgium's delegate, was filled with formalities of electing vice-chairs, testimonials to deceased country delegates, and a general report of FAO activities by Saouma.

Becker, Monroe, Ahalt, and I had arranged a meeting at three o'clock with Soauma, and he had four of his staff present. Though we intended an hour meeting, the purpose to clarify both concerns and opportunities for a good working relationship, it would last nearly two hours. I focused on zero FAO program growth, budget increases limited to inflation and unavoidable adjustments, such as in salaries or transportation. There were many clarifications and play-backs, to insure communication among people of different cultures and orientations, and even between our two executive departments, State and USDA. The meeting ended with good understanding, no animosity, and a mutually-held positive attitude.

Back to our hotel about six o'clock, a short rest, and Denney and I then took a long walk. We ambled through a residential area and across a park, picked up some cold pizza to eat as we walked. In time, we doubled back for an ice cream cone on our way to the hotel and were in bed by nine.

Tuesday, November 20. We scheduled delegation meetings every morning at eight o'clock, most at Ahalt's apartment, between our hotel and FAO. This let us brief each other on issues we had encountered, propose positions, decide which U.S. delegation person would lead for each topic meeting, and who else would attend. Because of past State/USDA stresses, we involved personnel of both agencies wherever possible. We would spend much of the day huddling with other delegations to find common ground on major issues.

Wednesday, November 21. This morning's general session was devoted to FAO's long-term strategy, plans for a 1992 international conference on nutrition, global work related to the environment and sustainable agriculture, and a study on the need for technical assistance to the Palestinian people in territories occupied by Israel, the West Bank, and Gaza Strip.

So it went for two weeks, with committee meetings, general sessions, and luncheons with mutual-interest delegations at restaurants, embassies, or at permanent delegate residences. I enjoyed Sunday walks through the residential and historic areas, one described later, and two evenings checking out Christmas offerings in elegant shops just below the Spanish Steps.

Protocol, Politics, and Pick-Pockets

As in business or scientific conferences within the U.S., what goes on in the hallway or at related social events is often more interesting and informative than what goes on in the formal sessions. Soauma hosted a private luncheon for the U.S. delegation after the first day's opening session and included his five assistant director-generals, (one a former USDA staff) and eight other upper level FAO staff, all U.S. citizens. We were in the top floor Moroccan Room, with pink and white mosaic walls and ceilings plus matching furniture and table service, all a gift from the King of Morocco. The menu: formaggio (cheese) soufflé, lamb, asparagus, and, for dessert, meringue gelato (meringue and ice cream). Now I *know* that Soauma wants to improve relationships with the U.S.

The second day included a luncheon for the heads of all major delegations, also hosted by Soauma in the Moroccan room. I walked up with John McGowan, head of the Canadian delegation and whose position in the Canadian Ministry of Agriculture parallels mine. We have much in common; early in his career he had been responsible in Canada for meat inspection and animal and plant health regulations.

Seating is important and is noticed. There were six round tables for eight. At Soauma's table (in this case, for nine) were the Council chair and the Lesotho delegate, seated to Soauma's right and left. I assumed the Lesotho delegate was placed there as a symbol of free, black, southern African countries. Next, to the right and left, were the Canadian delegate and me, delegation heads from Ethiopia and Egypt, then Iran and China. The Egyptian and Iranian delegates had been named vice-chairs of the annual meeting.

Japan, a major donor, was not at the table. There had to be a reason, but I knew not what. Ethiopia's presence and seating apparently acknowledges its many problems with FAO and other groups in carrying out food aid and development programs in their civil war circumstance.

I appreciated my visit with the Ethiopian delegate regarding the food aid needs I had observed in his country three years earlier, the International Livestock Research Station near Addis Ababa, and the traditional Ethiopian meal I had experienced.

After dessert, Soauma briefed the group on the FAO support staff strike, which had been evident. When we had arrived Monday morning, some FAO staff were milling around the building entrance and handing out a list of grievances. Their grievances included failure of FAO to provide a sixteen per cent pay increase, that per cent agreed to by an international civil service commission for all international groups located in Rome, as well as the per cent in Rome's private sector. By our second day, the protest group had grown to about twelve hundred and by the third, about fifteen hundred.

Through the first day's activities, there was evident concern among attendees that a PLO (Palestine Liberation Organization, not an FAO member) delegation would arrive, ask to be seated, protest Israel's treatment of the Arabs in occupied territory, and trigger emotional debate. It turned out that a PLO delegation did arrive and was given a place in the observation section. In short order, an obviously pre-arranged action was taken for FAO to proceed according to a resolution of a year earlier, Israel's delegate rose to remind all that it is a sovereign state responsible for all residents in its territory, and a PLO representative made a short statement of appreciation for the Council's concern for Palestinian people. All parties had been accommodated.

A major portion of any inter-governmental conference is drafting the meeting's final report, what is said about what was agreed to, and membership on the drafting committee is prized. In FAO, thirteen members of the drafting committee were chosen by region, the U.S. and Canada comprised one region and the U.S. had usually served. However, a Canada delegate had earlier called Denney to say Canada would like to serve this time, to give their new Rome representative the experience. Our USDA delegation was willing, even delighted; it is a tedious and exhaustive task. The committee would meet every evening beginning that evening, all day Saturday, perhaps Sunday, and may work until midnight through the second week. On every component, the degree of emphasis, choice of words, or relative strength of consensus reached would be debated, in several languages.

Several Department of State staff protested, felt Canada would not represent strongly enough some of our U.S. positions, and that a U.S. person ought to be the member. However, the U.S. and Canada were close on every issue and Canada's delegation would check with us on drafts of sections where we have strong feelings.

In the end, Canada did a fantastic job, perhaps got wording in the final report that a U.S. person might have had difficulty achieving. The Canadian delegate regularly gave us drafts for review. And, at the end, their lead participant was exhausted."

Time in Rome would not be complete without an encounter with pick pockets, including juveniles. Denney had spent much time in Rome and had warned me. On a Sunday afternoon, he and I had walked to a nearby business district and were returning to our hotel, each with a small bag of oranges or apples. We met a group of about a dozen eight- to ten-year-old "gypsie" children, and they began to surround us, some to detract and others to grab a billfold or watch.

I jumped out of their path, faced them, and raised my right arm ready to strike. They being children was of no consequence. Though they might not understand English, my words and set jaw conveyed, "Come on; make my day!" They backed off and departed.

Several months later, little more than a year after I had joined USDA, Yeutter and Crowder asked that I also take on a second job, heading USDA's Foreign Agricultural Service (FAS).

Chapter VI

An Agency Focused on Exports

"Several years before my time, a national tobacco association, to which FAS had provided funds to help promote tobacco exports, had used some of those funds to install a cigarette manufacturing line in Turkey. Now the association was seeking authorization to spend more FAS market promotion funds to install a second line in Turkey, and several letters from members of Congress urged approval. However, the request appeared to be in conflict with existing law."

The Foreign Agricultural Service, (FAS) an agency of about seven hundred staff, is known primarily for its agricultural attaches and export promotion staff stationed around the world. However, it also helps the U.S. Trade Representative's Office negotiate trade agreements with other countries, handles the logistics and financing of food aid, and can guarantee loans that banks make to importers of U.S. agricultural commodities and products.

Both FAS and OICD were international in their operations and the department was planning to combine the two into a single agency, so I could also start the process of merging some agency functions.

Two Offices and Two Staffs

The two agencies were both in USDA's South Building, the two administrators' offices on different floors and, fortunately, only about five minutes apart. However, each had different foci and cultures. Most of the OICD work and, therefore, staff interest, was focused on long-term development in target countries; most of the FAS staff effort was to facilitate exports of U.S. agricultural commodities.

FAS had two staff categories, Civil Service and Foreign Service, the latter requiring a year or more of State Department training on representing U.S. interests abroad. Whether Civil Service or Foreign Service, each person was a specialist in their discipline, such as dairy, pork, economics, trade policy, or import/export processes, and most had advanced degrees and dealt with U.S. commodity groups and exporters. Though a number of OICD staff had advanced degrees in a discipline, their work was largely contract management and program coordination and their domestic linkages were to other agencies. These differences were reflected in all aspects of agency operation and, especially, in staff evaluation and promotions.

I was fortunate in having highly capable and supportive people in both agencies. Four of the key FAS staff, Associate Administrator Steve Censky and Assistant Administrators Mattie Sharpless, Richard Schroeter, and Mary Chambliss would later sit in the administrator's chair. Assistant Administrator Chris Goldthwait, Sharpless, and another of my FAS foreign service officers, Allen Mustard, would be appointed ambassadors. Sales Manager Paul Dickerson, who also carried the associate administrator title and reported subsidized or loan guaranteed export sales proposals each morning to the under secretary, was one of the finest gentlemen with whom I have had the privilege of working. With my background largely in university and development work, I sorely needed these persons' experience and wisdom.

Here were some major issues at my arrival in FAS:

1. A congressional request for a comprehensive agricultural export strategy. Agency staff would work diligently on the strategy, but with a Democratic majority in Congress, the Republican administration was reticent to publish a completed product. As long as redrafting continued, and it did, the Democratic majority would have no document to criticize.
2. Language proficiency prior to attaché posting in a new country. The language proficiency requirement had been relaxed over time and studying the language after arrival in the country had become acceptable. I felt strongly that attaches should to be able to communicate in the host country language on their arrival.
3. In contrast to OICD, the volume of Congressional and clientele correspondence was awesome; one issue could trigger a dozen

letters. To both speed and make more efficient the response process, we would establish a correspondence office, with assigned specialists, specific protocols, and time targets.

4. Electronic communication with sister agencies, especially the Agricultural Stabilization and Conservation Service (ASCS), at this writing called the Farm Service Agency (FSA), and Economic Research Service (ERS).

I had been in the FAS job only a few days when I received a staff recommendation on what would be a politically sensitive issue.

A Second Cigarette Line in Turkey

Several years before my time, a national tobacco association, to which FAS had provided funds to help promote tobacco exports, had used some of those funds to install a cigarette manufacturing line in Turkey. It is ironic that Turkish tobacco had for centuries been considered one of the world's premier tobaccos, but in recent years Turkey had become a major importer of U.S. tobacco. Tobacco prices in the U.S. had dropped because of our anti-smoking movement, and that had made Turkey a potential market.

Now the association was seeking authorization to spend more FAS market promotion funds to install a second line in Turkey, and several letters from members of Congress urged approval. However, the request appeared to be in conflict with existing law. Market Promotion legislation indicated that where installations are deemed necessary to stimulate foreign purchases of commodities, they should be only "models." That one line had resulted in more U.S. tobacco imports by Turkey, and the tobacco association believed a second line would prompt more imports. But, the law's intent seemed clear.

The greater the political implication, the higher in the agency an issue goes for a decision. In this case, it would need to go at least to the under secretary. He might consult with the secretary, but the under secretary would likely "take the heat" if there were political repercussions. As a politically appointed administrator, I would share some of the heat, and a later story will confirm, but my Civil Service or Foreign Service staff would not.

My Commodity Division staff had drafted a rejection to the request and Assistant Administrator Mackie had brought it to me. He knew the political implications and asked, "Do you feel comfortable taking this across the street to the under secretary?" It looked solid to me and I respected the implied "one model" limitation.

Under Secretary Crowder knew it was coming and, when I handed it to him, said he wanted to study it a while. In the meantime, a full department response to interested members of Congress would be drafted, explaining why the request was to be denied.

Several days later, in our daily 7:30 a.m. staff meeting, Crowder handed back the tobacco draft, "Have your staff take another look at this." The unstated message, "Better find a way to justify this second line, perhaps it could be a different model. We may not want to take on the tobacco producers and their senators on this one."

In the end, following an appeal to Secretary Yeutter by Turkey's ambassador to the United States, using those promotion funds for a second cigarette line in Turkey was approved.

This issue would confront me a year later in two Senate hearings and neither would be pleasant.

Computers That Can't Communicate

When two key people fail to communicate, there is a problem. When the computer systems for two agencies that must work together can not communicate, the problem is serious. When neither the two systems nor the people in charge of each can communicate, it is time to solve the problem. That was the task my fellow administrator, Keith Bjerke of ASCS (Agricultural Stabilization and Conservation Service, now re-named Farm Service Agency), and I faced.

The Commodity Credit Corporation (CCC), functioning as a unit of Bjerke's agency, took title to and held in warehouses and storage caves—some of the latter in the Kansas City area— surplus grains, cheese, and other commodities. CCC purchased volumes of those agricultural commodities to "take them off the market," to help stabilize market prices. The commodities would be available for domestic food programs or, to a greater extent, our several foreign food aid programs.

My FAS staff received food aid requests from needy countries via AID and, once a request was approved by an inter-agency committee, worked with CCC staff to release the product from storage, then arranged shipment to the target country.

Data on volume, age, value, and location of these commodities should be accessible to personnel in both agencies. Unfortunately, as electronic data had developed, each agency had acquired different equipment and operating systems (software). Perhaps hundreds of thousands of dollars had been paid to vendors and consultants by each agency, and each agency had a store of data in their system. Each agency staff had familiarity and comfort with their system, but neither system could query the other for needed data.

There was also frustration in the USDA structure above. Bjerke and I both reported to the secretary, first Clayton Yeutter and then Ed Madigan, through Under Secretary Crowder. Neither Crowder nor his immediate staff could easily retrieve full and coordinated data. Bjerke and I had to solve the problem.

Bjerke's IT (information technology) leader was a well-trained young woman, a Ph.D. with corporate experience and, it is fair to add, confident in her opinions. My leader, responsible for agency administration, had no specific training in information technology. However, he was understandably loyal to his IT unit as well as to vendor judgments he had made or approved.

Though neither Bjerke nor I were IT-trained, we were fortunate in being decade-long friends through our membership in the Farm Foundation Agricultural Roundtable. Beyond a week-long IBM workshop at San Jose twenty years earlier, my IT exposure had been reading print-outs of computer-generated university data, encouraging and funding university staff for computer use, and a one-day short course while in AID on how to operate a PC. I had listened to operating systems being debated, our agency's VAX system vs. the system in ASCS, or MSDOS vs. FORTRAN vs. COBAL, but I was in no position to discuss the merits of any system or language.

We had both made repeated efforts with our respective groups to negotiate and compromise on a single operating system and to tell us what the conversion cost would be, but neither side would give an inch. Eventually we decided to get the two groups together in one room, invite open discussion, and listen. Bjerke and I would then jointly make a decision on a single system.

I do not know how Bjerke conditioned his staff for the meeting. In my agency, my leader gave me the opportunity at a weekly staff briefing that included about twenty unit heads, most of them users of computer data. When it came his turn to share current issues regarding his sector, he let loose a barrage of complaints and accusations regarding Bjerke's IT leader. It was over the top and out of line.

One of my principles of administration had always been that any admonishment of staff should be in their office or mine, not before their colleagues. But I could not let his barrage stand, further galvanize a negative attitude in my staff toward a sister agency and its personnel. I violated my principle, rather quickly and firmly.

Back in my office minutes later, I wondered if I had been too abrupt. In stepped Mattie Sharpless, my assistant administrator for the attaché service and one of those solid, common sense colleagues one appreciates and respects. Her comment: "Thanks, we needed those blunt words."

Any decision by Bjerke and me, however, would not be the end of the story. It had become clear that other agencies also had to be involved. However, Bjerke's staff and my staff knew there was no longer a fence around their respective systems.

I find in my files an October 30, 1991, letter to all FAS Staff, with copies to Bjerke, Crowder, and the director of USDA's Office of Information Resources Management, outlining nine steps that would be taken within FAS, presumably meshed with other agencies. Among them were replacing the agency's VAX system with a new client-based server system, installing PCs at every work station, and establishing a "local area network" within the fiscal year.

After the Wall Came Down

As electronic communication had developed in the late 1970s and 1980s, people in the Soviet Socialist Republics, also referred to as the Eastern Block of countries, became aware of the good life fostered by the West's free enterprise and resistance to the Soviet socialist system blossomed.

Separated by "The Berlin Wall" since the mid 1960s, the city of Berlin and the country of Germany were to be re-unified. In November of 1989, the East German government allowed citizens of East Berlin to both visit and host their relatives from the other side of the Wall. Soon The Wall was scaled by the masses and chipped to rubble. That same year, free elections were allowed in Poland.

The World Bank, private voluntary organizations, universities, and U.S. federal agencies all became involved in helping many Eastern Block countries adapt to the market economy, personal freedoms, incentives, and the rewards that can result. Though humans are a creative and competitive species, after forty to seventy years of central government ownership and/or control, the change to a creative and competitive economic system would not be easy. With centrally-dictated production quotas, prices, and product "allocations," few citizens had carried decision-making or management responsibilities.

A less-known part of that 1970s and 1980s communication had been between scientists on opposite sides of the "iron curtain," considerable financed by AID or the State Department and handled by the research division of OICD. By the time I added USDA's Foreign Agricultural Service to my OICD role in early 1991, FAS and other USDA agencies had also been asked by Congress and the administration to provide direct help.

Secretary Yeutter had gone to Poland two years earlier to discuss with his Polish counterpart, their Agriculture minister, how USDA could be of most help in moving Poland's agriculture to the free market system. The Ministry's first priority had been to send young, mid-career people from Polish agribusiness to the U.S. for short term training and experience. Next was forming joint U.S./Polish working groups to consider strategies for research, extension, infrastructure, and marketing. Retired Kansas State Extension Director Fred Sobering and two recently-retired university experiment station directors were soon on their way to Poland, and so was a team from USDA's Economic Research Service.

Our team, charged with reviewing work to date and also to be part of a "joint working group" with Polish counterparts, included Crowder, Assistant Secretary for Economics Bruce Gardner, Extension administrator Myron Johnsrud, FAS foreign service officer Guy Haviland, in-country FAS agricultural attaché Weyland Beegly (FAS had established a Warsaw office even before Yeutter's visit) and his assistant, Judy Phillips.

A special Congressional appropriation, "Support to Eastern European Democracies," had been made to USAID. Also, a portion had been allocated to USDA and some to VOCA (Volunteers for Overseas Cooperation in Agriculture) for a farmer-to-farmer program. Most of the USDA money was to be spent in Poland, some for Bulgaria, and the rest held back for other countries. My first visit was to Poland as part of the USDA leadership team.

A map of Eastern Europe, with current countries outlined and showing major locations within Poland, Belarus, Ukraine, Bulgaria, Hungary, and what is now Serbia, then a part of Yugoslavia.

Chopin and Old Warsaw

It was early on a Saturday afternoon, April of 1991, when we arrived in Warsaw, after an overnight flight to Frankfurt and from there by Polish airline. Within thirty minutes of checking into Warsaw's downtown Marriott Hotel, our Polish hosts had our team back in the van for a thirty kilometer drive west to Chopin's birthplace.

Our official work would begin Monday. In the meantime, our hosts wanted us to see elements of Poland's history and culture. Chopin's birthplace, a revered piece of Polish history, was a six-room cottage on three acres in a village of a half-dozen homes and one shop. Chopin's father was French, and a tutor to the children of the couple who had owned this former country estate. The manor house and other buildings were long gone; the cottage remained. The grounds were a virtual arboretum/garden, shrub and tree buds emerging, and a few ponds and streams, all to be enjoyed with strains of Chopin in the background. The-six room cottage contained just enough of Chopin's life, including the hand-written record of a classic he had produced at age seven.

The landscape to and from Chopin's birthplace was flat, all land not covered by homes was in orchards, just coming into spring bloom, or being tilled for vegetables and annual flowers. The soil appeared sandy; the sand and clean tillage suggested it could blow if spring winds were strong. There were a few tall trees and they, plus the small orchards, would make wind erosion less likely and less serious than on the open plains of Kansas or Oklahoma.

There was hardly time for a shower at the Marriott after the Chopin visit and before departing for "Old Warsaw," what had been the original walled city. It had been totally reduced to rubble by the German army when it was being forced out by Stalin's advancing forces in 1939 or 1940. Hitler had been incensed by the prolonged Polish resistance in Warsaw and was quoted, "Warsaw will never again exist."

Old Warsaw had been totally rebuilt after the war, the work based on photos and drawings of the original structures. Except for the churches, the new buildings may have different uses, such as museums, antique shops, and restaurants, but the market square and town pump were there and one can imagine former occupancy.

Enroute to a basement-level, evidently popular pizzeria, we detoured to a terrace view of the Vistula River. It was still full daylight at almost eight o'clock. Warsaw is at the same latitude as Edmonton, Alberta, and I was reminded of spring evenings in Brookings, South Dakota.

The next day, Sunday, our Washington group and Warsaw-based FAS staff, the latter including two Polish citizens, departed by van for a three-hour, one hundred eighty kilometer ride on two-lane blacktop roads to a famous horse-breeding farm near the Belarus border. Belarus was then still part of the Soviet Union.

A full breakfast buffet, including rolls, cheeses, cold meats, cucumbers, yogurt, fruits, juices, sausage, ham, bacon, pancakes, plus a chef that would make waffles or an omelet to order, had prepared us for a long day. That was fortunate; box lunches our FAS staff had ordered were not ready at our 8:30 departure time, so we left without them.

The soil to the east of Warsaw appeared less productive; less was tilled and more was devoted to cereals and pasture or hay. There was more clay in the soil and it appeared less well-drained. Likely because the soils were acidic, we saw no legumes. We noted a few scattered black and white, dual-purpose Friesian cows, beefier than Holsteins. Local staff told us that seventy per cent of the cows in Poland were in herds of one to three. Sheep were the predominant livestock.

On a Sunday morning drive through rural Poland east of Warsaw, we stopped to converse with farmers in the process of planting potatoes.

We saw a few orchards, plus scattered and increasing numbers of timber plots, both deciduous and white pine. In this northern latitude and short growing season, it is likely forty years to pine harvest, rather than the twenty in the U.S. Consequently, the pine is harder and, when finished, more attractive. We would later see the latter in a well-furnished deputy minister's office.

Poland is about ninety eight per cent Catholic, and many were on their way to church, by foot, car, or bus. Though we did not see many churches, most we did see in open rural areas were large, modernistic, and attractive.

Poland has a long history of breeding high quality horses and the farm we visited had provided many to the U.S., reportedly for prices up to several million dollars. The farm had been in operation since 1837, and built in part on Arabian stock from the African desert. All animals had been removed by the Soviets during their occupation and had not been returned. The manager, who had come in 1937 to serve the private owners, had remained during the war and later under "state" ownership. He had tracked down some of the earlier animals or their offspring and had gradually rebuilt a quality herd.

We gathered on the show field to look at eight breeding stallions, each of which had had two or three successful racing seasons, and a dozen mares, both standing and moving. Never had I seen such consistent high quality, ideal structure, and clean, easy movement.

A visit with the farm's veterinarian told me about that profession in Poland. He was a native of Warsaw and graduate of its veterinary school, one of four veterinary schools in the country. Before and during veterinary school, he had spent summers at the stable.

Each of Poland's forty nine vovoidships (provinces) formerly had twenty to thirty veterinarians, largely to administer brucellosis, leptospirosis, and tuberculosis control programs, with positive-testing animals destroyed and the owners reimbursed by the government. With the tight economy following break-up of the Soviet Union and personnel cutbacks in the bureaucracy, numbers of veterinarians were now down to two or three per vovoidship. A few of the veterinarians had chosen to start their own private practice, a new concept in Poland, and were not having an easy go.

Conversation continued over coffee and sweet cakes in the farm headquarters conference room. By then, it was well after noon and we would head back to Warsaw by a southern detour to see more of the country.

By mid-afternoon we began to miss those box lunches and were still three hours from Warsaw. McDonald's and Burger King had not yet arrived in Poland, and we found no restaurants open in the villages we passed through. Eventually, Phillips and I stepped into a state-owned shop, one of few that were open, to buy some bread and sausage to go with soda and beer our staff had placed in an ice chest in the rear of the van. The manager, a pleasant woman in her fifties, convinced us in Polish that she could have breaded pork steak, potatoes, and mild sauerkraut for each of us in ten minutes. She did that, and being "food of the region," the meal was far more enjoyable than any box lunch or McDonald's.

We continued back to Warsaw from the southeast, first through timber and grass country, then the last fifty kilometers, traveling northwest down the Vistula river valley, past orchards, some poultry production units, and more vegetable farms.

We had made one other stop during the morning, a state broiler unit, surprisingly empty. The manager was most distressed; he said that chicks cost him twenty cents and feed eighty cents per bird, both provided by the state-owned hatchery and feed mill, but the state-owned processor paid him only eighty four cents for the finished broiler at eight weeks. He was obliged to produce one batch per year and did that, but no more. It was a typical example of government control, with no competition and with each state-owned unit having both a monopoly and a quota.

Back at our hotel Sunday evening we gathered to discuss our Monday tasks, work with our Polish counterparts. For sustenance, we needed only a few potato chips and a coke. Then, it was eight hours of sleep.

Telephones and Pork Bellies

My task on Monday was to co-chair, with an assistant to Poland's minister of agriculture, a working group on infrastructure. Infrastructure, in this case, included sewage systems, electricity, and natural gas, most in "cooperative" ownership and distribution structures.

I would learn that only twenty seven per cent of Poland's rural homes, most in small villages, had a piped-in water supply and that the most recent record showed but 2.4 telephones per hundred rural residents. That was likely near the ratio in Iowa State's Pammel Court during my graduate school days, those phones in strategically-placed phone booths.

Poland's government had made infrastructure high priority, and both the U.S., under Public Law 480 (food aid), and the European

Community had provided food to Poland, that food to be sold to help finance that infrastructure. For example, U.S. pork bellies sent in 1989 had helped finance phone installations to about forty seven hundred rural homes. That would be a ten per cent increase in available phone service. The U.S. had also sent twenty million dollars worth of corn, the sale of which had helped finance some rural water systems.

At issue in our working group was whether USDA and our Polish Ministry counterparts had the authority to decide if future corn sales could finance more of these projects and, if so, which projects. The initial U.S./Poland agreement regarding food aid had not specified which unit in either government would decide the uses of the Polish currency earned. In Washington, AID and USDA staff had agreed on likely uses, based on what they knew as the needs. However, in Poland, three officials, the ministers of agriculture and finance and the coordinator of foreign aid, each believed his or her unit had the Polish responsibility. And each was pushing their favorite use. Also, a member of Poland's parliament, a strong-willed and politically powerful woman, was lobbying each official for a major share of the proceeds to go to the water and sewer projects. The net result was that much of the money, Polish Zlotys, was simply setting idle and drawing interest.

There was another problem. Just before departing Washington, we had learned the U.S. ambassador in Poland had withheld approval of USDA sending two more long-term extension advisers. Both had been hired for two-year assignments and had arranged leave-without-pay with their universities. The problem was that eight other U.S. executive departments, from Commerce to Interior, were sending advisory staff to Poland, and the ambassador felt his staff could not handle all the paper work, housing, health care arrangements, and other support for those two advisers and their families.

Lunch was across the street in a new Italian-owned and Polish-operated pizzeria, a brightly decorated, efficient contrast to the drab and dusty state-run shops in adjacent buildings. Poland entrepreneurs were on the move, changing the way things were done.

Natural gas was on the afternoon agenda and I would learn that so many gas lines crossed southern Poland that many villages were within ten kilometers of a gas line. Residents were seeking money to link those lines to the villages, having formed "social societies" to seek the funds and to plan both gas distribution and phone connections. The phone system was a government corporation called PPTT and, though the local society would provide the labor to build lines, the finished line would belong to the corporation; only the phone instrument would belong to the resident. Polish members of our working group, believing that a private entity would be more responsive to customers than the government corporation, were seeking advice on how they might privatize PPTT.

On return to Washington, an early priority for me would be to seek expertise in two USDA agencies, Rural Electrification Administration and Agricultural Cooperation Administration, as well as in the National Cooperative Telephone Association.

Poland's cooperatives were far different from U.S. member-owned cooperatives. Poland's cooperatives may have started out the same, but during the forty five years of communist domination, each had become central-government run. Member-owners had lost any semblance of leadership privilege and responsibility.

Polish citizens needed to regain that leadership privilege and responsibility, by law, by training, and by building motivation and confidence. Perhaps our discussions in this working group would help the process.

Tuesday evening was a U.S. embassy reception for official Washington visitors, as well as for U.S. private sector people who might be in Warsaw seeking trade or investment opportunity. Several key Polish legislators, ministry officials, and emerging Polish entrepreneurs were also guests. A highlight for me was to see and visit with a trade/investment group from South Dakota, headed by then Governor George Mickelson, who I had known well as an attorney in Brookings, South Dakota.

Because that "Support to Eastern European Countries" appropriation had named Bulgaria to be one of the recipients, and because my OICD agency was already involved with scientist exchanges and a fellowship program for young persons in that county, FAS Foreign Service Officer Guy Haviland and I boarded an early morning plane the next day, bound for Sofia, Bulgaria, but with a mid-day stop for several hours in Budapest, Hungary. Haviland was the type of person a new administrator needs, a long-time staff member who knows the agency and will "tell it like it is." He had no motive except to do his job and be available to help me learn and do mine.

In the next two days we would see more consequences of the Soviet system, and also cultural difference in peoples' responses to their new freedom.

The FAS budget did not allow an agricultural attaché in every country so, for Hungary and Bulgaria, the agency had hired a local person to gather agriculturally-related data and otherwise be available to represent U.S. agricultural interests, that person under the supervision of an attaché in a nearby country, such as Poland or Yugoslavia. We had been met at the Budapest airport by our young Hungarian staff member and we rode by taxi to his office. It was in the lower level of a late 1800s mansion near the far end of Andrassy Boulevard, a wide street that leads from the Danube River and downtown Buda to the site of Hungary's Millennial Exhibition 1896, billed then as a World's Fair. Our purpose was largely for us to meet the young man and understand his working situation, and for him to have a personal link to the USDA agency of which he was a part.

To return to downtown Buda, we rode the initial line of the world's second oldest subway system (after London's), built for that 1896 Millennial Exhibition. The subway car seemed no more than four feet wide and we traveled its two or three kilometers and in a tunnel that was only a couple inches wider than the car. In its adaptation to free enterprise and its material and social rewards, Budapest appeared well ahead of Warsaw. We were then off to Sofia, Bulgaria.

The streets and shops of Budapest in 1991. The shops were well stock with everything from clothing to fine jewelry, and busy with well dressed customers, little different from what I had seen in Rome in November.

What would I do with Two Hectares?

FAS work in Sofia was handled as in Budapest, a local person under the supervision of our Yugoslavia FAS assistant attaché, who had driven from Belgrade to meet us. After a three block walk with both men from our hotel past open shops, the four of us dined with several of Bulgaria's agriculture ministry officials. Our discussion focused on the assistance needs these officials saw and some options for USDA's help.

Of necessity, it included the living and working accommodations for personnel that USDA might send for short-term assignments.

Our second task in Sofia was to help interview about a half-dozen young men and women—faculty, graduate students, or ministry staff—who had applied for a Cochran fellowship to work and study in the United States.

Haviland and I were to fly back to Washington from Belgrade Saturday morning, riding to Belgrade with our Hungary attaché. A young woman, perhaps the most impressive of the several we had interviewed, had convinced our attaché that she should accompany us part of the way. She would show us circumstances of agriculture, land ownership, and other features in the small Bulgarian town and area of her youth. We would learn more of what is really going on in the country.

As we traveled, we learned that Bulgaria had retained sufficient land ownership records from the pre-Soviet time so that the original, small family parcels could be reclaimed by the surviving owners or their heirs. However, many heirs or surviving owners had refused to accept ownership. Why? "What would I do with one or two hectares?" "I don't want the responsibility." "I prefer a job with a salary and pension." "I have no money to buy seed or equipment." And, there were other reasons. For some of these people, the idea of ownership, management responsibility, risk taking, and the competitive spirit for profit, had disappeared. They appeared to feel, "Let the government make the decisions."

Credit for farms and for processing businesses was difficult to come by. There was also no private farm supply infrastructure. All agriculture had been in collective and state farms and government corporations, with inputs allocated, production quotas assigned, and prices set by officials.

We had met several young men the night before, however, who saw opportunity in the private sector, who were seeking to acquire or build processing businesses or farm operations, one having assembled considerable land. There was obvious opportunity.

Our young guide had called ahead, arranged for her mother to have an early afternoon meal prepared for us, the type of generous hospitality we would later encounter in Belarus and Georgia. On arrival at her home, we learned her mother had broken her leg that morning, part-way through preparations for the dinner, and was upstairs in bed. Though we begged our leave, our young hostess would not hear of it. While my colleagues and I admired the family vegetable and flower gardens, this young woman and a helpful neighbor completed the full meal preparation, including pork steak. They did this even though encumbered by an electricity outage, not uncommon in the country at that time.

Inside the entry gate of an agricultural cooperative in a small town west of Sofia, Bulgaria. The woman on the left and the man second from the right were cooperative staff. In the center is the Cochran fellowship applicant, Adelina Petrova. USDA's Assistant Secretary Bruce Gardner is on her left, and Assistant Agricultural Attache' Gregg Young from Belgrade on her right. At the far right is Guy Haviland, Washington-based foreign service officer.

Our young hostess then insisted that, since her home village was off on a country road kilometers from the Sofia-to-Belgrade highway, she should lead us by the necessarily circuitous route through farm country to that highway. On reaching the highway, we dropped her at a train station; she would take the train home and care for her mother before returning, somehow, to Sofia. It was more of that generous hospitality.

The evening drive to Belgrade was through beautiful farm country, fields lush with clover and alfalfa, young cereals, tillage and corn planting underway, orchards in blossom, and quaint villages with rows of white stucco or brick home with red tile roofs, each surrounded by deciduous trees with newly-emerged light green leaves.

We would overnight in a Belgrade hotel for a flight to D.C. Saturday morning.

Musical Chairs in the Foreign Service

In universities, the annual consideration of promotions and granting of tenure can be an emotional and difficult time for those involved. That emotion and difficulty are matched in the geographic reassignment of Foreign Service Staff in both AID and USDA's FAS.

It was early June and the week's major task was reassignment of those FAS foreign service officers who were completing three years in their current location, either in Washington or in a foreign post. Functioning as a committee, my assistant administrators and I would work to mesh the skills and desires of each person to the late summer openings. U.S. interests are paramount, of course, but the location and the job can have a large impact on the comfort and safety of the family as well as on an officer's future career.

Most foreign posts are limited to Foreign Service officers, but the officers are rotated back to Washington for three-year periods to insure they see themselves as an integral part of the agency and to give their families some living time in the U.S.

There are several reasons for the three years. Some posts mean difficult living conditions, perhaps limited education facilities for children or the need to send the children to a boarding school. Different postings and experiences broaden and educate the person. Also, if one stays too long in one country, one can develop an unconscious loyalty to that country and its needs. That must be kept in check.

A new Foreign Service officer can expect their first assignment in one of the Washington divisions, their second as assistant attaché in a two-person office overseas. That may be followed by a second three-year posting overseas, then back to Washington for three. After that, they might become an attaché in a one-person overseas office, back to Washington, and then back to a major foreign post.

In the mix, also, is a series of FAS Trade Development Offices. Whereas attaches are usually posted to an embassy in a country capital, trade development offices are in major port or trade cities, such as Milan, Italy, Casablanca, Morocco, or the city-state of Singapore.

We would have about sixty Foreign Service Officers to be rotated every year. Positions to be vacated by the expected reassignment or retirement, both in the field and in Washington, are usually posted in the fall and those to be reassigned submit their priority requests.

Of my assistant administrators, only Sharpless, who headed the attaché service division, was a Foreign Service Officer. She had been posted in Rome, Paris, and other locations, as well as Washington, before being named to coordinate and supervise all attaché posts. She would have one more year in this role, then rotate back out to an attache post. She had two deputies, both Foreign Service officers, one of them to be reassigned in the current effort.

I use the term, attaché, to describe the foreign post, but the word, attaché, is also a rank in the Foreign Service system. The beginning rank, assigned at the time of the first posting, is assistant attaché, next is attaché. That term is used for most one-person posts and for some second positions in multi-staff posts. A few earn promotion to the next higher rank, Agricultural Counselor. Perhaps ten or twelve hold that rank at any given time in the agency and fewer still, perhaps two or three, may hold the top rank, Minister-Counselor.

By the end of the week we had made most of our judgments, for review by the under secretary. He had earlier expressed his wishes on a few people and posts, such as that of a European Union trade negotiator then in Brussels, a senior and high rank officer that he wanted back in Washington to help him and the U.S. trade representative in their continued GATT negotiations (General Agreement on Tariff and Trade, a global effort codified by treaty). He had also suggested two or three of the senior attaches or counselors that he thought we should consider for the Brussels replacement.

About a third of the people were finishing Washington assignments, staff members in or heading offices in our trade policy, commodity, export promotion, or administration divisions. A few of those were ready for their first attaché post, others had had several such postings and were vying for what were considered the foreign "plums," two or three-member posts in Paris, London, Rome, or Ottawa. My predecessor as administrator, Rolland (Bud) Anderson, a South Dakota State alumnus, had Germany locked in by a commitment made when he left the administrator position. He was studying German and would go to Bonn but, with Germany's reunification, the embassy and office would soon re-locate to Berlin.

Staff in our personnel office, working especially closely with Sharpless, had laid out some preliminary suggestions and options.

I had first met Sharpless in the spring of 1970 in Paris. She was then a civil service staff member in the Office of Economic Cooperation and Development, a joint effort of Japan, the U.S., and major European countries' ministries of agriculture and focused on developing countries. University of Arizona's Dean of Agriculture Harold Myers and I, then dean at South Dakota State, represented U.S. colleges of agriculture at a week-long OECD conference on strengthening colleges of agriculture world-wide. Sharpless had requested and been detailed from a GS position in Washington; she had wanted the foreign experience.

The last afternoon Myers and I were in Paris, Sharpless led us on a shopping expedition that included coffee and pastries at one of the sidewalk cafes. I learned she had a college degree; she also had enthusiasm and sparkle. I was therefore not surprised when I saw her name on one of the doors in USDA's South Building in 1986, my first year in Washington with AID. Between then and my time as FAS administrator she had had another foreign post and when she next rotated back to Washington she had become assistant administrator for the attaché division.

I had also learned from Max Witcher, my head of the International Organizations division in OICD, that he had been the person who had convinced Sharpless, when she returned from that Paris OECD posting, to go to Cornell University for a Masters degree in agricultural economics and to qualify for the Foreign Service. During my time as FAS administrator, Sharpless was my most valuable adviser.

Back to the postings: Most of our judgments were made with unanimous or near unanimous agreement. A few, however, prompted rather intense debate. An officer then located in an export promotion office in Southeast Asia, had requested the export promotion office in

London. One of our committee would have none of that, "He has had two foreign postings and its time he comes back to Washington."

However, the officer's request rationale was that part of his family lived in England, they needed his presence and support, and he, the officer, was within eighteen months of retirement. Listening to the debate helped me make a judgment. I learned that in a previous posting season, either the secretary or the administrator had stepped in and approved a posting for this officer that this committee member had opposed. He was determined to even the score. However, the officer's skill and recent experiences, plus the London office's need for his skill and experience, pointed to London. The family issue just made London a win/win for both the program and the person.

A split vote was clear; I would simply need to make the judgment (it would be London) and, in time, defend it to the under secretary. As in a university, where a long-time staff member with established connections and who has lost an argument gets their "concern" to a top officer, a regent, or a legislator, I knew this issue, one way or another, would quickly travel across the street as a "concern" to the under secretary's office.

Another case was a young woman of Ukrainian ancestry and with the Ukrainian language who wanted the new Kiev post. Ukraine's agriculture potential and the degree of independence from the Soviet Union we then saw on the horizon had merited establishing that post. The problem was that she had a husband and a new baby and housing in Kiev was limited; the family would have to live in a hotel room.

"We can't send a new baby to Kiev," several suggested.

"But, she wants to go."

We held that decision for a few days. I wanted to visit with her personally, give her more time to learn all she could about Kiev living. In that visit, I would let her know that I would recommend Kiev if that is what she wants. I was sure that, with her husband's apparent support, she would reaffirm Kiev.

In drafting this item, I find in my daily log that her name was Mary Ponomarenko and that my visit with her was on June 9. The Senate confirmed my nomination to the assistant secretary post that afternoon. The next morning I was sworn in as assistant secretary, moved across the street to my new job, and an interim FAS administrator was named. (More about that move in a later section.)

I would later learn that Ponomarenko did not go to Kiev; the agency would use that position for an agriculture policy adviser to the Ukrainian ministry of agriculture for two years, after which another person was named agriculture counselor to Ukraine. It is my personal regret that I was no longer in FAS to support this young woman's desire. However, as I had learned in my university career, one does not get involved in their former unit's internal operations.

By the time of the next FAO annual meeting, November, 1991, there was a new person leading USDA. President Bush had asked Secretary Yeutter to accept chairmanship of the Republican National Committee and had named retiring Illinois Congressman Ed Madigan as Yeutter's replacement. Madigan chose to be in Rome for the first several days of FAO's meeting; he wanted FAO Director General Souma's support on a new and different matter.

The Secretary and the Secretary General

Madigan's agenda was to get Souma to support USDA Assistant Secretary for Food and Nutrition Programs, Cathy Bertini, to be the new director of another UN agency located in Rome, the World Food Program (WFP). Souma was one of three United Nations officers who would, as a group, make the selection decision.

The WFP distributes massive quantities of food to refugees in war-torn countries or victims of climate and weather extremes, the U.S. providing much of the food, and it was in the U.S. interest to have Bertini in that job. An effective administrator with unlimited energy and experience in the Department of Health and Welfare prior to her USDA post, Bertini was the type person WFP needed.

At several FAO events before Madigan's arrival in Rome, my OICD and State Department colleagues and I had been lobbying other country representatives on Bertini's behalf. She had also been in Rome during the week for receptions and meetings where those representatives could meet her.

Souma also had an agenda, to cultivate Madigan. The process would start with an evening dinner in Souma's FAO-provided home, an event requiring careful protocol. The U.S. would have four seats at the table, and it was important for Souma to feel honored by the four U.S. attendees being persons of the highest rank. Though State's seniority in UN dealings would call for two or three of those seats, no senior State officers were in town. Therefore, Madigan "pulled rank," and declared that he would be accompanied by Bertini, U.S. Ambassador to FAO Monroe (a State employee), and me.

It was a pleasant dinner, with many toasts to Souma, to Madigan, to FAO, and to the U.S. Perhaps because no business was discussed, it was a successful Step One for both Madigan and Souma.

Step Two would be Madigan's nine o'clock appointment the next morning in Souma's sumptuous fourth floor FAO office. Our USDA attaché, Ahalt, Ambassador Monroe, and I would accompany Madigan. As Souma motioned us into his office, Madigan signaled for the rest of us to remain in the outer office; he would go in alone. That was a surprise; rarely does a cabinet officer enter a formal meeting without a few aides in tow.

Less than fifteen minutes later, Souma's office door burst open, out stalked Madigan, with Souma close behind and pleading, "Wait! Wait!" Madigan did not slow his pace, motioned for us to follow. We headed for the elevator, Souma following with continued pleadings.

Our delegation barely in the elevator, Madigan pressed the Down button. On the first floor he marched through the building, and stopped only when we reached the front vestibule, where there were no U.N. personnel in sight.

"I had two choices," said Madigan, "Listen to Souma berate the U.S., or leave. I left."

Madigan had "studied his lesson" and planned his strategy. He had apparently believed there would be a better chance to get Souma's vote for Ms. Bertini by "being offended," than by being berated and then pleading Ms. Bertini's case.

A few weeks later, with Souma's being one of the "aye" votes, Bertini was named director of the World Food Program.

In the ten years that Bertini headed the World Food Program, the organization brought food to millions of hungry people in dozens of countries and gained global respect from donor countries as well as the global citizenry.

In October of 2003, for her outstanding leadership of WFP, Bertini was awarded the $500,000 World Food Prize in Des Moines ceremonies. To accept the prize and deliver the recipient's address, she flew from New York City, where she was then serving as deputy for administration to Kofi Annen, Secretary General of the United Nations.

To Move Across the Street?

On Sunday night in early December, 1991, the day after I had returned from that FAO week in Rome, Virgil Rosendale, administrator of USDA's Packers and Stockyards Administration, his wife, Thelma, and the Ackers hosted a holiday reception for our two agencies' staff and other USDA colleagues. As Sally Buikema, the secretary's appointments assistant, and her husband left the reception, she asked, "Has the Secretary talked to you about the Science and Education job?"

Charles Hess, former dean at the U. of California-Davis, had left the position to return to the Davis campus, and I knew several persons had been suggested as his replacement. However, I had had no contact with the Secretary about it and it had not been mentioned during our time together in Rome.

"He probably will," said Sally.

Monday morning came the call from Madigan, "Would you be interested in the assistant secretary spot, science and education?" As assistant secretary, I would be responsible for four agencies, Agricultural Research Service, with its one hundred twenty or more laboratories around the country, the National Agricultural Library, the Federal Extension Service, and the Cooperative State Research Service. The latter two agencies administer federal funds to land grant universities for research and extension, and a modest amount for agricultural instruction, plus research contracts for which any university could apply.

My response was ready, "I would be honored to do that job."

"Good. We'll proceed with that."

Though I relished the OICD and FAS assignments, each new and exciting territory and I would have many satisfactions and more stories to tell from each, the science and education role would put me back in more familiar territory.

The phone conversation was over, but I knew the process was not over. It would be in June, almost six months later, that I could be sworn in as assistant secretary and move across the street to an office that overlooks the mall. If the White House forwarded my nomination and I were confirmed by the Senate, I would have the ultimate job for anyone who has led an agricultural college, extension, or experiment station in a land grant university.

In the meantime, there would be plenty of work to do in FAS and OICD.

A Day's Agenda

As I scanned my log for names and dates for these memoirs, my eye settled on the entries of Wednesday, March 11, 1992, more than three months later. That day's encounters illustrate the diversity and fascination of daily work in my sectors of USDA.

Likely listed the evening before, were twenty items I needed to check on yet that week. Among them:

1. Tobacco information to the Secretary-General (FAO's Souma).
2. Preparation for House budget committee hearing.
3. Interviews for Jane Leo's position (a political appointee who had been moved elsewhere by the White House).
4. Resumes to Sally Buikema for an Economic Development Commission. (Having worked in five Midwestern states, I was often asked to suggest people for USDA advisory committees or even USDA agency positions).
5. Status of OICD funds – Miranda's continued tracking of OICD accounts receivable.
6. Recommendations to the under secretary on revised procedures for contracting (with commodity organizations for sharing the cost of promoting their exports).
7. Office space and likely programs for Bulgaria.
8. Report from Nicaragua (OICD's Richard Rortvedt's second review trip under President Bush's Caribbean Initiative).

9. Personnel structure (a staff proposal for merging OICD and FAS personnel offices).
10. Applications for Fruit and Vegetable ATAC (one of several FAS "Agricultural Technical Advisory Committees," on which we depended for advice on product qualities and volumes, for both export and import). In this case I had attached the name, Eddie Kimbrell, a highly respected staff member in USDA's Food Safety and Inspection Service and who had been a senior my first year teaching animal husbandry at then Oklahoma A&M. I trusted Kimbrell's advice.
11. Briefing of Frank Frazier for his meeting in the Secretary's office. (Frazier was executive officer for a poultry association and had invited me to join an informal D.C. agriculture luncheon group during my time with AID.)
12. Gary Madson or Gene Bailey (of USDA's Congressional Relations office) regarding Senate courtesy calls (that I should make to members of the Senate Agriculture Committee regarding my nomination).

Appointments and phone visits during the day involved:

- A phone visit with Assistant Secretary for Administration Chuck Hilty on moving some FAS units to the International Trade Center then under construction just north of the Mall.
- An OMB (Office of Management and Budget) proposal that the Commodity Credit Corporation (CCC) provide a $4.3 million share of the estimated $17.2 cost of the new "LandSat" program (a satellite that could help assess crop conditions and production potential in countries around the globe, information FAS had responsibility to know.) Though CCC was considered a part of and administered within a sister agency, ASCS, the role of FAS in handling food aid out of CCC stores made me one of the responsible officers, a vice president of CCC.
- What my staff in our FAS High Value Products division (meat, fruits, canned and frozen product) had learned about the Soviets buying some high value products from the European Community. It is well to know what your competitors are doing.

- A draft publication showing FAS' new mission and goals statement (which my assistant administrators and I had written in a day-long workshop).
- A visit with Export Credits staff on why some food aid destined for Armenia was going via Turkey and was stuck in a Turkish port.
- My OICD staff's need for help from USDA's Food Safety and Inspection agency. I suggested they contact Dr. Bill Dubbert, FSIS assistant administrator (who had been my classmate in both Animal Husbandry and FarmHouse Fraternity at Iowa State. A few days later I would attend an award ceremony in the USDA atrium where Dubbert would be named as one of the years' ten outstanding USDA staff, among the agency's one hundred thousand employees).
- Chris Goldthwait, Export Credits and acting sales manager regarding ten million dollars in food aid going to each of Zimbabwe and Romania; Ukraine had requested three hundred million in food aid, Russia six hundred million. Goldthwait was reviewing authorizations under several titles of food aid legislation.
- Pushing Lebanon to purchase U.S. wheat under our export enhancement program, in which FAS could "subsidize" the sales price quoted by U.S. exporters or guarantee loans that U.S. banks would provide to the importing country. In many of the countries, the purchaser would be a government-owned company.
- Granting such credit (guaranteed loans) to former Soviet Republics if they would buy U.S. grains or other products.
- Staff preparation for a meeting of OECD countries (the earlier-mentioned organization for Economic Cooperation and Development). A focus would be on what all can and should do for Eastern European's "emerging democracies," the former Soviet republics.

At 3:34, my log shows a visit with Deputy Secretary Ann Veneman in her office about my future job, Science and Education. Among the topics:

- Leadership of a department effort regarding an infestation of the "white fly" in U.S. fruit growing regions had been pulled into the Secretary's office because it was felt that Science and Education agencies had not communicated sufficiently with other USDA agencies.
- I should work closely with JoAnn Smith, assistant secretary for marketing, on developing a USDA biotechnology council.
- Persons I might consider for my S&E deputy position. Madigan and I had agreed that I should choose my own deputy, and the current occupant would be headed to Rome to replace Ahalt. I wanted a good scientist with private sector experience; I knew USDA and universities, and moving new technology to the private sector needed more attention. I also had a person in mind, Dr. Dale Wolf, a Nebraska graduate, a Republican, and retired as DuPont's agriculture vice president.
- Other current personnel in the S&E assistant secretary office. One was described as having good relationships with Senator Cochrane and that could be beneficial, but "he needs to be kept in harness." (I would find that to be true and, fortunately, I had also established a good link with Cochrane through the fellowship program in OICD that bore his name.)
- My plans for coordinating programs among my three larger agencies and including the administrator of the Economic Research Service in all staff meetings. Though ERS was under the assistant secretary for economics, its research was closely related to that of my agencies. (In a later administration, ERS would report to my re-named position, under secretary for science, education and economics.)

At five o'clock, my two associate administrators, Steve Censky and Chris Goldthwait, the latter in an acting capacity after Dickerson had resigned to re-join the private sector, briefed me on issues each had handled during the day. They ranged from a drafting error in a GATT document, to an agreement with the Red Cross for some food distribution, and a request from Azerbijan, another former Soviet Republic, for food aid and technical help.

My last entry was at 6:20 p.m., a phone call from Bruce Blanton, an assistant to Under Secretary Crowder, asking about a 1985 department reorganization plan. On that I could be of no help. Perhaps it was still on a shelf somewhere, awaiting approval by a Congressional committee.

A footnote at this writing, February, 2015: The 2014 Farm Bill called for USDA to "incorporate all international functions into one division" and that would have to include elements of additional USDA agencies, Food Safety and Inspection (FSIS) and Animal and Plant Inspection Service (APHIS), both involved in monitoring, enforcing, or helping negotiate features of trade agreements. Some countries try to limit imports from the U.S. by unduly imposing "sanitation" requirements, even demanding "inspection and approval" of plants from which exports come. APHIS gets involved because a product, such as apples, may be accused of carrying a disease the importing country fears. Each country and its commodity organizations, including the U.S., seek ways to protect their own industries from competing imports. It could also include elements of the Economic Research Service (ERS). To form that "division" could create a unit so large as to be cumbersome to manage.

It will be interesting to see the outcome.

CHAPTER VII

FOR AN OFFICE ON THE MALL

"Mr. Acker," said Senator Leahy, with deliberate courtesy but a tinge of concern, "I have here a letter regarding a cigarette line in Turkey, a staff letter to you recommending that the line not be financed by your market promotion program. However, Under Secretary Crowder or Secretary Yeutter apparently made the opposite decision. Which position did you support, that of your staff or the decision that was eventually made?"

My answer had to be, "Senator, with all due respect, that is a question that I believe would be inappropriate for me to answer."

The room, always respectfully quiet, went dead still."

I find in my log a February 27, 1992, conversation with Buikema that my nomination and others advanced by Madigan had not yet left the White House. Betty Jo Nelson, then administrator of food stamp and related programs, had been chosen by Madigan to replace Bertini as assistant secretary for food and nutrition programs, Dan Sumner would go from deputy to assistant secretary for economics, and Jim Huff, handling rural electrification loan programs in Mississippi, would head USDA's Rural Electrification Administration.

Buikema suggested it may require prodding by Senator Cochran of Mississippi for the White House to move on Huff, and perhaps I should suggest Senator Dole's office do the same regarding my nomination. It would be good if all four went to the Senate at the same time.

By March the several USDA nominations had been sent forward by the White House and were now in the hands of the Senate Agriculture Committee and its staff.

Any Minorities in Your Country Club?

That question was in a phone call from a Democratic majority staff member for the Senate Agriculture Committee. I knew what he was looking for, something to embarrass President Bush and his administration. If a nominee belonged to a country club that would not admit blacks or other minorities, that would be a good reason to reject and, at the same time, get column inches of publicity across the country suggesting Republican bigotry.

It works both ways, depending on which party is in the White House and if the opposite party controls the Senate. Cabinet, sub-cabinet, certain administrator, all ambassador appointments, and a number of top military nominations must be confirmed by the Senate. Before the Senate votes, the appropriate committee considers the nomination, holds public hearings, and may or may not recommend confirmation to the full Senate.

Democrats had the Senate majority, so the Senate agriculture committee chairman was long-time Senator Patrick Leahy of Vermont and the staff functions were led by the committee's "majority staff." For most Senate committees, two thirds of the committee staff are named by the majority party, one third by the minority.

I had completed another set of forms for the committee, paralleling those I had completed for the White House two years earlier. But these new forms were more extensive, ten pages plus twelve of attachments covering land owned, to whom rented, USDA "corn deficiency payments" by year, cash rents received, and a complete financial statement. All of this was to be accompanied by a copy of every paper I had ever written for publication, whether for scientific or education journals or for industry publications, and any copies of speeches I had given. There may be in one of those papers or speeches a statement that could be used to embarrass the nominee or the president.

Fortunately, I had maintained a rather complete file, arranged sequentially in a series of notebooks. On our next trip to the farm, I brought back several boxes, far more weight than should have been allowed on the plane. The copying cost to the Department was rather large; I was not about to send up to the Hill my only file copy.

In the meantime, I had met with the committee staff to tell them about my career, my philosophy about science and education, and my view of the assistant secretary position. I was also asked a series of questions on leading Democratic issues, such as the environment, affirmative action, and conservation.

It had been a comfortable conversation; on none of the issues was my posture at odds with majority party thoughts. We had built miles of terraces on our Iowa farmland, I had written an editorial for a national conservation journal, and I had named the first woman to be county extension director in South Dakota, a woman as interim director of Extension in Nebraska, and the first black vice president at Kansas State.

However, I knew the majority staff would keep looking.

In time, a staff member apparently noted on one of the forms my membership in the Atlantic, Iowa, Golf and Country Club. I had joined the club several years earlier because we spent some week-ends at our farm (and because the annual cost was only fifty dollars for one who lived more than fifty miles from Atlantic).

"Ah, ha!" Perhaps this is one of those country clubs that does not admit minorities.

I was ready for the question. Just the day before, our mail had included a club membership list, and I had noted that Frances Diaz, a native of Guatemala, was a member. Diaz had been a technician in the swine nutrition group when I was working on my Masters degree at Iowa State, and had followed my major professor, Damon Catron, to Atlantic to work for Walnut Grove, the local feed company.

I could easily respond, "Yes."

A week later came another call from committee staff, "We called the Atlantic Country Club and the person who answered the phone told us they did not have any minority members. You said it did."

"I will bring you the membership list," I said. I mentioned Diaz' name and suggested that whoever answered the Club phone may have equated the word, minority, with black or Afro-American. They would not think of Diaz, a long-time member of the community, as a minority.

A week later came another call. "Can women own stock in that Atlantic Country Club?" It appeared to be a never-ending game.

"I do not know, but I will find out," was all I could say. That night I placed a call to Chuck Kinen, listed in the club directory as Club president. He was one of the Kinen twins I had picked up each week-day morning at the last stop on my Wiota school bus route my senior year, and by then a leading salesman for Walnut Grove.

"I don't think they can," Chuck said. "Seems to me this came up a few years go and we checked the by-laws. I'll find a copy of the by-laws and get back to you."

I told Chuck why I was calling and that if he was correct, I would probably need to resign from the club.

"Maybe it is time we took a look at that at our annual meeting," Chuck said. I agreed, but consideration at the club's annual meeting would not do me any good.

The next morning the Atlantic Club's by-laws appeared in my office fax machine. They only stated that every male member had to own stock. I called Kinen again, read the statement and asked, "Might there be some widows whose husband had owned the stock and the widow now owns it?"

Chuck's response was quick, "Why would they want to? We buy back the stock and the widow can continue as a member."

Regardless, the by-laws' wording seemed to satisfy the majority staff, and I would not need to resign from the club. There were no more phone calls, just waiting for the next step, a public hearing before the Senate Agriculture Committee.

There could still occur some event, a statement by me or an action by FAS, that could be used as an excuse by the majority party to deny my nomination. Consequently, I would give no speeches, would not travel outside Washington on USDA business, and would not be publicly identified with any major FAS decisions. My associate administrator would represent me at a spring attaché conference in Southeast Asia and other staff would handle speech requests or be quoted in agency announcements.

Party Games Continue

The Senate Agriculture Committee had scheduled a morning hearing in late March on FAS' Market Promotion Program. Some senators had questioned the program's value, relative to cost, while other senators wanted the total committee to hear commodity groups tell why the program should continue. Chairman Leahy would not be present for the hearing (on less than headline issues, committee members are often absent), so Alabama's Democratic Senator Howell Heflin held the gavel.

First on the schedule was testimony by commodity leaders, all expressing support for the program's continuation. Then it was my turn, to briefly encourage continuation and to answer any questions the senators might have.

Heflin turned to Georgia's Democratic Senator Wyche Fowler for the first question. Fowler began by referring to that second cigarette line for Turkey. He mentioned support letters from House and Senate members, the initial denial on the recommendation by staff, and the subsequent approval following the Turkish ambassador's visit with Secretary Yeutter. His question to me was, in essence, "Why the reversal?"

Fowler had obviously been provided copies of the agency's internal letters. My response could only be, "As in any agency, there are levels of recommending and decision-making authority. At each it is simply a matter of judgment, in this case the secretary's final judgment.

Fowler pressed, quoted a statement in Assistant Administrator Mackie's initial letter on why the request should be denied. Did I support that?

I could only say that wording of the legislation left that implication.

Then came the question, in essence "Did you support the recommend by the staff you oversee or the decision by the Secretary?" It was then obvious this exchange was not about the Market Promotion Program; rather, it was part of the game regarding my Science and Education nomination.

I had already mentioned the levels of decision-making authority which, of course, the senator knew. This was a foul question, designed to publicly pit me between my staff and my superiors in USDA.

From the transcript:

"Mr. Acker: Senator, I would respectfully respond that I think it would be inappropriate for me to pit myself against some other member of the – (interruption)

Senator Fowler: Is that the Fifth Amendment, Mr. Acker?"

Mr. Acker: No. It is just I - - (interruption)

Senator Fowler: So you are not taking responsibility for a decision of your own administration (FSA staff) recommending it up higher to the Secretary of Agriculture?

Mr. Acker: Well, I certainly take responsibility to see to it that the decision-makers above me have all of the pros and the cons. And I might elaborate - - (interruption)"

So it went for what seemed like twenty minutes, more than ten pages in the hearing transcript, with the senators' repeated efforts to separate me from Secretary Yeutters' eventual decision and, in the end, accusing me of "failing to take responsibility."

Interim Chairman Heflin then turned to South Dakota's Democratic Senator Tom Daschle. Daschle is a South Dakota State graduate and because I had served there as dean, I thought that he would abandon the obvious game and shift to issues of the market promotion program. Instead, he continued.

Again from the transcript:

"Senator Daschle: You are going to be before this committee for confirmation as Assistant Secretary for Science and Education — — and I will have before me the transcript of your answers (to Senator Fowler) and your refusal to respond to what your position was — — I would be very interested in knowing if at one more level (assistant secretary) you are going to tell this committee that you are going to be unwilling to take personal responsibility for your actions. If so, I question if we should confirm you."

Eventually, after one or two more Democratic senators had had their time with me, Heflin turned to Republican Senator Mitch McConnell of Tennessee (at this writing, January, 2015, the new minority leader of the Senate). Most of the Democratic senators had risen from their chairs to depart; they had played their role.

Again, excerpts from the transcript:

"Senator McConnell: Thank you, Mr. Chairman. Mr. Acker, are you having fun yet?

(Laughter)

Senator McConnell: I would just like to say — I am sorry my colleagues are no longer here. I frankly am not here to either criticize or defend —. I do not find it at all incredible that you are not willing to announce when you differ within the Department with a decision that is ultimately made by the entire Department.

Mr. Acker: Thank you, sir.

Senator McConnell: I know that I would not be real happy if my legislative assistant, whom I frequently over rule, called the press and said, you know, I told that so-and-so not to take this position, but he insisted on doing it anyway against the best interests of the people of Kentucky. So I must say, I don't find it all incredible that you are not willing to come up here before this committee and announce those occasions upon which you might have differed internally with the decision subsequently reached by the entire department. That is not unusual. It is not inappropriate. And I don't want you to feel bad about that. I certainly hope that (when in) a very responsible position — you don't come up here and nail your superiors on every occasion upon which you might have some minor or major difference (and that) would subsequently kill your confirmation. It shouldn't. I am confident that every member of this committee periodically overrules advice of subordinates, and we do not expect them to go out and announce those differences to the press."

That day's phone log shows a 4 p.m. phone call to Jeff Hall of McConnell's staff to thank him for his good briefing of McConnell prior to the hearing, plus, "And, be sure to thank your boss!" The reader will also understand why I was rooting for McConnell in his tight race for re-election from his home state of Kentucky in the fall of 2014. I was pleased to see him win re-election and, with Republicans gaining a majority in the senate, his becoming majority leader.

A personnel nomination also opens the door for a senator to make some demand on the president in exchange for a needed vote, perhaps a grant or loan to one of his or her constituents, letting a contract to a military equipment supplier in the senator's state, or at least some special attention by the White House or executive department to the senator's "concern." During the days after the Market Promotion Program hearing, my log shows sixteen entries regarding Senator Fowler's chief of staff, Bob Redding. The senator apparently had concerns about our agency's market promotion agreements with the National Peanut Council, and parallel organizations that promote Vidalia onions, pecans, and tobacco.

Perhaps the senator felt FAS had not been generous enough in the dollars allocated. Or, perhaps he felt our staff had been too strict in auditing program expenditures. Interspersed were conversations on those issues with USDA Congressional Relations staff Gene Bailey and Gary Madson and with Under Secretary Crowder.

Which Nominee Will be Borked?

The Senate Agriculture Committee hearing for the four nominees, Nelson, Sumner, Huff, and me, was set for the afternoon of May 19. An election year would be a logical time to make a political issue out of a nominee's statement in the hearing, or referred to in the hearing. It could get considerable media coverage and, especially, embarrass a president running for re-election.

Some readers will recall the eventual Senate approval of nominee Clarence Thomas to the Supreme Court in 1991 or the Senate rejection of nominee Robert Bork in 1987. Both left stains on what should be a respectable process for assessing the qualifications of a president's nominee. In the case of Bork, Senator Ted Kennedy's public statements in opposition—and spread widely in the media—were so obviously irresponsible that the case became infamous. The phrase, "to be Borked," became a standard reference for an unjustified Senate rejection.

Being one of four nominees to be considered by the Senate Agriculture Committee, the majority of the opposite political party from a president campaigning for re-election, I wondered, "Which one will be rejected?" "Which one will be Borked?"

It would not be Sumner, an academic on leave from a university. His role was only to give economic advice to the secretary and others, so he had little political liability, little potential for exposure and embarrassment.

It would not be Huff. Before taking the Mississippi position where he handled low interest federal loans to local rural electric cooperatives, he had been with a private utility. No one could be against loans for electric cooperatives in rural areas and Huff would have no Washington experience scars.

Certainly, the Democratic majority would not reject a woman. Nelson should sail through.

During much of my year in FAS, Washington newspapers and other media, nation-wide, had given rather full coverage to a failed Atlanta, Georgia, bank which had financed the sale of U.S. wheat to Iraq several years earlier. FAS had guaranteed the bank's loan and Iraq's failure to pay for the wheat and subsequent failure of the bank had been costly to the U.S. Though that had all happened long before my time in FAS, it would be fertile territory for the committee hearing. Also, the exchange during the MPP hearing a couple weeks earlier could be repeated. I had better be well prepared.

There should be questions regarding science and education. Why is USDA financing research on transgenic fish production? Will you recommend additional funds for historically black institutions, the 1890 land grant universities in the southern states? Does the Agricultural Research Service need all those one hundred twenty research facilities located across the country? There were dozens of worthwhile questions in this arena, and I had studied briefing books prepared by agency staff and had spent several half days discussing program details with them on likely issues.

There was another matter: Committee Chairman Patrick Leahy, known for strong partisanship and for using his prosecuting attorney skills to the fullest, had missed the MPP hearing. This hearing would be his chance.

Stay Right Where you Are!

The committee room, 328A of the Russell Senate Office Building, was packed. Though our key USDA colleagues had to be at their desks doing their day's work, we nominees spotted family or friends in the audience and I was complimented to see with my wife, Shirley, several of her colleagues from the White House volunteer office. Except for Gary Madson of USDA's Congressional liaison staff, few in attendance had been at the late March MPP hearing.

Chairman Leahy called the meeting to order, declared the purpose of the hearing, to determine the fitness of four nominees advanced by the White House for responsible positions in USDA. The four of us were at a table facing committee members. After generous introductory and endorsing comments for each nominee by home state senators, in my case both Kansas Senator Bob Dole and Iowa Senator Chuck Grassley, those home state senators not on the committee departed and questioning began.

The questions to Sumner and Huff were brief and perfunctory, usually led by Leahy and followed by both majority and minority members.

Then it was my turn and Chairman Leahy turned to me.

"Mr. Acker," said Leahy, with deliberate courtesy but a tinge of concern, "I have here a letter regarding a cigarette line in Turkey, a staff letter to you recommending that the line not be financed by your market promotion program. However, Under Secretary Crowder or Secretary Yeutter apparently made the opposite decision. Which position did you support, that of your staff or the decision that was eventually made?"

After the rather routine manner of Sumner's and Huff's questions by committee members, this type question caught the audience's attention. At least Leahy had put it more concisely than had Senator Fowler several weeks earlier.

My answer had to be, "Senator, with all due respect, that is a question that I believe would be inappropriate for me to answer."

The room, always respectfully quiet, went dead still.

The senator's face showed shock. "You mean to tell me that you won't stand up to tell us your own opinion?"

There followed the same general sequence as in the earlier MPP hearing. "Do you not have the courage to state your convictions?" "Are you not willing to assume responsibility for your actions?"

Though my responses to each of the questions may have varied in words, they were little changed from the first and often interrupted by Leahy's next question.

With an evident show of frustration, Leahy turned to his Democratic colleagues, and each followed the same line. My responses were little changed, and it continued for another ten or fifteen minutes.

In time, I motioned for Madson to step over to my side; he had been through many such nomination hearings. "Your advice, Gary?" I asked.

His response was quick and clear, "Stick right where you are!"

From then on, my response would be, "With all due respect, Senator —"

It is fascinating to watch the "senatorial courtesies," for senators of a president's minority party, in this case, Republicans, to let the majority party members run their course. Not until every Democratic senator present had had their swing at me, did a Republican senator raise his hand or be acknowledged for a question or comment in my support.

When their time came, each was generous in their statement, repeating, in essence, the rebuttal and defense that had been so eloquently stated by McConnell in the MPP hearing weeks earlier.

Though I had experienced legislative committee hearings in South Dakota, Nebraska, and Kansas, as well as numerous Congressional committee hearings in my AID and OICD roles, and had had my share of intense conversations with individual legislators, regents, alumni, and, especially, athletic boosters, I had experienced no grilling that compared in intensity or propriety to those of the MPP or nomination hearing.

Surprisingly, I would not be the only one on the grill that afternoon. Betty Jo Nelson, nominee for Food and Consumer Services assistant secretary, was intensely grilled by Leahy and his grilling followed up by others. Their issue seemed to be the senators' displeasure with the allocation and distribution a few years earlier of emergency food supplies by her agency.

Though I had not worked closely with Nelson, I had gained through Bertini and others much respect for her work in the department, including her agency's handling of food distribution in domestic emergencies, and was surprised by the intensity of the questioning.

The four of us shared a car back to the department after the hearing. Nelson declared that if not confirmed, she was ready to leave her current administrative post and head back to Wisconsin. That would be a tragedy for the department and the programs she had been nominated to lead. No one was as well equipped to take over for Bertini.

Back to Wisconsin Nelson would return. Shirley and I were at the National Arboretum on Tuesday evening, June 9, for a dinner recognizing new inductees to the USDA-ARS Scientists Hall of Fame. I was called out from the dinner for a phone call from Gene Bailey, assistant secretary for congressional relations, to tell me he had just gotten word that, on the recommendation of the Senate Committee on Agriculture, Forestry and Nutrition, Gardner, Huff, and I had been confirmed by the Senate.

At the Secretary's staff meeting soon after eight o'clock the next morning, there were two-minute swearing-in ceremonies for Gardner, Huff, and me. When the meeting adjourned, I walked down the hall to my new office that overlooks the Mall and the Washington Monument.

USDA Secretary Ed Madigan, on the right, swearing in the author as assistant secretary. In the middle is Ann Veneman, then deputy secretary and who would become secretary in the George W. Bush administration nine years later. More than five months had elapsed from the day Madigan has asked the author to take the assistant secretary position. (USDA)

Huddling in my assistant secretary office with, from the left, Assistant Interior Secretary and former Kansas Governor Mike Hayden, USDA Assistant Secretary for Administration Charles Hilty, and Extension Service Administrator Myron Johnsrud, June, 1992. We were likely sharing "war stories" about our Senate confirmation hearings or other dealings with Congress. (USDA)

I had learned that Dr. Dale Wolf, who I had in mind for my deputy in the assistant secretary's office, was by then lieutenant governor of Delaware. Regardless, I checked further and found his term would end in December or early January, and called him about interest in the position. I could afford to wait for Wolf until January, assuming my Senate confirmation and President Bush's re-election. Unfortunately, Wolf's friends were urging him to run for governor and he declined consideration.

I still wanted a solid scientist from the private sector and was alerted to Dr. Bruce Stillings of New Jersey, a Republican and who had been research vice president for two well known companies in the food industry, Nabisco and Reckitt-Coleman. Stillings would, after my confirmation, get White House approval and come on board. Though our time together would be short, with Bush failing in his re-election bid that fall, Stillings was the right person. His personality, ability to focus on issues, and his experience in the food industry made him valuable to me, to my agencies, and to other of USDA's food-related agencies.

After his time in USDA, Stillings would return to the private sector, becoming senior vice president for an organization of food industries, cocoa, chocolate, and confectioners.

Creative or Illegal?

Though the lead person in a federal department may change, the pace of issues to be handled does not slow. There were several on my new desk or in my new secretary's hands that needed attention; some sort of "welcome to the office" event would come later.

I did find time late morning to move a few books and personal items from my FAS office in the South Building, but before heading home that evening, I would face an especially disturbing issue in one of my new agencies.

My four o'clock visitor was a key person in the agency that distributes federal research funds to land grant universities. He was one of the more enthusiastic of the people I looked forward to working with, one with a strong scientific and administrative background in universities prior to joining USDA. He was eager to share with me how his agency had been creative in helping the director of the southern association of experiment station directors, and who accompanied him. I listened.

From the time of the 1887 Hatch Act, USDA had provided federal funds to share the cost of each state's agricultural experiment station research, those funds allocated according to each state's farm population and farm numbers. In recent years, Congress had also appropriated additional money to USDA for competitive research grants. Every station wanted their share of the grant money and wanted to see the total research "pie" increased.

To lobby for the latter, four regional consortiums of state experiment stations had formed and an executive director named for each region to present their case to USDA and Congress. Each region's stations provided some state or private funds for the regional director's salary and travel expenses.

Because this regional director, located on the Texas A&M campus, needed more money to do his job than his member stations had provided, the agency had made a "research grant" of federal funds to

Texas A&M, and a parallel amount had apparently been transferred by A&M to the regional director's office.

One of the first rules I had learned as a new dean and experiment station director twenty six years earlier had been "Do not use state appropriations to lobby your state legislature and do not use federal money to lobby USDA or Congress."

There was no need to embarrass my agency person in this setting, so I only listened. However, as soon as the two left my office I called our general counsel's office and described what I had just heard. I knew the steps I needed to take, but I wanted to be solid with the law.

The general counsel's response: "No question. Out of bounds."

I next wanted to find out if this "creativity" had been used for only this one regional association or if it had been extended to others. I called Kurt Feltner, director for the north central association at his Kansas State office. Feltner had joined the Kansas State agronomy department while I was associate dean and I had sold him my hail-battered 1955 Ford for three hundred dollars when we left Kansas for South Dakota. In the interim, he had been on the faculties of Montana State and the University of Vermont, and had returned to Kansas State to serve several years before becoming a regional director.

I told Feltner only that I needed some background on this regional office-USDA relationship, and asked him a series of questions about fund source, how he and his counterparts in other regions functioned, especially in use of state or any federal funds. His answers were clear. No federal funds were involved in the North Central regional office; it was strictly state-financed. And, he assumed that was the case for the other three.

Early the next morning I had my agency person back in my office. I replayed what he had told me the day before, and told him I was drafting a letter for him to cease and desist from the process he had described.

I was to learn in the next week that this was not the only impropriety by his agency. The general counsel's office had been quietly investigating others for some time.

This man's scientific creativity, enthusiasm, and energy were outstanding and he had had success in several administrative roles. But he was dumbfounded at my reaction to his creativity, essentially "laundering" money through a university, and the posture of the General Counsel's office.

My thoughts: When a person "crosses the line" a bit between right and wrong on some item, likely "to get needed things done," he or she may be tempted to cross the line further on a future issue. In time, in his or her mind, the "line" has moved. It is no longer located where society or the law had placed the line. To make decisions or take actions that most would call improper will have become, to him or her, normal and proper.

I am not naive enough to believe this is the only case of government "creativity." In hundreds of federal agencies and programs, with university or other grant recipients eager for more funding, and considering the competitive and creative nature of humans, such are inevitable. But this one would stop.

There was a follow-up, politically practical issue to consider. Should this person be relieved of his administrative and financial responsibility, and any improprieties found by the general counsel office made public, especially just a few months before an election? Regardless of how long this had been going on, public exposure would bring splatter to the current administration.

Bill Clinton would defeat George H.W. Bush in the latter's quest for a second term and Tom Urban, then CEO of Pioneer Hi-Bred International, Des Moines, would be a key member of Clinton's USDA transition team, a small group that would identify issues of which the new administration should be aware. It would be my privilege to brief Urban on science and education agency issues and to answer his questions. In preparing for that transition team's work I had placed fifteen items in a notebook for my successor, including the complete correspondence file on this case.

While writing this section, I find in my personal files a copy of my January 19, 1993, letter to Secretary Madigan, his and my last full day in the office, expressing thanks for the privilege of serving as his assistant secretary and including that "about $30,000 has been returned to the department by Texas A&M." I had also learned that during the following year, this person was transferred to an important research unit outside Washington, where his *scientific* creativity and vigor would be of continued value to USDA and U.S. agriculture.

My Home Area Colleagues

The author and his wife, Shirley, flanked by three young USDA staff at a welcoming reception in my new assistant secretary office. On the left is Chris Nissen, Agricultural Marketing Service (AMS) and native of Atlantic, Iowa, the author's home town. Lower right is Donna Rock, an intern with AMS, native of nearby Oakland, Iowa, and distant cousin of the author. The tall man in the right rear is Tom Rial, also native of Atlantic and on the author's OICD staff. More detail regarding each those three young staff is given in the text that follows. (USDA)

Rial was an international training specialist for OICD's Cochran Fellowship Program. After OICD and FAS merged, retaining the FAS name, Rial helped broaden the Cochran Program to more of the newly independent, former Soviet republics. He later moved to USDA's Agricultural Marketing Service to lead that agency's work in those republics and, in that role, gave transportation and marketing assistance to U.S. shippers and exporters. That experience, in turn, opened doors to the private sector and, in 1997, Rial left USDA to work with such organizations as the Iowa Soybean Association and the

Greater Des Moines Chamber of Commerce. His foreign contacts and experience in multi-country trade requirements and constraints, such as those of Japan, China, Russia, and Cuba, then led him to international freight transportation. He is now with a New Jersey international freight transportation company, managing the Midwest sales office in Des Moines.

Rock had joined AMS as an intern after graduating from the University of Kentucky. Later, in one of several USDA reorganizations, she moved to USDA's Animal and Plant Health Inspection Service and, since 2000, has been with USDA's National Finance Center in New Orleans. Although headquartered at New Orleans, she "teleworks" for the Office of USDA's chief financial office in Washington. At this writing she works at home three days a week, and drives the sixty miles to her New Orleans office the other two from her acreage across the state line in Mississippi.

Though born without arms, this has proven of little consequence in her professional career and personal life. For example, I had called to bid her goodbye at the close of her internship, learned she had already moved to a different assignment, and I had to ask of her office mate, "How does Donna handle the computer?" Her response: "No problem; she just places the keyboard on the floor and types with her toes." Rock had earlier shared with us that she had no problem driving; her feet had been her "hands" since birth.

Chris Nissen had been injured in a freak accident while a high school junior and since then has spent much of his time in a wheel chair. He earned two degrees at the University of Iowa and, after completing his Masters in Business Administration, was offered a job with what is now the Marketing Order and Agreement Division of AMS, USDA. That division administers producer and processor-financed "market order" programs—including quality standards and quantity adjustments the industry wants to make under the authorizing legislation—for a variety of agricultural commodities.

After completing an AMS middle management development program (soon after Shirley and I had left Washington), Chris applied for and was named to a supervisory position in a field office in Winter Haven, Florida.

While completing this section, February, 2015, I had the opportunity to have lunch with Chris in Ft. Myers, Florida, where he had brought his personal van for some repair work. He is now Regional Director for that Southeast Marketing Office in Winter Haven but, since 2012, the term, Southeast, is hardly descriptive. He manages five people plus two field offices that oversee market order programs for Florida and Texas citrus, Florida avocados and tomatoes, cranberries and tart cherries produced in several states, southeastern potatoes, and Vidalia and Texas onions.

Chris tells me that, although traveling with a disability has its challenges, he enjoys being located "in the field" with opportunity to interact directly with his staff and the industries as well as, sometimes, his travel to Washington headquarters. Most weeks he "teleworks" one day at home, the other four days he goes to his office by public transportation. Especially, he gives credit to his wife, Heidi, who he met at the University of Iowa and who has been a substantial contributor to his career, and to his father, Richard, who was able to travel with him after his retirement from teaching mathematics at the Atlantic school.

My Day in a Wheel Chair

To increase sensitivity of USDA employees to their colleagues and clientele who may have physical limitations, it was suggested that several of us spend a day "in others' shoes," to experience some of their daily life. Some who volunteered for the experience chose to spend the day blindfolded, their ears plugged, or one arm locked to their side. I chose to spend a day in a wheel chair.

Though it took me some time to get familiar with the chair and to negotiate my way around my office suite, those were the simple tasks. Mid morning I headed to the Men's Room. Instead of a wide, right angle entryway, common in buildings of recent design, entry was through a heavy, spring-loaded door. I first tried to shove it open with one hand, but it sprang closed before I could get both hands on my wheel rails. After several failures, I kicked open the door, my hands ready on the wheel rails, and wheeled in before the door could spring closed. Had my legs been paralyzed, I would have been out of luck.

I found no "handicap stall," large enough to handle the chair. I could use an existing stall only by pulling the stall door open and propping it in place with the chair. To later reach the paper towels, I had to stretch, push myself up with one hand.

To depart, I pulled open the door with one hand and rolled the chair against the open door with my other hand.

The physical difficulties were awkward, but not surprising. What did surprise me were others' behaviors toward one in a wheel chair. I had been invited to a late afternoon pre-Christmas reception in my former South Building FAS office. As I wheeled myself through the overpass above Independence Avenue I met an OICD staff member with whom I had worked closely, and my mind was poised for a "Merry Christmas" greeting. However, our eyes did not meet; we passed each other, she without glancing my way.

As I have related that experience to others, I have heard repeated confessions, "You know, unfortunately, I tend to do the same." They sometimes follow up, "When meeting a wheelchair-bound person I sometimes feel uncomfortable; I certainly do not want to stare. So I may just focus on my path ahead."

Perhaps I had been fortunate. From my early youth, my father's cousin, so physically malformed that he had to be lifted up stairs, and a blind family friend were so often in our home and at our table that to both seek and extend a greeting seemed normal.

At the reception, I rolled myself through FAS staff and guests, the latter mostly Washington-based commodity organization officials and foreign country attaches, to exchange greetings. Some asked, "Why the wheel chair?" But I would notice other former colleagues off to the side, reticent to ask me and likely asking each other, "What happened to Acker?"

I recommend such an experience to others.

Earmarks and Line Items

In my book, *Can State Universities be Managed: A Primer for Presidents and Management Teams,* I wrote about working with then Senate Majority Leader Bob Dole and his staff to get written into federal appropriation bills a large sum of money to help build what would eventually become the Bob Dole Communications Building at Kansas State University. To obtain such a "Congressional earmark" or "line item" for Kansas State was part of my job. In time, nearly six million dollars in federal funds were provided for that building.

In the first budget I handled as assistant secretary, I had three pages of such line items to administer through my four agencies. Most I considered worthy, research and education endeavors near the top of any list that our staff in human nutrition, biotechnology, veterinary medicine, or agriculture would recommend. A few, however, would be of little value in advancing the U.S. food system or U.S. agriculture; some were hardly related.

I find in my files Pages 30 to 33 of a report by the House subcommittee on appropriations for Fiscal Year, 1992, showing one hundred forty two line items for the agency that distributes money to state experiment stations, CSRS. Each item is identified by the state to which the money would go. Here are a few:

Aflatoxin (Illinois)	$134,000
Alfalfa (Kansas)	125,000
Alternative crops (North Dakota)	700,000
Alternative Pest Control (Arkansas)	1,400,000
Asparagus yield decline (Michigan	94,000
Broom Snakeweed (New Mexico)	200,000
CRP acreage usage (Missouri)	50,000
Dairy goat research (Texas)	75,000
Expanded Wheat Pasture (Oklahoma)	337,000
Floriculture (Hawaii)	296,000
Food irradiation (Iowa)	237,000
Human nutrition (Louisiana)	800,000
Leafy spurge bio-control (Montana)	125,000
Maple research (Vermont)	99,000
Mink research (Oregon)	46,000
Peach tree short life (South Carolina)	192,000
Sand Hills grazing management (Nebraska)	99,000
Swine research (Minnesota)	140,000
Water conservation (Nevada)	200,000

There was also a CSRS construction list of thirty three capital projects, feasibility or planning studies or for construction. They ranged from $225,000 for a Vidalia Onion Storage Research Facility at the University of Georgia's Tifton Station to $10 million for a Food Toxicology Center at Michigan State.

This construction list was in addition to projects that experiment stations had already planned for CSRS-provided money allocated annually to state experiment stations under 1960s legislation. (In the book, *From Troublesome Creek,* I tell how I had to employ South Dakota's attorney general to convince our state architect that those USDA construction funds did not require that the contractor pay federal minimum wage rates.)

I also find a Fiscal Year 1992 construction list for the Agricultural Research Service, considered USDA's "in-house" research agency, but with facilities in many states. The money would be for feasibility/planning or construction. The list included:

Rice Germplasm Center at Stuttgart, AR	$ 729,000
U.S. Salinity Laboratory, Riverside, CA	5,300,000
National Pork Research Facility, Ames, IA	1,800,000
Northern Regional Research Center, Peoria, IL	1,825,000
Natl. Ctr. for Warm Water Aquaculture, Stoneville, MS	1,100,000

Most of the ARS construction projects had been recommended to Congress by USDA through the president's Office of Management and Budget (OMB), and were needed to keep established research facilities up to date and fulfilling its mission. The National Pork Research Facility was an exception.

ARS did not want the pork research facility, believing its existing Meat Animal Research Center at Meade, NE, was adequate for accommodating all the scientists, animals, and product research that ARS' operating budget could handle. The desire for this facility had been advanced by the leadership of the National Pork Producers Association. They had successfully lobbied Congress for that $1.8 million dollars for planning and were determined to get construction funds in the next fiscal year appropriations.

It was in my first months as assistant secretary that I would meet with the delegation of pork producers. Though they knew I could not lobby Congress for the construction funds, should I be asked for my judgment by a member of the appropriations committee, they wanted my response to be positive.

I had asked my staff to find out how many dollars of public money, state and federal, were then being spent for research and extension education on swine production and pork as a product. The data turned out to be about one dollar per hog marketed in the U.S. Should I be asked for reaction by a member of Congress, I wanted to know that figure and I felt the delegation should know it.

We would be long back on our Iowa farm when, in the mid 1990s, Shirley and I attended the dedication of a new ARS structure on the Iowa State University campus; it was connected to an existing ARS Soil Tilth lab. Though ARS/USDA had continued its opposition to the national pork center, Congress had appropriated the construction money and *instructed* ARS to proceed with construction.

However, ARS did not have funds to staff the new building and Congress had not followed up with additional operating money. According to Dr. Dave Topel, then Iowa State's dean of agriculture, ARS *gave* the building to Iowa State for one dollar, and it would be used by Iowa State's experiment station.

The pork industry was not left in the lurch. Long-time and strong swine production and pork product research and education has continued by Iowa State's and other states' experiment stations and extension services, their programs often enhanced by contributions from the National Pork Board and state pork producers' associations.

Back to the one hundred forty two CSRS line items: Each had an interest group and political support. Aflatoxin, produced on mold-infested corn when there was too much rain during harvest, had become a serious problem for Illinois corn producers. Illinois is a major corn-producing state and had a strong producer organization. Alfalfa is a major crop in Kansas' river valleys and perhaps had not received the research attention over the years as had wheat and grain sorghum. There was considerable CRP acreage in Missouri. Perhaps Missouri conservation clubs wanted to find out if adding diverse species of grasses and herbs in CRP seeding mixes, or other management practices, would increase the pheasant or quail population.

Most every experiment station has a list of research needs that have not been funded. A station director or advisory committee member may suggest to a key member of Congress that such be included in committee budget deliberations. Elected representatives and senators want to help their university, its research program, and the agriculture/rural sector and may ask, "What are your priorities that have not yet been met?" It is all part of a democracy's political process.

We Have Been Acquainted

Considerable of ARS' research is conducted on land grant university campuses, and Iowa State had long hosted ARS scientists and their work in corn, soybean, soils, and entomology. Long time corn geneticist, Dr. Arnel Hallauer, among the inductees to the ARS Scientist Hall of Fame dinner at the National Arboretum dinner mentioned earlier, had been stationed on Iowa State's campus and I was visiting his laboratory. Shirley had accompanied me from Washington for this Friday visit and we would spend the week-end at our farm.

Hallauer was a Kansas State graduate, had earned his graduate degrees at Iowa State, and had been with ARS for thirty years, first located on the North Carolina State campus, then back on the Iowa State campus. He had formally retired from USDA after thirty years service, but had continued his ARS-financed work as an Iowa State employee and distinguished professor.

Hallauer's research has resulted in more than thirty inbred lines that by 1990, according to an Iowa State document, were "so widely used they have found their way into most of the commercial corn produced in the North American Corn Belt." As part of that work he had also developed more efficient *ways* of developing inbred lines, methodology put to work by other corn breeders in both public and private breeding programs.

In describing his work to us, Dr. Hallauer gave much credit to his technician, a Mr. Jim Sears, who stood nearby. A man in his mid fifties, Sears looked familiar, but I could not identify how I might have known him. When Hallauer had finished his presentation and we were free to move around the lab, I went up to Sears, "I'm sure we have been acquainted."

"You bet we were." Sears responded. "You were my adviser."

I later learned that I had been Sear's adviser during his first two years in the Animal Science curriculum, but he had transferred to Agronomy for his last two years. In the meantime, I had moved up one flight in Iowa State's Curtiss Hall to head the College's Farm Operation curriculum.

I commended Sears for his contributions to Dr. Hallauer's work. He had been the one supervising part-time student workers and insuring that identities of all materials were maintained, that thousands of seeds got planted on time, the grain harvested, and agronomic and other traits recorded.

But Sears was eager to talk about our earlier acquaintance, "You know what you said to me one day?" he asked.

"What was it I said to you?" (Most interviews arranged by the College placement office were in a small room at the end of hall just outside my Farm Operation Curriculum office. Apparently frustrated after an interview, Sears had stopped in to talk with his former adviser.)

"I was in your office trying to decide what to do. I did not have an opportunity to farm and I had not found the right job. You said, 'Jim, I think you ought to consider going into research.'"

Sears continued, "I left your office thinking, 'What is he talking about? I'm not interested in research.'"

Sears then described a sequence of jobs, working for a vegetable processing company in Illinois, then a seed corn company in eastern Iowa. After his father was temporarily sidelined by an injury, he operated the home farm for a year. He had kept looking for the right thing and learned of a temporary job in Iowa State's corn breeding program. "I remembered what you told me that day, and I applied," he said.

He then followed up, "It has been the best job I could have had. It has been fun, a tremendous experience."

As Sears talked, a more detailed memory emerged. I could visualize Sears in his early twenties, recall him as an excellent student, friendly, but not one I would easily see in a sales type position. Whether it would be in banking, a USDA service agency, or the private sector, most of the jobs for which our graduates were being interviewed in that little room just outside my office involved some form of salesmanship. Sears was more analytical. He was also very open, and got along exceedingly well with others.

Perhaps my observations and impressions, plus Jim's apparent frustration or indecision, had triggered what he had remembered, "Jim, you ought to consider going into research."

My thoughts as we left Hallauer, Sears, and the laboratory: Too few people in this world have the good fortunate of a career as successful and rewarding as those two. Though Hallauer had had the public recognition, it would be difficult for me to differentiate between the two in terms of personal success and satisfaction. And, each had contributed mightily to the quality and productivity of U.S. corn hybrids.

Thoughts that Remain

On January 23, 1993, my office books and memorabilia and our personal items from the rented apartment overlooking the Washington Parkway loaded in our son-in-law's pick-up, Shirley and I were on ice-covered I-88 in western Maryland, headed toward our Iowa farm. After the mid-day's sun melted the ice and we could relax, we talked about our six-year Washington experience, what we learned and the impressions we would retain.

Shirley had appreciated the excitement of her varied work in the White House Volunteer office, learning and teaching calligraphy, and the several travels with me to food production, re-forestation, food-for-work, and other programs in African and Central American countries.

I had appreciated the privilege of six years in a totally different work environment, a contrast from a university campus, more nationally- and globally-focused work.

Though the word, bureaucracy, triggers thought of redundant processes, roadblocks, and frustration, those were not uppermost in my mind. I had encountered those before; the Washington bureaucracy was simply larger and more complex.

Rather, here are some of my thoughts that day and that remain:

1. Cabinet level departments and the independent agencies are filled with dedicated and hard-working people. Though I would

usually be in my office by 7:30 and sometimes earlier, many colleagues would already be at their desks. When I would leave my AID, OICD, FAS, or assistant secretary office, often six o'clock or later, some might be awaiting a fax or phone call from overseas or responding to one. Yes, some people were less productive than others, but we had that in universities.

2. Virtually every decision that is made within a federal department or agency is, to some degree, political. At the same time, most decisions of consequence are also a matter of judgment: "Is this project or effort within the spirit of the law passed by Congress and signed by the president?" "Is it a worthy investment?" or "Considering the benefit to business sector A vs. the likely negative effect on business sector B, is implementing this program of net benefit to the country?" or "Can I take the political pressure from A (senator or commodity group, perhaps) after I accede to the political pressure from B?" I recall, also, that some of the decisions I faced as a university dean or president were not void of political pressure.
3. A seemingly foolish program, at least in AID or USDA, is not likely the result of the agency worker's idea or opinion. Rather, it likely exists because Congress passed a law or resolution that requires or encourages it. Further, Congress likely passed that law or resolution because an industry, organization, or influential interest group lobbied for it. Yes, exceptions do exist. Some federal agencies, such as EPA or OSHA, may attract zealots to their staff, people who will use the wording of any legislation to advance their personal cause.
4. It is a rare cabinet officer who is allowed to lead his or her department largely on the basis of his or her competence and experience under, of course, guidance from the president. I have empathy for cabinet officers who may feel forced to "salute and follow" when they get a call from a White House staffer. (For more insight, I suggest the recent book, *Duty*, by former secretary of defense, Robert M. Gates, Alfred A. Knopf, 2014.)
5. The suggestion that there is a fourth branch of government, Congressional staff, is valid. The Office of Personnel Management recently reported that the Senate had more than seven thousand staff, the House more than twelve thousand.

The figures calculate to seventy six per senator and twenty eight per House member, people who work directly for the members or their congressional committees. Not only do many of these staff have their own "constituency," there is plenty of opportunity for a committee staffer to insert a line or a line item, or modify a line, in a several-hundred-page bill. Most members of Congress spend their time in committees, conversations, or raising money, and have little time to read final bills.

6. Working in the Washington bureaucracy is a heady experience. It is where power exists, having steadily migrated in recent decades from local and state governments to Washington. For some people, it is difficult to leave. It is not uncommon for a replaced senator, representative, or agency head to remain in D.C. as a lobbyist. Though some may earn six figures and more, I have known some who would stay for only a desk, a phone, and a chance seek clients.
7. Every federal program is an invitation to fraud. In the agencies in which I worked, the approval processes for food aid or export subsidies, plus a watchful domestic constituency, minimized fraud opportunity. However, I shudder at the opportunities in money distribution programs, such as loans or grants to the private sector, Social Security, or Medicare.
8. Though there have been highly publicized cases where an administration has abused its authority via sympathetic staff in a key agency (such as the Internal Revenue Service in recent years or the Federal Bureau of Investigation in an earlier administration), most career staff try to be apolitical. They provide both the public and the administration, regardless of political party, the data as it exists and they administer programs as the law provides. John Lee, head of the Economic Research Service during my time and under several administrations once told me, "Every new administration wonders whether they can trust us to give unbiased information. After about six months, however, they realize that we just give them the facts."

To get away from the bureaucracy and the people density of Washington, Shirley and I would usually devote Saturday or Sunday to a drive into the Virginia or Maryland countryside, or even into West

Virginia or to visit a distant cousin on the central Pennsylvania farm from which my Acker ancestors had departed by wagon for Iowa in the early 1880s.

With such friends as the Rosendales, he an Illinois farmer heading USDA's Packers and Stockyards Administration, or with other friends, we picked peaches on a Virginia mountainside farm, visited the Wyeth art museums or Longwood Gardens in southeastern Pennsylvania, saw the miniature horses at Chincoteague Island, or ate crab cakes on Tangier Island. The latter two are islands off the Virginia tip of the DelMarVa Peninsula, the first reached by car and the latter by ferry.

Direct flights from Ronald Reagan airport to Kansas City made it rather easy to spend week-ends at our Iowa farm. Our calendar shows that we made forty five such trips during our six years in Washington. For several years we kept a car in the back yard of fraternity brother Ken Bruene's acreage a few miles from the Kansas City airport and it was less than three hours to our farm.

There were, of course, many week-end interests inside the District of Columbia, including an excellent zoo, tours of the Old Executive Office building, which was built in the 1800s for the Departments of State and War, and the many monuments and memorials. There was even a Saturday tour of foreign embassies, the latter arranged by a coffee group Shirley had helped organize in our Crystal City apartment building. Our six years in Washington provided rich experiences.

CHAPTER VIII

TO OPERATE OUR FARM

"Five minutes later, I discovered that I was midway across the field and dragging only the tongue of the harrow! The tongue had broken as I had turned at the field edge. Inside the insulated cab and listening to Agri-Talk on local station KJAN, I had not heard the tongue snap, and my tractor engine had not missed the harrow's weight.

"Armstrong will come driving over the hill," I thought, "and see me dragging a seven-foot tongue stub across an open field with a sixty five-horsepower tractor. That will be too good a story for gregarious Armstrong to keep to himself."

Though Shirley had agreed to the goal of operating our own farm, there seemed to me another issue. She deserved a home that she could design. In our married life we had owned five different homes and she could decorate them as she wished. However, two thirds of our married life we had lived in homes we did not own, twenty-one years on university campuses, including eighteen months in Iowa State's Pammel Court, and six years in a rented, Washington area apartment or house. I asked her where she would like to build a new home. Perhaps she would prefer one of the university towns where we had lived, our home town of Atlantic, or even Des Moines. Her response was quick, "We should build it at the farm; that is where you will be."

Between that November, 1992, election and early January, I had daily USDA administrative chores and some specific projects to wrap up, but we also found time to think not only about that house we wanted to build and, especially, our future farm operation. The farm would be different from what I had left forty five years earlier to enter college.

Fortunately, we had the Iowa farm home, which we had used many week-ends and during vacation time while at Kansas State and in Washington. During those years, we had added a double garage and insulated the house, so we would have a comfortable home while planning both the new house and our farming operation. Having expected Bush to get re-elected, most of our leases were locked in for the 1993 crop year; we had only one hundred fourteen acres uncommitted and on which to "practice."

For the total acreage I would eventually operate, beginning with the 1994 crop season, or even to handle that small acreage the first year, I would need more tractor power than the twenty-three horsepower Ford 1600 I had purchased fifteen years earlier to trim roadsides and waterways. If I could find what I needed before December 31, according to federal income tax provisions, I could take a full year of depreciation. Perhaps that depreciation would help justify a *new* tractor. I would find and buy mostly used equipment but, a new tractor was Number One on my list.

A New Tractor by Fax.

Perhaps a salesman needed to fill his year's quota of tractor sales. Or a dealer may need to sell more equipment by December 31 to qualify for his manufacturer's sales incentive. Such incentives were not uncommon in farm equipment and automobile businesses.

It was not until the Christmas holidays at the farm that I could check out models at local dealerships and I eventually settled on a Case-IH 5140 with an air-conditioned cab and front-wheel assist. The latter would make it a four-wheel drive with only the touch of a lever. I made calls to several dealers, even one at Harrisonville, Missouri, where I had seen a 5140 during a fall visit to Kansas City. As we left the farm and drove toward Murfreesboro, TN, to spend New Year's week-end with daughter LuAnn, I was still considering price offers.

It was mid morning December 31, in a phone visit with the Case-IH dealership in Audubon, Iowa, that I reached a purchase agreement. I told the salesman I had to complete the sale yet in 1992, all necessary paper work completed and signed.

"But you are in Tennessee and I'm in Audubon" he exclaimed.

"No problem," I said, "You have a fax machine and we will find one here in Murfreesboro. You fax me a bill of sale. I'll sign the bill of sale and fax it back to you." I do not recall if I wired a down payment or put a December 31 check in the Murfreesboro post office before it closed.

The 5140 would be delivered to the farm in late January.

More Sales per Crop Acre

Scott Deter, manager of the Deter family-owned General Motors dealership, called in October our first year on the farm with a question. I knew Scott as a Rotary club member, and, with his young daughter, at the First Presbyterian Church. I did not know then that he would eventually become my son-in-law.

Scott was working with a new computer and had a floppy disc with 1987 Census of Agriculture data. Always inquisitive, Scott had been scanning through Iowa's state and county data. His question was, "Why does Sioux County have so much higher farm sales than Cass County." The difference was more than three-fold.

Why did Scott call me? I had become part of a newly-formed, local Rural Development Action Committee focused on trying to increase the county's agricultural intensity. In the years since my youth, Cass County had become a corn-exporting county; most livestock and poultry enterprises had disappeared from area farms. The county was missing a lot of economic activity, such as milk and egg handling, transportation, veterinary services, feed manufacturing and sales, and other jobs associated with animal operations. Cass and neighboring counties had once been corn-importing counties; most farms were now simply crop operations, with a two-year, corn-soybean rotation.

I had a ready answer for Scott. In late summer, I had joined a Farm Credit Services tour of several northwest Iowa counties; we had seen cattle feedlots, swine, egg, broiler and turkey operations, and livestock equipment manufacturing. From almost any location during our tour we would see numerous animal operations. Many were two-generation, father and son or father and daughter.

Main streets in Sioux Center and Orange City were thriving. There were new churches and schools. One local resident observed that with such high employment in the countryside, required by those animal operations, school buses rarely got above twenty miles per hour on the country roads; they would be stopping at the next farm home to pick up more kids.

I considered the change in my home community. As a school bus driver my senior year, I had picked up twenty two students in my seven-mile circuitous route to Wiota. In the early '90s I could have gotten all the school-age kids on that route in the extended cab of my pick-up.

I told Scott: First, Sioux is a larger county. Second is Sioux County's large animal population. Livestock and poultry convert the grain and forage to higher value products. Though Sioux County was a large grain producer, because of high quality soil, it was also *importing* grain for those animal operations.

Obviously on Scott's mind: Higher farm sales would mean purchase of more Chevy pick-ups, Buick autos, and, likely, a few Cadillacs.

Scott's question prompted me to study the data for other counties. Perhaps exposing the data comparisons would encourage local producers to move back into animal enterprises. Perhaps local lenders, as well as main street business and professional people, would encourage them. It would mean more farm income, more year-round employment. It would also mean more business on main street, more bank deposits, and more sales and property tax to support schools and other government services.

An Ohio friend had asked me a month before at a meeting in Minneapolis what the "4x4" on an Iowa farm pick-up stood for. I bit, "What does it stand for?"

"Four weeks in the spring and four weeks in the fall."

Yes, that rather well described what I saw in our area. Only a few weeks of labor during the year are required to plant and harvest corn and soybeans, especially for producers who hire commercial applicators for weed and pest control. Little labor is needed beyond that.

The USDA data gave credit to each county for only that portion of "production" that occurred *in* the county, crops and animals grown and sold and, in the case of imported feeder pigs or feeder cattle, *only* that portion of the final sale weight that had been *added* while in the county. Because counties vary in geographic size, I chose to calculate dollar sales value *per crop acre*. That allowed business intensity comparisons between or among counties.

Were the differences among counties in sales value per crop acre due *only* to animal operations? No. Soil maps and corn and soybean yield data showed higher soil productivity in Sioux and its neighboring counties than in Cass and its neighboring counties. A higher proportion of the former counties' crop land was devoted to those crops and less to pasture. My "educated guess" was that about two thirds of the difference among counties in dollar sales per farm acre was due to the differences in number and size of animal operations.

USDA's Census of Agriculture is taken only every five years. From the time Scott asked that question, I would use the data, or five-year updates, as a challenge to farm and community audiences in southwestern Iowa at any opportunity. In the following table are the data for 1992, million dollar sales value, farm acres, and sales value per farm acre, plus the latter for 2012, for my home county, Cass, and adjacent counties, plus two counties to the north, Sioux and Carroll. The latter two provide a challenge for the others.

Dollar Sales Value per Farm Acre, Selected Iowa Counties*

County	Million $ Sales Value 1992	Farm Acres 1992	Sales Value per Farm Acre, 1992	Sales Value per Farm Acre, 2012
Shelby	124	362,900	$ 344	$ 943
Audubon	94	277,000	343	1,027
Pottawattamie	180	554,300	325	872
Cass	96	344,800	278	787
Montgomery	63	257,700	244	773
Guthrie	84	361,800	235	490
Adair	74	353,700	212	582
Adams	46	262,900	175	525
Carroll	196	348,200	338	1,506
Sioux	422	465,900	906	3,329

* Data from USDA. Farm acreage for every county had changed by 2012, as land may have been converted to or from other purposes. Calculations for the last column were from 2012 data.

11-4-14

By his question, Scott gave me the basis for much of the Rural Development Action Committee's work as well as for those presentations. Eventually gaining him as a son-in-law was a bonus.

A Rural Development Action Committee

It had been Garry Pellett, manager of a crop input business with seven locations in Cass and nearby counties who had initiated that Rural Development Action Committee. He had watched other parts of the state increase their farm dollar volume, was concerned that his area had not kept pace, and had pulled together a small group to try to get the ball rolling.

We were hardly settled after our move to the farm when, in early April, I had been invited to join Pellett and several others at his company headquarters on Atlantic's West Second Street. I find in my files a March 26, 1993, summary of an earlier meeting by that group. It was addressed to "Rural Development Action Committee" (RDAC) and it mentions Rick Pellett, Bill Pellett, County Extension Director Rich Hall, Tony Hermann (then with DeKalb Seeds), Janell Hansen, and Randy Euken. It said the group "would become a steering committee with representation from many groups with ideas for rural development and that it could also work with the Cass County Development Committee (CCDC), Atlantic Industrial Development Foundation (AIDF) and the Atlantic Chamber of Commerce." Marie Klinefelter of CCDC, at this writing, Mrs. Marie Rourick, AIDF board member Leanne Pellett, JoAnne Poeppe, Royal Bierbaum, and Maynard Hansen—as well as others—would be part of later meetings.

It further stated, "The group would probably be loosely structured initially, to encourage brainstorming and nontraditional thinking" and would not, itself, be part of financial transactions.

Apparently recognizing that I was then unemployed, it included, "All present agreed to ask Dr. Acker to come to the next meeting and to possibly chair the group."

Impressed with what the group had in mind, I was pleased to help. An April 14 meeting was my first with the group, and minutes describe an active discussion. Excerpts: "In trying to bring in value-added industries to the area, do we screen or do we promote anything that is presented to us?", "CCDC can be of benefit by targeting firms, construction, and product development", we need to "create an environment that stimulates creative ideas" and need to get "the word out to people, a news release telling about the group and what it is doing, ask to be on the meeting agenda for different boards, and get the Board of Supervisors involved."

The group's mission statement was refined to read: "Expand rural development opportunities through improved and increased dollar value of agricultural products and systems while maintaining and improving quality of life." Noting the dust and odor from grain processing businesses in major Iowa cities, and debates regarding the large swine units then recently built in north central Iowa, it had seemed to me that the phrase, "maintaining and improving quality of life" had to be included.

The goals were also refined, to enhance communication between rural and urban interests, to gather and nurture ideas and concepts, and then to promote and assist in their development.

Garry Pellett would be vice-chairman and Rich Hall secretary. Bill Pellett suggested we get subcommittees going to address the ideas already of interest, specifically beef and hogs. Euken and Bill Pellett would form a group focused on cattle feeding opportunities, Hall and Rick Pellett would work on hog production opportunities, and Hermann and Garry Pellett would focus on alternative or specialty crops.

Over the next several months, others stepped forward with ideas and suggestions, including Fred Kay, opportunities in poultry, Larry Kay, specialty crops, and Steve Olsen, alfalfa as a high-value crop. Other names are mentioned in bi-weekly meeting minutes and notes, including Don Sonntag, Varel Bailey, and Ray Underwood.

A year or so later, the leadership of CCDC and IADF moved to form a single entity to replace those two development groups. It would be county-wide, but would also acknowledge by its name, Cass-Atlantic Development Corporation (CADCO), that Atlantic was the site of major monetary support and larger potential for business development. In time, Dan White became CADCO's executive officer, a small state grant for RDAC's work was obtained, and Norman Mills, retired from a career in the feed industry, became a part-time RDAC coordinator.

From this apparent enthusiasm and strong start of the RDAC, it would be interesting to see what would develop. See later chapters, especially Chapter 11.

Thirty five years earlier, when I was advising Iowa State University students planning to farm, Iowa's average farm size was less than two hundred acres. I recall telling my advisees, then all young men, that to provide the level of living they and their spouses would likely need to raise and educate a family, they should be thinking about a considerably larger operation than Iowa's then-average acreage. Though animal enterprises would add dollar volume, they should also be thinking about more acres.

I would also suggest that the traditional goal, to "own our farm debt-free before we die," may therefore not be realistic. They should count on renting considerable land and/or plan to carry some level of "perpetual debt" on owned land. Those twenty-one-year-old students might have had four to five hundred acres as their target, but well before they were forty years of age, some would be operating more than a thousand acres and/or be handling large livestock or poultry enterprises.

As we had left Washington, I had wondered if our thousand-plus acres would be enough to bring the return to labor and management that a younger farm couple would have needed to raise and educate a family.

With our age and our land investment, I was also considering return on equity. I hoped to achieve a higher return on our land investment than if the land's value were invested in stocks, bonds, or a mutual fund.

As I had done in preparing for other new jobs, I had studied "the data." Farm Business Association records in both Kansas and Iowa had shown that financial return to labor and management on reasonably well-managed operations had narrowed from about twenty per cent of gross sales in the early 1960s to approximately eleven per cent in the early 1990s. I was familiar with association data, had for years used them as a base for speeches to farm, service clubs, and other groups.

Second, farmers in the 1990s needed to pay more attention to the impact of tillage, fertilizer rates, herbicides, insecticides, or manure handling on water quality, as well as native plant diversity, wildlife populations, and their neighbors' comfort.

The Business Plan

It seemed essential to write a farm business plan. It would include the enterprises that our land, skills, and borrowing capacity could handle, a set of goals and the strategies to achieve them. It should be detailed; at age sixty two, if I failed, I would not get a second chance.

One of our early actions was to invite Steve Olsen, to whom we had been renting an adjacent five hundred acre unit, to join in the operation of our total acreage. An Iowa State graduate and son of one my fellow 4-H members, Steve had taught vocational agriculture, then started farming at an unfortunate time, the early 1980s. Extraordinarily high interest rates had taken away both potential profit and ability to pay off operating loans. We proposed that we purchase his equipment and lease his small cow herd. He would have a steady income and the Olsen family could remain in the home they had occupied since early 1984.

I also needed Olsen's help on the business plan; I could read publications for advice, but he was current on farm equipment and practices. I find in my files an eight-page business plan we put together, but I provide here only a condensed version. Some enterprise and strategy explanations follow.

Talycoed II Business Plan

Goals:

1. 8 % return on assets. Considering start-up costs, 6% in 1994, 7% in 1995.
2. $500 gross product (hay, grain, and animal gain) value per farm acre; $300 for 1994, $400 for 1995.
3. Maintain and enhance natural resource base, the soil, water, and pasture grasses.
4. Neat and attractive farmstead and fields.

Enterprises and income sources:

1. Corn – approx. 500 acres, most following beans or alfalfa.
2. Soybeans – approx. 500 acres.
3. Alfalfa – target of 200 acres, 50 planted each year.

4. Beef calves. – target of 100 cows.
5. Conservation Reserve Program – 167 acres then contracted through 1998.

Strategies:

1. Focus on highest economic yields.
2. Hold crop machinery investment to $150 per crop acre.
3. Minimum tillage to help hold rainwater and soil.
4. Rotation grazing, to maximize grass production and beef gain per acre.
5. A written marketing plan, to include forward contracting and/ or hedging.
6. Carry hail and/or multi-peril insurance on a portion of the crop.
7. Nutrient applications within 115% of expected crop nutrient removal.
8. Employ a crop adviser to minimize herbicide/pesticide use and cost.

Alfalfa as a cash crop was not common in Iowa, but Olsen was enthusiastic about alfalfa and evidence suggested it could compete with corn and beans in profit potential. Alfalfa would require a large per acre investment to establish a stand, yield potential would be reached only in the second year, and there was no ready cash market as local elevators provided for corn and beans. However, plant pathologists and entomologists had suggested that a third crop in the rotation could help break the life cycles of corn-specific and soybean-specific pests. Also, once established, alfalfa's annual input cost would be low and, as a legume, alfalfa fixes nitrogen from the atmosphere, so we would need less nitrogen fertilizer for a following year of corn. Further, being an additional enterprise, alfalfa would spread the risk. We seeded one hundred twenty five acres of alfalfa in the spring of 1994.

Research showed less soil loss and more build-up of organic matter in the soil with no tillage, planting directly into the previous year's crop stubble, and I was sold on the concept. However, it had not worked for Steve on the poorly drained, creek-bottom portion of the land he had been renting. With crop residue remaining on top, there were few days each spring when the soil below was dry enough for planting or warm enough for good seed germination. With post-harvest cultivation, however, the exposed black soil would absorb more heat from the spring sun and dry more quickly.

We compromised on zone tillage, a six-row rig that tilled an eight inch strip in corn or bean residue. The machine on the market included a liquid fertilizer tank and we could also mount a six-row planter on the rear. It let us do the whole job of tillage, planting and fertilizing in one pass across the field. The tilled strip would absorb enough heat for germination, and the untilled strip, twenty two inches with rows thirty inches apart, would hold most of the rain and soil on the hillsides.

Some may ask why we should limit fertilizer to 115% of the nutrients leaving the field in grain. A fifty-bushel soybean crop will leave about fifty pounds of nitrogen in the soil for next year's corn, and a bushel of harvested corn will take with it only about a pound of nitrogen. Nitrogen not used by the corn plant either escapes into the atmosphere or, more likely, percolates down toward a water aquifer or to field tile drain lines that empty into a pond or creek. We wanted neither.

Avoiding the Iron Trap

It was the limit of one hundred fifty dollars machinery investment per crop acre that may have worried Olsen the most. Once we tallied the cost of the new zone tiller and planter, his equipment we were purchasing, the drill and rake needed for alfalfa, my new Case-IH 5140 and cultivator, and half the value of a Chevy pick-up (the other half I should attribute to personal use), there was no budget left for a combine.

"Can we count on getting a custom combiner when the beans are ready?" Olsen would wonder. Mature and dry soybean pods can easily shatter. And, if corn is not combined when ready, there is risk of ear drop.

However, the association data told me that, to achieve decent profit or return on equity, one had to be cautious with machinery investment. I had already signed a two hundred thousand dollar note for equipment and operations. I was not ready to pay six per cent or more interest on another eighty thousand dollars for a combine we would use only four weeks of the year.

Custom combining had been common in the wheat belt for decades, crews moving with wheat maturity from late May in Texas to September in North Dakota. Our beans would mature in late September and there should be custom operators available. In time, I learned that neighbor Don Jensen was using a custom combiner from Kimball, Nebraska, and we worked out a mutually beneficial arrangement. Bean varieties mature at varied times and his operator's two machines could keep pace with both our maturing fields. For corn, when Jensen's drying bins were full, his operator moved to my fields. By the time our drying bins were full, Jensen's dried corn had moved to storage bins, and the operator moved back to Jensen's.

By arranging a custom combiner, Olsen and I were free to haul the grain from the combine to the elevator or to our own storage bins. No additional labor was needed and the custom operator even provided a grain cart for our use. Note the loader on the front of the tractor; it was needed to load and stack hay bales, clean feedlots, and handle snow.

Operating a combine is more fun than hauling grain to the elevator or to drying and storage bins. Steve did not completely miss that fun; on several days he managed to trade spots with the custom operator.

In Belarus, Cold Hotel and Warm Hospitality

Most beginning farm couples would be in their twenties. We were in our early sixties and carried experiences that would yield unexpected requests. During our first November back on the farm, Shirley and I would travel to another of the former Soviet Republics, my role to help tell college students what private farming is all about.

Shirley and I left on our coats as we unpacked in our fifty-degree Orbita Hotel room in Minsk, Belarus, after a twenty-hour flight from the U.S. We were glad to see a down comforter, a woolen blanket, and large pillow on each of the twin beds.

We found a bit of heat drifting from a recessed radiator below the window. We stacked two chairs over the luke-warm radiator and against the window drapes to block some of the cold oozing in alongside the window sash. Then we crawled under the down comforters and slept.

Next door, my college classmate and former Shelby County, Iowa, county agent, Dale Seebach, and his wife, Carol, were likely doing the same.

Seebach and I had been recruited by VOCA, Volunteers in Overseas Cooperative Assistance, to spend a month in what had been known as White Russia, now Belarus, to lecture students at Belarus Agrotechnical University (BATU) on private farming and how it functions.

We had been well warned by Washington VOCA staff. Belarus was in deep economic trouble, having lost its guaranteed trade, energy, and communication linkages with other former Soviet republics. We should take warm clothes and dry, packaged food items. We should expect cold rooms and no or few restaurant services.

Part of a Minsk apartment complex in November. Note the snow, heavy coats, and caps, and the bus stop shelters. Private cars were rare, not affordable.

After solving visa problems on arrival at the Minsk airport, I had changed twenty U.S. dollars for a stack of Belarus rubles, about four thousand rubles per dollar. Inflation was approaching one thousand per cent per year; ten days later we would get forty five hundred rubles for a dollar.

We were met by a VOCA office assistant and driver and taken in two small cars to this hotel, perhaps five km. from city center. Our planned hotel in city center had *no* heat. We breakfasted the next morning in our room on dried fruit and granola from our suitcases, then walked to an adjacent supermarket to purchase a loaf of dark bread and to seek, without success, bottled water "without gas" (non-carbonated). Then, at a small shop just off the hotel lobby, we found fruit nectar, UHT (ultra-high-temperature pasteurized) milk, and coke, all imported from Western Europe and for which we paid with dollars.

Late morning at a downtown office we met VOCA's country representative, an Iowan, Richard Selby, and Dr. Larisa Tericova, BATU director of international programs. She and her interpreter drove us to the BATU campus and an early afternoon luncheon. Considered special guests, we were accommodated in a dining room just off the student/faculty cafeteria, windows lining one side and colder than our hotel room.

The menu: cabbage borsch, beet/cabbage salad, a hot dog cooked in butter, French fries, and hot tea. It was excellent food and flavorful. Within our hosts' resources, we were being treated beautifully, and felt complimented.

Next was a meeting with BATU's vice rectors and department heads to "equalize expectations," discuss just what our lectures would cover. All discussion had to be handled through Tericova's interpreter, the head of BATU's "Rural Languages" department. Seebach and I asked what they expected from us, and their response surprised us, "Lectures in ecology."

My response that neither of us considered ourselves ecologists was met with expressions of shock and irritation, and it took minutes of laborious interchange through the interpreter to clarify that their concern was ecological management of soils, including minimum tillage and chemical use.

The primacy of ecology also became clear, the recent Chernobyl disaster. Chernobyl is but a few kilometers south of Belarus' Ukrainian border. Nuclear fall-out had drifted northward, causing at least temporary abandonment of up to one-fourth of Belarus' productive land and, of course, family relocations. Many Belarus deaths and maladies had been attributed to Chernobyl. Perhaps the abandoned soils could be re-claimed, made "ecologically sound."

In time, we agreed on a list of ten topics on which we would lecture. However, Seebach and I also needed some understanding of the students to whom we would lecture, as well as the problems and potential that any current Belarus' private farmers faced. Only then could we prepare fully useful lectures.

The impact of Chernobyl was the topic of the day in Belarus. A local women's group, learning that two American educators were in town, had pressed the VOCA office for us to schedule time with them before we headed back to our hotel. Their concerns were intense, largely the long-term effects of nuclear fall-out on their children's health. We had no data on the form or degree of fall-out in southern Belarus, so could be of little help. We could only empathize.

We did learn that this and other groups had raised funds to send some of the children to rural camps in the northern part of the country or to Italy for brief "vacations" away from any radiation risk.

In a follow up meeting with the vice rectors and department heads the next day we re-emphasized our desire to visit a farm, but met disinterest or objections. It eventually dawned on us that, 1) our hosts may not know of a private farm and 2) BATU may not have money for fuel to drive us there, if and when they did learn of one. A private farm would be rare, and any that existed would have been recently established.

Our BATU hosts would come through, but only after firm insistence by Seebach and me that our first lectures would be *after* at least one visit to a private farm.

Two per cent Interest and One Hundred per cent Inflation!

Some kilometers outside Minsk we twice reversed direction on the highway, our driver asked directions of truck drivers, collective farm workers, and villagers and, finally, wound through a village adjacent to the highway and about a mile beyond drove into a farmstead. The farm was fifty hectares, equivalent to about one hundred acres. Twenty three hectares had been "allocated" by the government from a state or collective farm three years earlier and another twenty seven hectares the year of our visit. Personal land "ownership" was generally less than a hectare surrounding one's residence, and that usually in a village.

Government policy encouraged private farming, but that policy was opposed by many, especially the state and collective farm managers. Once allocated by the government to a private farmer, the land could not be sold, but could be passed on to succeeding generations. Our host therefore felt secure in making an investment in a house and facilities. However, since the land had been only "allocated," the farmer did not hold a merchantable title and it could not be used as security for a loan.

He was about forty years of age, formerly a truck driver. He had grown up in a village, his father a teacher, and he had long wanted to farm. We asked why and he quickly replied, "To be my own boss."

His wife was at a nearby agricultural institute for a two-week course in artificial insemination, an eighteen-year-old daughter in training for another occupation, a seventeen-year-old son was in an agricultural training program, and an eight-year-old daughter in primary school.

A split-level house, perhaps two thousand square feet, was under construction, using tile, brick, and concrete. A cement block barn with a pre-stressed concrete, flat roof held twenty four small-type Holstein and Friesian cows, several calves, a dozen sows with litters of six to nine pigs, two horses, about twenty sheep of mixed breeding, and about twenty five hens of mixed colors. Our host told us the cow herd had averaged ninety six hundred pounds of milk per cow the past year. He felt the herd's production could be improved over time by use of artificial insemination.

In the barn was also a feed room, with a twenty five-horsepower electric grinder, a milk tank and washing room for his pipe-line milking system, a utility room, and temporary home/office.

The local state veterinarian and his assistant came by for what appeared to be a routine check of the dairy herd, but perhaps prompted by our visit. The veterinarian told us the major cattle concerns were a "blood cancer," leucosis, and reproductive problems.

Major crops were potatoes and barley. Potato sorting and bagging equipment was in the yard and a pile of barley was in a corner of the machine shed. There were also four tractors, from twenty to one hundred horsepower, a pick-up, truck, combine, field cultivator, disc mower, and spring-tooth harrow.

With land allocated at no cost, a government operating loan of two thousand rubles per hectare at two per cent interest for three years, and inflation at one thousand per cent, he had a great deal! He had paid off his loan with cheap rubles, was debt free, and had money left over to build the house.

The private farm south of Minsk, the farmer's house under construction and some of his equipment.

We asked this private farmer about his most serious problems. His response was quick, "Access to tractor fuel, fertilizer, agricultural chemicals, and knowledge." He had obtained semen for his cows and some technical help from an agricultural research institute in the area, but said that an extension education system like in the U.S. would be helpful. The vice rector commented that he had been to Canada a year earlier and recalled that farmers there and in the U.S. "had access to forty different businesses that could provide inputs and services."

We asked our host what advice we should give to university students to whom we would be lecturing. He responded, "Do not be afraid."

On return to Minsk we invited the vice rector and interpreter to be our guests for lunch at one of the few open restaurants, 7-Fridays. The vice rector declined; he said he did not often get a chance to eat at such an expensive place and asked for a rain-check. We dropped him at his apartment and at 7-Fridays the five of us had delicious mushroom/vegetable soup, fish filet in batter, peas, pickled cucumbers, and a sauerkraut/coleslaw dish, all for a grand total of thirty six thousand rubles, less than nine U.S. dollars.

Bread on the Hour

Free for the afternoon, we headed with our spouses to the "Italian store" to look for "biz gas" and found none, so purchased a liter of lemonade, a carton of fruit nectar, and two candy bars with U.S. dollars. In a different "Dollar shop" we found some biz gas, oranges, musli breakfast cereal, and cheese, and then continued shopping in a supermarket, upstairs in the same building.

We exchanged our plastic bag of earlier purchases for a numbered wire basket. We found plastic bags of zwieback, a family favorite, in a large bin, bags of sugar cookies (thicker, darker, and less sweet than those in the U.S.), loaves of freshly baked dark and white bread, yet warm, not wrapped and on open shelves at the rear of the store.

We were told that ingredients and baking capacity were so limited that customers would often be standing in line at those shelves for each hour's bread production. On an earlier shopping trip, Shirley and Carol had stood in line for bread; we had happened to be in this supermarket at the right time.

We searched for a small jar of jelly or fruit sauce and the only thing smaller than a gallon was a half pint of applesauce for babies. Like every other jar in the store, it had a pressed-on metal lid and a plain brown label.

Our basket of groceries at the check-out counter cost about three thousand rubles, less than one U.S. dollar, and that included the add-on cost of a plastic carrying bag. We then returned the shopping basket at the entry counter and retrieved our earlier purchases.

Dinner for the Seebachs and Ackers that evening in our room was dried fruit from our suitcases, apples our BATU host had brought us from her garden, applesauce (the lid pried off with my knife and eaten with a shoehorn from our airline kit), and part of an Italian chocolate bar.

We had wondered about the "Italian store," and other evidence of Italian presence. We learned that the Italian military had occupied this area during the latter part of WWII and, after Perestroika, Italy had been one of the earlier and larger contributors of loans, grants, and advisers to Belarus. In addition to being a part of later European Community aid, Italy had contributed development funds directly and there had resulted several joint ventures and trading businesses with Italians.

A Pin for your Good Work

We had pressed our BATU hosts to let us see both a private farm and a collective farm, so we might be best equipped to adapt our lectures to the students' backgrounds or experiences. We were now at a collective farm near the city.

The artificial insemination technician, a woman in her fifties, had been showing us the record system that helped her achieve a seventy per cent conception rate in the dairy cow herd on the first insemination and another twenty-five per cent on the second. It was a large, rotating wheel, divided by months and the days within months, on which hung a numbered tag for each cow. Outside the wheel, on solid background, were the time periods for the estrus cycle, pregnancy, lactation, and dry period. By moving the wheel a notch each day, she could see how many tubes of semen she would need the next day, as well as the status of each of the herd's four hundred Holsteins.

From the left, our BATU dean, the artificial insemination technician, and the collective farm manager. Note the wheel the technician had devised to keep track of each cow's spot in the reproduction cycle and her schedule of tasks.

The farm director praised her work, told us she inseminates twelve and eighteen hours after detecting estrus. She had worked at the farm twenty seven years and was to have received a Soviet medal after twenty five. However the Soviet Union had dissolved just before that and she did not get her medal.

Though we saw few cows that would approach twelve hundred pounds in weight and few showed the glossy hair coat we would like to see, the director told us the herd was averaging ninety six hundred pounds of milk per cow per year. It had been above ten thousand pounds, but production had dropped since Chernobyl, due to lack of forage "from the south," and less motivated labor. I wondered, "What motivates in a collective if there are no more medals?"

The barns were clean, cleaner than at the private farm we had visited, and some lime had been scattered on the barn floor, a sanitation practice common on U.S. dairy farms in the '30s and '40s. We saw the same neatness and cleanliness at the farm's seed cleaning and storage unit, which apparently sold barley and other seed to other collective farms.

The vice rector had told us this collective was also the "university's training farm" and, of course, had the equipment and enterprises related to BATU's curriculum. However, we did not encounter any university students as we walked and visited. The director, crop and livestock managers, and agricultural economist, the latter a young woman with a masters degree in agricultural economics, each had questions for Seebach and me about U.S. farms and farm policy.

We quizzed the agricultural economist about comparative profitability of enterprises, asked for any data comparing this unit with other collective farms. Her response was that, though they had much data, galloping inflation made it of little value and emphasis was on just finding enough money to pay workers' salaries.

With all of the enterprises, fertilizer, chemical, or processing plants and collective farms being state enterprises, I wondered how decision-makers could make reasonable price or quota adjustments in the absence of an open market and market-reporting system, either public or private. Time and translation limitations precluded our really digging into that issue. In a country trying to move toward some form or degree of free enterprise and profit motivation, I would not envy the management task.

This farm was facing yet another problem. It was in a Minsk city expansion area and, according to our hosts, had lost much of its land for "new mansions for high-placed bureaucrats who had become wealthy." Was some "privatization" being achieved by granting land or business ownership to certain officials? I would later see evidence of that in Ukraine.

Just how should a totally socialist country move nationalized real property to the newly-allowed private sector? The several countries of Eastern Europe were a series of experiments, each struggling through the process in its own political way.

I also wondered, "With U.S. farms moving to larger units for more efficiency and competitiveness in a global market, was it really wise to break up these collective farm holdings into individual, small units? Might it be better, long term, to give or assign each worker shares of ownership in the farm, retain and enhance any existing efficiency of scale, and prepare—or replace— management to focus on efficiency, marketing, and profit?"

The Seebachs and Ackers still had to think about dinner in our hotel rooms. We stopped at an adjacent, state-owned poultry unit and in its sale shop purchased six hundred grams (more than a pound) each of two types of ready-to-eat chicken sausage. We would find it flavorful and with good texture.

Lecturing in an Overcoat

Fifteen students and three faculty, all in heavy clothing and some wearing gloves with the fingers open so they could take notes, awaited our first lecture. The classroom was frigid, but I had on long underwear, a heavy woolen suit, and an overcoat. Even more revealing of Belarus' circumstance, most of the students would take their notes on envelopes or scraps of paper. I do not recall seeing a spiral or three-ring notebook.

Neither Seebach nor I knew the Ukrainian language and only a few of our audience would handle English. We had been provided a retired military translator and he had picked up our lecture notes at our hotel room the evening before so he could familiarize himself with the words. We were cautious and sparing in our word choice, often avoiding complete sentences and choosing words less likely to be misinterpreted.

Presentations would take far more time than for home audiences. I would state a concept, perhaps using a blackboard or overhead projector to illustrate, and our translator would follow up in the Belarus language. Any questions would, of course, be a two-step process and so, too, our answer. Here are some of the lecture topics we chose for our eight 90-minute lectures.

Gaining Assets to Farm – assign or lease land, borrow money, buy or lease equipment.

Goals and Strategies – return on investment, yields, protecting the soil.

Decision-Making in a Risk Environment – lists of risks, choosing low-risk enterprises.

Economic Principles in Farming – fixed and variable costs, law of diminishing returns.

Record Keeping – for crop inputs, yields, prices, animal production, income, and outgo.

Producing for the Consumer – product quality, direct sales, sanitation

Farm Organizations – to share information, seek inputs or markets, influence laws.

Ecology of Soil Management – soil structure and organic matter, soil organisms.

Attendance at our daily lectures, at 11:30 some days and 4:30 other days, was voluntary and varied from four to twenty six, and we were distressed by the low attendance. However, we were repeatedly assured that we were providing exactly what the students needed. Unfortunately, most students and faculty were preparing for December final exams. The original request by BATU to VOCA had been for volunteers the month of October, but process delay and our schedules had precluded our arrival until mid November.

Our first day, with the fifteen students, we asked about their backgrounds. Here is what we learned:

Raised on or had worked on a collective farm – 13
Is now a private farmer – 2
Had worked for a private farmer – 3
Wanted to be a private farmer – 12
Planned to work on a collective farm -3
Had read some English - 4
Had completed secondary school – all
Now enrolled in BATU – 11
Had completed the university – 2

Three students stuck with us throughout. One was a thirty five-year-old who had a vegetable seed business. The second, in his mid-thirties and working in the Minsk tractor plant, had children from ages eight to sixteen and said he wanted to come to the U.S. to drive a tractor on a U.S. farm. The third was a shy man in his early twenties who indicated he had enough money to travel to the U.S. for some farm work experience.

Our interpreter and his colleagues in BATU's foreign language (English) department invited us to an afternoon tea. They not only valued conversing in the English language, several were hoping for travel to or perhaps graduate study in the United States and asked for help in preparing their resumes.

BATU was a specialized institution, and could be described as a U.S. university department of agricultural engineering, plus components of mechanical and electrical engineering, soils, and the milk and milk handling sections of dairy and food science departments. We saw no evidence of an agricultural economics faculty. A livestock engineering laboratory, for example, included twelve students at work in a room with a stationery forage cutter, a hammer mill, a potato steamer and mixer (potatoes are chopped, steamed, and mixed with barley or other grains for hogs), and other such equipment. Equipment was well built, similar to what we used in the 1950s or '60s. A second laboratory had a one-stall milking parlor and milk processing equipment.

In the BATU library we found several books that outlined record-keeping systems and gave some attention to the management function. At BATU, as elsewhere in the former Soviet system, it appeared that concepts of supply and demand, diminishing returns, substitution, or competitive opportunity were not commonly held. Where government allocated resources and set quotas and prices, and where decisions are heavily influenced by personal or party politics, they would be of little use.

Government policy was to encourage private farming, but BATU needed to reach elsewhere for concepts. That is why we had been invited, but Seebach and I, together, were only a "drop in the bucket," relative to need.

At BATU, there was no attention to the biological aspects of animal and crop production, such as genetics, variety development, animal reproduction, physiology, or nutrition. We were to learn that these disciplines were taught at a second agro-technical university about three hundred kilometers west, in the city of Grodno and near the Polish border. We decided we wanted to visit Grodno.

Who Tells You What to Plant?

That question to Seebach and me was from one of twenty three private farmers who had gathered on the Grodno Agrotechnical University campus to hear us. It was our last day in Belarus and we had driven with our VOCA representative those three hundred kilometers to Grodno. Grodno's dean had learned we were in country and his request that we come to his campus had meshed with our desire.

Travel had been slow on the rough, two-lane road, with no time or place to stop for lunch, and we had arrived just in time for a five-minute visit with the dean before a scheduled 3:15 lecture. The dean had just returned from visiting land grant universities in Utah, Oklahoma, and Tennessee, and told us he had "so many ideas that he could not sleep nights." In January, he would start a supplemental short course for their fourth- and fifth-year students who wanted to become private farmers.

Seebach and I were hardly able to get through our twenty-minute presentation, concepts we felt important and with a few slides. Our audience was bursting with questions. "How big is your farm?" "What do you grow?" "How do you borrow the money you need?" "Where do you get your seeds, or fertilizer, or chemicals?" That was good; more learning occurs in response to questions, and our answers were easily understood and accepted.

However, when we answered the next question, "Who sets the price?" with "Only supply and demand," facial expressions ranged from surprise to wonderment. We had to explain. The Belarus government had always established prices, and the relationship of supply or demand to price just did not fit the paradigm. There were follow-up questions, "Doesn't the government set the price?" How do you know if your price is the right price?"

The next question was, "Who tells you what to plant, the government?" When we answered, "No, we do," we had more explaining to do. We talked about supply and demand, relating how high supply and/or lower demand prompts us to increase or decrease acreage of a crop, perhaps shift acreage among crops.

I recalled a conversation of two years earlier in Poland, where a state meat market manager was worried that his product was piling up. We suggested he lower the price. His response: "If I lower the price, I won't make a profit." I assumed he would just report spoiled product to his superior. Avoiding spoilage by selling at a lower price did not fit the paradigm—or, perhaps, the price had been *set* by government policy.

We would have more experience with residue of the Soviet system. At 4:45 we had to close down our discussion and find a place to eat. We had had no lunch, for me only a candy bar I had carried in my pocket. We scouted Grodno, but no restaurants or cafes were open, not even a bakery or sausage shop. At restaurant doors, locals would tell us, "No food until six o'clock." That had been the government policy and had remained. There was yet no evidence of business competition to serve the public.

What we had seen on the drive from Minsk gave us no confidence we would find a place to eat in the three hundred kilometers back to Minsk. We had no alternative but to wait, and at six o'clock we were at the door of Grodno's downtown hotel dining room.

With our flight back to the U.S. scheduled for the next day, we assumed Shirley and Carol were pacing the floor at our Minsk hotel. However, I had a good nap while on the road and we pulled in about midnight.

In both Belarus and, later, in Georgia, conversations often included reference to WWII. In the case of Belarus, it was a village to the east of Minsk where all residents were killed and the village burned to the ground by the German army because of some residents' resistance activities following occupation. We were taken to that village to view the memorials.

Only the Tongue of the Harrow

Back on our Iowa farm in early spring, it was alfalfa seeding time and I was preparing the seedbed. For good germination and, eventually, a thick stand of alfalfa, seed-soil contact is critical. This meant two trips over the land with a disc to loosen the soil as well as to cut up the corn stalks and leaves from the previous season, one trip with a Logan harrow to smooth the surface, then one with a heavy culti-packer. Our drill would place the alfalfa seed a half-inch deep and we would then harrow and culti-pack again. This day, pulling the harrow with my Case-IH 5140, I could be embarrassed.

The Logan harrow was new to me, three sections of what appeared to be oversize cyclone fence connected to a foldable front beam. From that beam, a ten-foot tubular steel tongue extended forward, reinforced only by two short braces at forty five degrees back to the beam. That left about seven feet of tongue between the braces and the tractor, with stress concentrated just ahead of those braces. We had seen a fresh weld at that point when we had purchased the harrow at a farm sale in January.

Shirley had called to tell me that former Kansas Farm Bureau President Junior Armstrong and his wife had stopped by our home and were driving up to visit with me. Five minutes later, I discovered that I was midway across the field and dragging only the tongue of the harrow! The tongue had broken as I had made the turn at the field edge. Inside the insulated cab and listening to Agri-Talk on local station KJAN, I had not heard the tongue snap, and my tractor engine had not missed the harrow's weight.

"Armstrong will come driving over the hill," I thought, "and see me dragging a seven-foot tongue stub across an open field with a sixty five-horsepower tractor. That will be too good a story for gregarious Armstrong to keep to himself."

I spun the 5140 around, headed back to the harrow and was unhitching the tongue from the tractor, positioning it back in place, just as Armstrong pulled up.

Armstrong was sympathetic, offered that breakdowns always happen in the busy season. I kept him focused on our conversation and the broken tongue; I was not about to let him notice those tractor tracks out to the middle of the field and back.

Steve Olsen planting the seed, spring of 1994, for the one hundred twenty five acres and, in time, the tons of alfalfa that we would sell as a cash crop.

Collision in the Corn Field?

The concrete highway between Atlantic and Wiota, laid down in the early 1930s and now identified as Highway 83, had served its time. One of my first community involvements soon after we moved back to our farm, had been to join some community leaders to meet with Iowa's Department of Transportation Commission in Des Moines to press for that section's reconstruction. One commission member was a Kansas State graduate and perhaps my presence would help focus his attention to the need.

I do not know if my presence had helped, but by the spring of 1995 re-construction was underway and Highway 83 traffic had been detoured north to I-80. However, many Anita and Wiota residents driving to Atlantic used a shorter route, a township road that ran along the south edge of our farm.

The reckless speed of a small car leading a cloud of road dust yet a quarter mile away pulled my eyes off the blinking lights of the corn planter monitor. I was making the first pass around the field, planting the six "end rows" along the field edge.

This otherwise rarely-used township road, dirt the first three quarter mile toward an intersection at the corner of our farmland, and gravel past our farmland, was now a busy, informal detour. As the car passed the intersection and hit the loose gravel, it began to fishtail. Watching the fishtail rhythm, I thought, "He's going to hit me."

There was no field fence, only a shallow ditch between the roadway and my big Case 2290 diesel, its faded yellow and orange reflecting its thirteen years, and my new forty thousand dollar tiller, fertilizer applicator, and planter.

If that little Plymouth should fly across the shallow ditch and hit my four tons of steel, seed corn, and liquid fertilizer, there might be nothing left but crumpled plastic, glass shards, and a bare chassis. Perhaps Monday's Kansas City Star or the K-State Collegian would carry a small item, "Former K-State Head Injured in Cornfield Collision." It would be more a human interest story than hard news.

He had lost it; the Plymouth was airborne! But, it was in the air only a few seconds. Its right fender hit the ditch bank below where the fence had been, it did a double reverse somersault, and, by some miracle, landed squarely on all four wheels, inches behind my planter and facing the direction from which it had come. Had it been in the Olympics diving competition, it would have earned at least a silver medal.

I shoved the Case into neutral, jumped down from the cab, and raced back to the settling dust. The car's rear hatch was open, two windows had popped out, and a clear plastic bag containing what appeared to be a tuxedo and shirt was lying on the ground.

I had expected to find a bleeding driver under one of the wheels or, perhaps lying lifeless over in the ditch. However, still in the seat, shaking, and clutching the steering wheel with both hands, was a boy of about sixteen. I would learn he was on his way to Atlantic to return the tux he had rented for his Friday night Junior-Senior prom in Anita, then to his five o'clock job at Burger King. He had not left home early enough and feared he would be late for work.

"Are you O.K.?"

"I – I – I think so."

By that time the dust had settled, "Do you need to call someone?"

"I need to call my mom."

I ran back to the tractor, reached up into the cab for my portable phone, then yet a half-pound instrument.

Still in his seat, "Mom, I just ruined your car."

Fortunately the car was not a total loss. The boy was shook, but physically O.K. My corn planting was delayed only for the time it took to make phone arrangements for him and the car.

We finished planting the field about midnight.

After the White House Volunteer Office

By now in our new farm home, Shirley found time to get back to one of her long-time interests, painting. Though she would miss her friends from six years in the White House Volunteer office, painting could be "all-consuming." She had studied under one of our art faculty during our time at Kansas State and she and a friend would escape to the Flint Hills to do water colors. During our time in D.C. she had taken classes in calligraphy and had also taught calligraphy.

She had now moved to a far more complex and ancient art, fired oils on porcelain. In addition to perspective, color, and shading, porcelain art demands attention to the effects of firing temperature on individual pigments and their oil carriers. After each application of paint, starting with the lighter colors, the piece is fired at a temperature above 1400 degrees.

Mention of porcelain or china painting usually triggers thought of flowers on dinnerware. That was Shirley's starting point in the mid 1990s after our return to the farm. She was soon creating her own designs and using a variety of stock, from boxes to vases to floor and wall tile. Her love of nature prompted her to move to landscapes and scenes, then to birds and animals. Soon she was winning blue ribbons in State Fair and other competition.

By that time she had become a member of the Cass County Arts Council, was named to the Iowa Arts Council by Iowa Governor Terry Branstad, and would serve two terms on the board of the Wesley Foundation, which owns and operates retirement and extended care facilities in five Iowa communities, including our home town of Atlantic.

Through all of this, she continued to try new ideas in porcelain painting. To provide extra texture to some pieces, for the bark of a tree, for example, she experimented with a thin layer of fiberglass, which fused to the porcelain during firing. To create something new is her satisfaction.

With the help of local photographer, Kerry Barrett, a CD of her many pieces was put together and next, with the help of electronic publishing, there would come a book, *Fired Oils on Porcelain, Selected Work of Shirley Hansen Acker.*

CHAPTER IX

THE FARM AND MORE

"I awoke Monday morning to no electricity, no convenient food in the apartment except a bag of M&Ms with peanuts. Maglakelidze had taken us to dinner the night before and I had gotten back to my apartment after the supermarket had closed. My maid, a mid-forties pediatrician at a state hospital and needing more income than her salary, would come to introduce herself and pick up any laundry and a grocery list. She arrived but, to communicate, she phoned her son to translate for us. I gave her a ten-dollar bill to buy a few groceries for me at the supermarket."

My crop consultant, Doug Pedersen, had given me two pieces of advice when I had engaged his services, 1) Start planting corn on April 20 regardless of temperature or the weather forecast, and 2) Buy a cultivator.

Late planted corn and beans generally yield less. Members of a Top Producers' workshop I would later attend at Purdue calculated the cost of delayed planting at three to four hundred dollars per hour, depending on size of planter and acres to be planted. These calculations would confirm Pedersen's planting date advice.

With only a six-row planter for nine hundred acres of corn and beans, we tried to keep the planter going from near sun-up to late at night. Steve and I would spell each other for meals and for his work with the cattle. In this case, with rain forecast, I had napped late afternoon, had spelled Steve about nine o'clock, and would plant through the night.

Out of Diesel at 2 a.m.

Just before midnight I finished planting beans on the north farm and pointed the old Case 2290 and tiller/planter toward home. I would fill the planter boxes and the tractor's fuel tank and move on to a one hundred twenty-acre tract that adjoined our farmstead.

Our house was dark, but under our security light I filled the planter boxes with bags of beans from the pick-up Olsen had driven down for me and headed to the field. In my rush, I forgot the tractor fuel.

After I planted the end-rows, the tractor lights and my familiarity with the land (I had worked every inch of this home farm in my youth) led me to the far end of the longest terrace, one my father had built with his F-20 and moldboard plow forty-five years earlier. That terrace would guide my side-hill planting pattern.

"This all-night work is not so bad," I thought. The tillage coulters were working well and the planter's monitor lights were blinking with regularity (each of the six monitor lights blinked as a seed dropped past a sensor in the tubes below the planter box). The ten o'clock news, radio talk shows, and my watching both the monitor and trailing equipment kept me from getting sleepy.

I had just dropped the tiller and planter into the ground below that terrace and was only two hundred feet into the field when the Case engine sputtered. The clue was unmistakable, out of diesel. I grabbed and turned the key, swore silently about forgetting to fuel up, and hoped I had killed the motor before the line from the fuel tank had completely drained.

Though I had my phone, I was not about to call for help. Shirley, not enthusiastic about me working through the night, would be asleep. Steve was three miles away by road and also long in bed.

It was pitch dark, no moon. I stumbled through a half mile of corn stalks back to our shop, put a five-gallon can in the back of the pick-up, along side the bags of seed, and filled it with diesel. Hoping my clatter had not awakened Shirley, I drove back up across the field, poured in the diesel, and climbed up into the tractor cab.

If I had failed to kill the motor in time, I had a big problem. There is no "choke" in a diesel, as in a gasoline-powered vehicle, to suck the fuel from the tank to the motor. If the fuel line is empty, one has to bleed the air out of the line so the fuel in the re-filled tank will flow down toward the engine. It is a tedious and time-consuming job, even in daylight.

I turned the key to heat the glow plug and held it long enough to be sure the plug was red hot. I made a silent prayer and turned the key to "Start." The engine coughed — and coughed — and coughed — and started!

Steve Olsen and our son-in-law, Terry Nygaard, pouring soybean seed into the planter boxes, the planter mounted at the back of the zone tiller. Note the corrugated coulters or discs that do the tillage, and the liquid fertilizer tank above.

Perhaps not recognizing that I was now busy farming, or not believing I would be foolish enough to do it, several former colleagues suggested me for a variety of tasks. One of the more interesting was to serve as an expert witness in a Mississippi court case involving division of state appropriations between that state's two land grant universities, Mississippi State University at Starkville and Alcorn State University, located between Vicksburg and Natchez. Like Iowa State and Kansas State, Mississippi State had its roots in the 1862 Land Grant Act. Alcorn State's base was the Land Grant Act of 1890, which provided federal funds to help establish land grant colleges for southern states' black students under the "separate but equal" philosophy of the time.

By the 1990s, both universities had long been open to all students, regardless of race, but the Alcorn student body had remained predominately black. Trustees of the Mississippi University System believed it could not afford two colleges of agriculture. At the same time, fans of Alcorn State said that their university had not been fairly treated and that a higher proportion of state appropriations should go to Alcorn. Representatives of Alcorn and at least two other predominately black universities had filed suit against the System trustees and the case had been long in court.

My job was to gather data that would help the System trustees justify the allocation decisions they had made and, as an expert witness, present that data in court. I would make several trips to Starkville and Alcorn to become sufficiently acquainted with both so that I would be credible in my judgments and in court.

I returned from a week-long trip to Mississippi in late June to find a flourishing crop of cattails in several acres of the more poorly drained, creek bottom land we had planted in May to soybeans.

Cattails in the Soybeans

I had addressed part of the bottom land problem the previous fall, building about two thousand feet of diversion terrace to catch water draining off the adjacent hills. However, there had been considerable spring rain, too few sunny and windy days, and we had had to almost "mud in" some of the soybeans. The tractor and trailing equipment had left tracks in the soil surface, and more rain had followed.

Though the soybeans had emerged and were four to five inches high, cattail seeds from previous years had had a head start. They were twelve to eighteen inches tall and beginning to head.

"Oh, oh," I thought, "If my friends in the local NRCS office come by to see if that diversion terrace had held during the spring rains and see those cattails, they might declare this acreage a "wetland," to be forever maintained as such.

I called Pedersen, "What will kill the cattails in my soybeans?" He did some checking and reported, "I found nothing that is guaranteed to work and the product that might work would cost more than you would want to spend."

That prompted an inspiration. I attached my five-foot rotary mower to the little Ford 1600, set the blades just above the tops of the soybeans and, straddling the soybean rows with the Ford, mowed off the cattails. Within a week, with the warm June sun and plenty of soil moisture, I had an un-broken field of soybeans. No one would notice the cattail stubs between the bean rows.

What Would you Hear?

Our Rural Development Action Committee had been at work about a year when one of my young farmer friends said to me, “If your committee really wants to increase farm income, help us develop our marketing skills.” Soon, Hall, Garry Pellett, Ken Kay, and I got together over lunch at the Casa Grande on West Seventh Street to discuss what we could or should do. Farm publications told us every farmer should have a written marketing plan. Each of us had attended marketing meetings and Hall, as County Extension Director, had arranged many. Most had emphasized price protection, either forward contracting a portion of the expected crop, selling futures contracts, or using options, puts and calls. Most farmers had attended the same sessions, had read the same publications we had read and more. Something else must be needed.

Our discussion eventually came around to decision-making, the willingness to commit to a forward contract sale, to buy a futures contract, or, even at or after harvest, to “pull the trigger,” make a sale. We talked about what and who influence that decision-making. If we could have some positive impact on those two issues, *willingness to make a decision and who or what influences that willingness,* we should.

Hall suggested his wife, Deb, then Extension Director in adjacent Adair County, and who had conducted workshops on the topic. Perhaps they could work as a pair to lead a workshop. We then identified a dozen young farm couples to invite to our home for an evening in late December. Our letter of invitation said the purpose was to “help identify the skills, knowledge, and support that farm couples need” in marketing. Nine couples accepted our invitation.

After some initial discussion by Rich on market information sources, pricing methods, and local markets, Deb broke the attendees into three groups, and directed each group to *list their sources* for marketing advice. After ten minutes, we re-assembled for reports and discussion. Some of the sources reported: spouse, trusted friend, charts, father, Extension, tax consultant, and DTN (electronic real-time price data to which some subscribed).

Next, each group was asked to identify their *barriers to trying new things* in marketing. The top three were fear, money, knowledge, and "will my banker or partner agree." Among others: what neighbors will think, emotions, cash flow, lack of a plan, and the up-front cost of hedging options or contracts.

The third instruction to each group was to answer, "*What will I hear* (from any party) if I sell and the market goes higher?" Shirley and I had listened in on the group discussions, and this one brought out the most animated responses. Here are some examples:

> I told you so!
> I got a dime more.
> You should have known better!
> Why did you do that?
> There goes the van!
> How does it affect your average?
> At least we broke even.
> Hard come; easy go.

Among the statements reported by the three discussion groups, six were positive, three were neutral, and *twenty nine* were negative.

That high ratio of negative feedbacks told why we sometimes have trouble making a marketing decision. No one wants to risk negative feed-back from one close to us, especially our spouse, partner, neighbor, parent, or banker. When we avoid a decision, we *avoid negative feedback.*

However, I was once told, "To not make a decision is to make a decision." When faced with alternatives and one avoids choosing, one is *making a decision* to avoid the decision.

Our reason for inviting couples is evident. Whether it is the wife or husband who does the marketing—and some observe that the wife is usually more analytical and better at marketing—the feedback by the opposite party is critical. A negative response plants fear of facing the next decision point. A neutral or positive response does not instill fear; a positive response will likely give some confidence for making the next decision.

We may have done some good that evening for those nine couples. Most of the credit goes to Deb and Rich Hall.

There would be more follow-up and involvement by the RDAC marketing group. I find in my files a January, 1996, letter from Rich Hall to county producers announcing a five-session, hands-on workshop on developing and implementing a grain marketing plan. Sessions would be from 4 to 6 and 7 to 9 p.m. and RDAC would serve soup to the attendees between 6 and 6:45. The workshop instructors would be Iowa State Extension specialists, Dr. Dennis Thomas, whose home farm adjoins ours, and Lynn Benson, one of my former Iowa State students.

I find in my files a one-page alfalfa marketing plan but, though I recall having drafted a grain marketing plan my first year back on the farm—and followed it rather closely—it is not to be found.

I was not without some grain marketing experience. The years that our land had been rented to others on a crop-share basis, I had usually forward contracted to local elevators forty to sixty per cent of my expected bushels of corn and beans, doing it in several increments between planting time and the beginning of harvest. On becoming administrator of USDA's Foreign Agricultural Service, with responsibility for market-influencing subsidies or credit guarantees for grain exports, I could not have a financial interest in U.S. crops, so had shifted to cash rent.

I recall that my grain marketing plan back on our home farm included early season sales, selling in increments of five to ten per cent of expected yield, beginning at planting time or before, and updating that expected yield in response to rainfall, temperature, and other factors during the growing season. My records show that for the 1994 crop, my first two corn sales were January 4 and 5 at $2.45 and $2.44 per bushel. The market moved down during the year, I sold in nine increments, and my last sale was at the end of harvest, mid November, at $1.88.

In 1996, I sold our corn in fifteen increments, the price ranging from $2.10 on February 7 to $3.00 on September 19. My last sale, at the end of harvest, was for $2.41. I sold our beans in seven increments that year, two sales during the day on March 5 at $6.80 and $6.85, two on April 2 at $7.25 and $7.35, and the last two after harvest, October 22, at $6.43 and $6.45.

Yes, prices may change during the day. My tractor radio would give me hourly price reports and I made many phone calls from the tractor cab. Today, my smart phone or I-pad would make it easier.

Carrying Cash to Georgia

Less than two years after our time in Belarus, I was on my way to another former Soviet republic country, Georgia. The World Bank has asked USDA to recommend a consultant to review Georgia's agricultural research and education programs, and I had flown to Washington in early June to discuss the task with Bank staff. Depending on my recommendations, the Bank might extend a loan to Georgia to help make program changes.

On a Saturday, July 1, 1995, I was sitting in the Vienna, Austria airport terminal with sixty five hundred dollars in crisp U.S. bills, a few fifties, but mostly twenties, tens, and fives, stuffed randomly in two money belts, my pockets, a carry-on bag, and briefcase. I had been warned that Georgia banks and businesses would not take worn bills, so had asked our local Whitney Bank to gather those new or near-new bills. Waiting for my flight to Tbilisi, Georgia, I noted that eleven of the twenty four flight destinations shown on the departure board were cities I did not recognize. They had been behind the Iron Curtain and not part of my daily awareness.

Though the project appeared fascinating, I had been given a depressing picture of Georgia conditions by Bank staff—electricity a few hours each day, hot water once in a while, no air conditioning, high crime, and no check or credit card system. I would need to carry cash to the country for all expenses, and sleep on my money belt.

I had asked if my wife could accompany me, at our expense, of course. Bank staff members were shocked, "Oh, that would not be safe or comfortable for her."

I responded that she had traveled with me to many countries, including twice to Nigeria, a country that many categorize as unsafe. My hosts reinforced, "Next to Georgia, Nigeria is a picnic!"

The task also appeared daunting for the limited time budgeted, thirty days. The Bank could give me little knowledge of existing Georgia institutions and programs, only that there appeared to be two public and several private universities in Georgia, more than fifty agricultural research stations or institutes operated under the Ministry of Agriculture, Georgia Academy of Agricultural Science, or the Georgia Academy of Science, and no Extension entity, per se. There was an assumed presence of technology specialists in the Ministry units responsible for state farms and commodity processing, as well as on some state farms and in the processing units themselves. And, there were reported many technical colleges or schools.

I had another concern, "I would arrive alone in Georgia with no knowledge of the language, no acquaintances, and no knowledge of the city."

"You will be met at the airport by our Bank man in Georgia, George Maglakelidze." That name rang a bell. Atlantic farmer friends Bill and Leanne Pellett had told me about their hosting a young Georgian several years earlier. I was sure it was the same name. A visit with Bill a few days later would confirm their guest had been George Maglakelidze.

I would be embarking on the busiest twenty five days I would have since my first days as a Kansas State president or Nebraska vice chancellor, and would be doing most of my work through an interpreter in a country with no dependable electricity or phone system. Except for the name of Maglakelidze, what the Bank staff had told me, and a few Georgia documents they provided, I knew only that I had a reservation at Metechi Hotel in Georgia's capitol city, Tbilisi, at an estimated one hundred seventy five dollars per night.

My seatmate in the flight from Vienna to Tbilisi was from Williams College in Massachusetts and a bank consultant on his way to review Georgia's civil service system. I slept for two hours, awoke to a lunch my seat-mate had held for me, lettuce salad, roll, generous portions of cold lunch meats on a bed of potato salad, cole slaw, and cake. Through the window I watched snow-capped peaks of the Caucuses, then ripening cereal corps in fields too large for the one to two-hectare private farms of which I had read; they were more likely state farms. Then it was over another mountain range to arid land much like that of central South Dakota and eastern Montana, dry range land and wheat fields on plateaus with erosion-carved breaks at the plateau edges.

Maglakelidze met my plane at the Tbilisi airport and we drove dimly lit, wide streets to the Metechi hotel in the heart of the city, as attractive in all respects as any in Washington and with a seven-story lobby.

After six hours sleep, I was down early Sunday to a breakfast buffet of a dozen fruits and juices, yogurts, a half dozen cold cereals, about ten hot dishes—even an omelet chef—and uncounted pastries and breads, all impressively presented.

At the buffet and during two hours reading in the lobby, I saw no more than eighteen residents. I was told three or more floors of rooms were never used. Tourism had been a big business, mostly from other Soviet republics, but the move away from the single Soviet currency, Georgia's economic collapse, and electricity and water interruptions appeared to have killed tourism.

Maglakelidze arrived early afternoon to help me check out housing options for the month. First, we looked at two guest houses, each with rooms at eighty dollars per day, and then an apartment a Bank consultant from London, Peter Marion, would abandon. His wife and family had arrived for a two month stay, so he had leased a home in a nearby village. The apartment would cost two hundred fifty dollars for the month, included three rooms and bath, and I could continue the maid Marion had arranged. It was only about three buildings from Maglakelildze's home, so I could ride in his car to and from work.

The entrance to the apartment was first through a drab walkway to a no-grass, one-tree, ten-vehicle courtyard, then up a stained and dirty outside and inside stairway, past two or three steel apartment doors, each with evidence of three or four locks. It was depressing. However, the apartment was clean, contained old but fine antique furniture, and two book-cases stuffed to the ceiling and edges. (I would find but one title in English, Wonderworld of Tropical Bonsai.) There was an electric water heater, which I would keep plugged in so it would heat any time the electricity was on, a four-burner gas stove and, for an afternoon in the high 80s, a pleasant cross breeze through the steel shutters.

I gave Marion five $50 bills and he wrote me a receipt. I dropped my suitcases and briefcase in the living room and Maglakelidze and I checked out a nearby supermarket while Marion and his family packed and loaded a rented Volkswagen van for their move to the village.

I awoke Monday morning to no electricity, no convenient food in the apartment except a bag of M&Ms with peanuts. Maglakelidze had taken us to dinner the night before and I had gotten back to my apartment after the supermarket had closed. My maid, a mid-forties pediatrician at a state hospital and needing more income than her salary, would come to introduce herself and pick up any laundry and a grocery list. She arrived but, to communicate, she had to phone her son and he handled the translation for us. I gave her a ten-dollar bill to buy a few groceries for me at the supermarket.

Maglakelidze picked me up and took me to the Ministry, perhaps two kilometers from the center of Tbilisi. It was a faded yellow stone rectangle with courtyard, also grassless and filled with cars. There was no evidence of recent paint, floors were almost encrusted, and office doors bruised. It was 9:45, some workers were in the hall visiting, some at desks, and some arriving. It was not a bustling place. I was reminded that salaries were low, two to six dollars per month, there was little money for cars, fuel, paper, or other expenses. I would learn that field research facilities were virtually shut down for lack of budget, so there probably was not much work that could be done. We stepped off the elevator at the fifth floor and walked past offices occupied by a European Union aid team. In the World Bank project area, floors had been sanded and finished, and offices freshly painted. Desks were simple, painted black or white, and with open sides.

Maglakelidze's driver took me to a downtown Telex office to fax a letter home that I had arrived, then to the consular section of the U.S. embassy to check in and record my apartment and office phone numbers. I visited the adjacent AID office, met three staff who gave me a quick briefing on some food aid and rural projects they finance through U.S. PVOs, such as CARE, and I was given an engraved invitation to a fourth of July reception at the embassy, noon to two o'clock the next day. Having had no breakfast, I bought a loaf of bread at a vendor's booth and enjoyed it on our way back to the Ministry.

I bought a coke at a vendor's apartment building window across the street from the Ministry, found my assigned desk in a room I would share with two young interpreters and a computer operator, and started reading a few documents Maglakelidze had given me. I then charted a schedule of work, to include visits to as many of the research institutes as I could get to, the agricultural universities, and at least some of the secondary or post secondary schools of agriculture across the country. Only after such visits, conversations with any private sector agricultural leaders to whom I could connect, and ministry staff, could I develop recommendations for the system.

Also high priority was to identify a Georgian to work with me and, hopefully, to lead the implementation of any of my recommendations that the World Bank would fund and that Georgians would accept. First, I needed lists and locations of those institutes, schools, and private entities. I also needed a driver and interpreter. Maglakelidze had told me he had a person in mind for the latter, a young woman who had been an exchange student in Minneapolis and a family friend.

I could find no water fountain, but a secretary shared a bottle of water from her desk; I drank from a cut-off glass coke bottle. Mid-day I bought a can of lemon Fanta and a sandwich, a small hamburger inside a segment of a bread loaf and garnished with onion, at a nearby vendor. For the next day, I would bring a bottle of water from the apartment, and maybe a thermos of tea.

Some workers began leaving at four o'clock; I departed at seven with George. My apartment was clean, but the ten dollars had not been enough for the grocery list. There was bacon instead of cooked ham and the hydrator contained miniature pears and some apples. A loaf of bread and a box of Kellogg's corn flakes were on the table, plus a list of items with the cost shown. I walked downhill the two blocks to the supermarket for milk, juice, cheese, and cans of corn, pork and beans, and sauerbraten. I added corn to a partial can of beef stew Marion had left, decanted off the fat, and supplemented that with a pear, apple, and bread, then M&Ms for dessert.

I spent an hour on my Tandy (the Radio Shack computer I had purchased eight years earlier, storage capacity about twelve pages of text) recording my day, read some Tom Clancy, and was in bed at ten o'clock.

I awoke my second work day to no electricity and a sore back. The mattress was like a hammock; I would try the floor the next night. The water was still hot, so I shaved with a blade and it was refreshing. Not knowing when the electricity would be back on, I fried the entire two hundred fifty grams of bacon. I found some coarse sugar for the corn flakes so, with bacon, milk, and juice, I had a good breakfast.

I had not accomplished as much as I had hoped on Monday. Maglakelidze and I were to have spent a couple hours discussing priority visits and persons who might be my counterpart. However, he had gotten tied up. A copy machine had arrived without the cover, a fax machine without cord or instructions, and several computers without printers. And, as in most formerly communist countries, no one would do anything without checking with the boss. Maglakelidze had been sought for everything from "Can I have Mike drive me to the embassy?" to "How high do I install the coat racks?"

Scientists Design; the Ministry Implements

This morning I was determined to get priority items discussed, some interviews set, and one or two completed, so I pressed Maglakelidze on these issues en route to the office and he suggested we get together five minutes after arrival. After twenty, I crowded into his office and we covered several items, but I soon learned to depend on his office manager, Tata Jaiani, who had worked for a deputy minister and knew how to get things done. She and a young man by the name of Vakhtang Gegelia, Maglakelidze's Ministry counterpart, scheduled for me a noon meeting with the deputy minister of education, under whom some of the agricultural secondary and post secondary schools operated, and he would drive me there.

The deputy was tied up with the minister, so we met with a subordinate directly responsible for post-secondary vocational and specialist schools. There had been sixty such agricultural schools, now down to thirty two, and she gave me a list of eleven she felt worthy of investment. The deputy minister, a former dean of education, confirmed that list on her arrival, and I admired their sense of reality.

I had written criteria for the Georgian I needed to recruit and work with me: Respected in the research/education community, comfortable on farms and in food processing plants, focused on the future, and able to handle the English language. I shared these criteria with my hosts and asked if they would suggest to me three names, with supporting information, by July ten. I would ask the same of every key person with whom I would visit.

Day 3. I rode with Maglakelidze and an interpreter to the Academy of Agricultural Science at the edge of Tbilisi, a three story, stone building just off the highway, and surrounded by fence and tall grass. An hour and a half with the Academy vice president, Robert Andguladze, was friendly and open. He emphasized that the academy coordinates all agricultural research, most in Academy institutes but also including that at universities. Another hour included the academy president, a former rector of the Agrarian University, who said Khrushchev had dissolved the Georgian academy after he had told Georgia to produce only corn and academy scientists had said that was not wise. I suggested that Roswell Garst, my western Iowa neighbor, may have planted the corn idea in Khrushchev's mind when Khrushchev visited Iowa in the summer of 1956.

Though these men emphasized the need for business management on farms and in the food industry, they made no mention of a knowledge base for teaching and developing that business management skill. They explained that their animal and plant scientists and economists would *create the model* farm or business, and those models could then be *implemented* across the country by the Ministry. The Soviet top-down paradigm remained.

I received a similar message later in the day from the director of the vegetable and wine institute regarding grape production by newly independent farmers, and with one addition. He suggested a law requiring that newly independent farmers continue to grow grapes, in order to preserve Georgia's wine industry. As state farms were broken up, persons to whom land was assigned had apparently torn out some vines and were raising other crops and livestock. Georgia had lost its captive wine market to Russia and other former Soviet republics, so demand for Georgian wine and the value of grapes had dropped.

Though all with whom I visited appeared dedicated to democracy and determined to see Georgia through these difficult times without reverting to communism and Moscow control, many still held the "top down, central government knows best" philosophy. Whenever I asked how the ideal production or business models would be utilized, the response was generally that they would be "given to the Ministry of Agriculture and Food Industry to implement." There was no suggestion that the private sector would help develop the models, or that farmers or processing managers would be approached with an education effort.

However, farmer and industry organizations with which I met said that an extension effort was badly needed. Those who had seen the U.S. system would refer to input, demand-driven education. One mentioned "like the Maine Potato Board."

Day 4. The most impressive visit that day was to the Agricultural and Biotechnology Research Institute, an impressive five-story, two-block-long structure. It was to have been the Soviet center for basic biological science to serve agriculture, and had been built just before the Soviet break-up. There was one car in the parking lot, grass growing through the asphalt, and the general appearance was that of an abandoned building. Inside, except for one man in the lobby, appearance was the same. The second floor office of the director was attractive but spartan; the secretary had no evidence of work on her desk. The director greeted us warmly, escorted us down the dark hall to a well-appointed and furnished conference room. At one end was a small table for six, set with small china plates, wine glasses, and a large bowl of fresh fruit.

I explained our purpose and we took a thirty-minute tour of the building. The one research project, test-tube propagation of virus-free potatoes, had a controlled-light laboratory for growing the potatoes, a second room for tissue preparation, and a third room with three workers washing glassware. We walked through three other labs, all vacant and with unused equipment, boxes of test tubes, and other unpacked supplies setting on the floor. There were two floors of such labs; the other floors had vacant offices.

In addition to research at academy and ministry institutes and universities, I found that the state operated a wheat industry facility with its own research program as well as a school for wheat production. The facility's director is on the left, Maglakelidze on the right.

With free fall of the Georgian economy, scientists received only two to three dollars per month and worked their own plots. Those who were at work, at least those who put in reasonable hours, were doing it because of dedication and loyalty. For most, work was only from nine o'clock to two or ten o'clock to three. There was no money for supplies or travel, and electricity was off much of the time. The potato research lights at the biotechnology institute were dependable because "the director is a good friend of the man who controls load shedding for the city." In one institute, the first two professors (scientists) we saw were playing chess in an office. Most were reading at their desks or visiting.

Georgia's Ministry of Agriculture and Food Industry had a different purpose than its U.S. counterpart, USDA. In communist countries, the Ministry had been the "corporate headquarters" for collective and state forms and for the government-owned wineries, flour mills, fertilizer, and other food and agriculture manufacturing businesses. The conduct of research had been in the separate Academy of Agricultural Science and its institutes. Universities were generally limited to teaching. Institute scientists, however, may carry the professor title, and they may have a "faculty senate" or association, functioning in many ways similar to a U.S. university subject matter department.

Academic departments in U.S. universities sometimes have too little inter-department communication or cooperation, and may even battle over subject matter turf. In Georgia, separateness was even greater; the institutes were all at physically separate locations, though most were in the capital city of Tbilisi. Each also had its own network of experiment stations and farms around the country.

I had assured Maglakelidze that the Bank sent along plenty of cash for me to hire a car, driver, and interpreter, so money should not be a limiting factor. I had agreed that all drivers and interpreters should be paid the same, so he was handling all such arrangements.

Late in the day he brought in the interpreter he had arranged, Magna Magradze. She was a bright young woman, and handled English well. She took home with her an organization chart of institutes and a list of schools to translate for me, and to also check earlier translations that had been done. Two translators may use different English spellings, so it was difficult for me to know if similar names that may appear on separate lists were one school or two. Magradze would prove to be excellent, both in translation and in helping me "read between the lines," peoples' attitudes and reactions that are not always easy to read in an unfamiliar culture.

Tata had arranged for me to travel with Ministry staff to visit a highly respected technical agriculture school in western Georgia on Saturday. I was delighted; I wanted to see the country and the school, and week-ends in the city could be boring.

Georgia's Schools and the Family Pig

Saturday, Day 6. We were in the humid, flat land of western Georgia, not far from the shores of the Black Sea. I had been picked up at eight o'clock by Mulhaz Shelia, head of the Ministry's Department of Schools, his eighteen-year-old son, Sandros, a good student of English and who would be my interpreter for the two-day trip, and a driver named Zugar, all in a shortened version of a Jeep Cherokee.

Zugar's foot seemed fixed to the floorboard; we passed every vehicle and oncoming traffic just moved to the side. He even zipped through police checks, with a beep of the horn and a wave to the police. I learned later that he was an aide to a senior and powerful member of parliament from western Georgia, so he knew the right people and they knew him.

Our route was up through the long, wide semi-arid Kura valley, past large fields of wheat, grapes, and apples, evidence of collective or state farms, to a five thousand foot mountain pass. We then glided down into the valleys of the Ovirili and Rioni, the latter flowing to the Black Sea. Just before the pass, we had stopped at a roadside market area, with public toilets and perhaps fifty tables and stands offering vegetables, fruits, nuts, cookies, and bread. I filled my sport jacket pocket with peanuts. In visits to Tbilisi area institutes and at the office, lunch was never mentioned, so I had been carrying a sandwich and a bottle of water. I had the bottle with me on this trip but not the sandwich.

We had gotten a late start out of Tbilisi, having gone to the far side of town to load a thirty gallon plastic drum of wine behind the back seat. And, we had stopped midway to siphon out some of the wine into jugs for a priest friend of our driver. Considering the distance, I knew that any lunch at our destination would be well beyond noon.

The Rioni valley was more lush, warmer, and with more rainfall. In both valleys there was evidence of irrigation systems, mostly elevated cement troughs on cement bases, but not in use. A few orchards and vineyards appeared abandoned; medium height corn plants were yellow from lack of nitrogen and a wet spring. Any grass had been grubbed to the ground by small herds of seemingly small, thin cows and their calves. There were no fences; a herder was often seen in the vicinity of the herd, perhaps watching from under a tree.

Our destination school was near Didi Jahaisi, a village comprised generally of homes on about two hectare (five acre) fenced plots. The houses were set back a hundred feet from the road, flowers or a garden were closer to the road, and the house would be surrounded by intensive cropping. Peppers, citrus, plums, eggplant, tomatoes, and corn appeared to cover every inch of the property. Most also had a cow, two or three hens, and one or two of what were referred to as "family pigs," all of which utilized any spare forage.

Several pigs of varied sizes and ages were foraging along the village road, each wearing a collar and cross stick that prevented them getting through neighbor's fences. Later in the evening, I would see the "family pig" standing by their home gate, waiting to be let in.

On arrival at the school director's home, the first step was siphoning wine for the director out of the thirty-gallon drum into five-gallon glass jugs. The director's home was elevated about ten steps, and we walked into a forty-foot long room, windows all along the north, a sink in the left, inside corner, and a dining table, set for six. Lunch was bread, cold chicken, eggplant, and, of course, wine.

Then came a walk around the grounds, property of the school. The grounds included the former home and a "museum" of the man given credit for founding the school in the 1920s, a famous Georgia "revolutionary" by the name of Nikoli Nikoliasis. The walk ended with a visit to the toilet, a typical outhouse, and I then stretched out on a bench for fifteen minutes.

It was three o'clock when we got to the school, itself, built by the Soviets in 1982 and already in terrible condition. Stucco was falling off the exterior, doors sagged, and windows were broken. I was told the broken windows resulted from students rushing out in panic at the time of an Armenian earthquake, which had reached into Georgia.

In questioning, I learned the course content of two curriculums, fruit and vegetable processing and farming, and I was impressed. Secondary school ends with grade eleven. Secondary graduates would enroll in this school, earn a diploma after two years and then go to work or go to the Agrarian or other university. In one of the classrooms sat three students and a young woman, an economics instructor, each at individual tables adorned with table cloths and a flower, and I visited briefly with each. The instructor had a university specialist degree, comparable to our masters' degree, and appeared enthusiastic. The students, two men and a woman, were shy but obviously bright. The woman wanted to be an accountant; the men were aiming for the university.

Future employment was uncertain. Virtually all employment had been at state grain, wine, milling, mineral water, or milk corporations, or on collective farms. Now, with no property ownership law having been passed by parliament and no decisions made on privatizing government corporations, the future for all was in limbo. It was assumed the corporations would be privatized and few were now being aggressively managed.

The state farms had been mostly broken up and the land assigned to families but, except for individual homes, no formal property ownership existed. Also, no land surveys existed; pre-Soviet boundary records had been, for the most part, destroyed by the Soviets. Where land had been assigned, disputes abounded. Even if an ownership law were to be established, there were no reference points for legal descriptions or boundaries. As in Belarus, without ownership, there could be no transfer of title, so land could not serve as collateral for a bank loan. A lender would have no way to obtain title to the land if a borrower defaulted

In Tbilisi I had seen plenty of private enterprise, street-level apartment building windows where one could buy sodas, candy bars, bread, and cigarettes; sidewalk vendors; and gasoline or diesel tank trucks parked along the highway, each with a hand-painted, price per liter sign. Though private enterprise was increasing, lack of action by parliament was a brake on human initiative.

The above was likely half the problem; the other half was lack of petroleum or energy generation, price gouging by other republics that had energy for sale, and a civil war in northwestern Georgia, apparently fomented by Russia.

A few had gotten rich in the previous five years, bringing in petrol or getting control of land, even if not real ownership. There may have been some "sweet deals," involving licensing and import regulations, but generally the morale was low and a common comment was "We can't do that because - - - ."

Back to the school: Classrooms were neat and clean and I commended the director. However, the building structure was terrible. Floors were wood but not hardwood; they were chipped and pieces were missing or loose. The basketball court was of six-inch boards, not even tongue-in-groove, and loose; they tilted as I walked.

I would later see evidence of high quality Georgian construction and craftsmanship. What I saw at the school was blamed on the Soviet system; workers would steal material and short-cut construction, and suppliers, other state corporations, would substitute shoddy materials. It was an embarrassment to Georgians, and also contributed to low morale and feeling of futility.

We finished our visit to the school at six.

I had pressed to talk to farmers and at least drive by two other near-by ministry schools, and my host director asked, "Tonight or tomorrow?" Assuming a late supper, I said, "Tonight," and an hour later, after dodging potholes, stopping for a funeral procession (all on foot, children dropping flowers at the head of the procession, followed by young men carrying the wooden coffin lid, then the open coffin holding a white-haired, aged woman, and mourners) we found the school.

As we drove toward the next school we also passed several individual pigs, each standing at a gate by the side of the road. My host explained that many families maintained a pig to utilize table scraps. During the day the pigs were allowed to roam the neighborhood for whatever they could find, but always came home in time for their evening meal.

The school's vehicle gate was locked, but we walked through a pedestrian gate to what appeared to be an abandoned facility. We walked by two aged tractors, one with a flat tire, a six-row planter and cultivator, and a piece of dirt-moving equipment. We looked through a window at machine tools, including lathes. As we walked, we encountered the school director, mid-fifties and unshaven. He told us the school had a capacity of three hundred and that, when in session, they had two hundred thirty enrolled. He described three dormitories in bad condition, a dining hall, and a physical education building. He said they had four combines, three that worked, and two trucks, in addition to the tractors I had seen.

I had begun to wonder if there was a lawn mower in Georgia. In northern Europe or the U.S., even if staff had no money for their projects or classrooms, most would keep their facility reasonably well tended. This was more evidence of futility.

Back at the director's grounds and home, by then nearly eight o'clock, I was asked if I wanted to visit Nikoli's museum "tonight or Sunday." Georgians honor their ancestors and heroes and a visit by me was expected. It had been a long day and I knew the dinner would be long, so suggested Sunday. I then learned the docent had been waiting all day for us to visit, so I said, "Let's go see it."

Though it was still daylight, the many surrounding trees and the window drapes made it difficult to see the many photos and documents. However, we looked at every one, including those that covered the lives of Nikoli's son and daughter, and even visited his wine cellar and livery stable. Georgian's honor their ancestors and heroes.

Dinner at the director's home started well after nine o'clock, and included our driver, plus two instructors who had brought an accordion and drum. The menu: small cold fish, a hot mushroom dish, fresh tomatoes, cucumbers, cheeses, breads, probably twenty five dishes on the table. And, there would be at least twenty five toasts during the evening.

The director served as Tamada, head of table. The Tamada gives the first toast and grants permission for other toasts. Tradition also calls for "bottoms up" on the first and last toast, but I had learned there may be many "last toasts." For toasting, it was tradition to use hollowed animal horns, large and small. The host may fill one with wine and challenge a guest to drink it empty. Near the end of the evening our host brought out a photo of the school's late founder and we toasted him. He then brought out his parents' photos and we toasted them. He asked about my parents and we toasted them; he asked about my wife and we toasted her. Toasting lasted until midnight. Georgians honor their ancestors and traditions.

Standing for one of many toasts. I learned quickly; I filled the horn myself, holding the open end toward me, then tilted it slowly to "drink."

The New Internet in 1995

A few days before I had departed Iowa for Georgia, I had heard Jim Kinney, operator of a computer store in my home town, Atlantic, tell the Atlantic Industrial Development Foundation directors that Atlantic could be, if it wished, the smallest city in the world with an internet connection, and that the cost for a business to connect would be in the neighborhood of thirty five dollars per month, much less for an individual. Though I had used my Tandy notebook for eight years, I knew little about the internet. I only knew that, once words were digitized and cable or satellite infrastructure became functional, information could be searched for and/or transmitted and at low cost with the touch of a few keyboard keys

I had seen no computers at the Georgia universities, schools, or institutes I had visited, only at the private Tbilisi Business School. What a great boon the internet could be for Georgia's scientists. I wondered if there might be an internet connection somewhere in Tbilisi and discovered that the interpreter at a desk adjacent to mine knew the president of a new internet franchise in downtown Tbilisi. Magda, my interpreter, made an appointment for us that afternoon.

We found the business in a three-room ground floor office next to "Andropov's Ears," a series of narrow arches constructed as an art piece while Andropov was Soviet Premier. The office had been open only a month and had Gateway 2000 equipment and one apparent customer, the Georgia parliament. USAID had provided money for the parliament's connection and perhaps had subsidized the franchise start-up.

The franchise president, George Kashia, estimated that for the Agrarian University to connect, the subscription would be about fifteen hundred dollars per month for one terminal, or six hundred dollars per month for part time, three to four hours per day. Of course, any number of faculty could use it.

The problem would be phone lines. Lines existed, of course, but connections were poor and a dedicated line would be needed for internet to be functional. This would have to be provided by the state phone company and Kashia's cost estimate was a thousand dollars per mile. I asked about linkage to a college or extension center in western Georgia, more than one hundred kilometers from Tbilisi, either a dedicated line or a separate downlink?

"Oh," he said, "that cost would be prohibitive!"

I had only understood the potential; this visit was my first direct exposure. Kashia tried to demonstrate searching for information, but he found only a few lists of U.S. or German institutes and a few short lists of documents. I typed in "Kansas State University," and found a description of the university's high-energy physics lab. For Iowa State, I found a list of extension topics, such as weather, market reports, and scheduled training meetings. Each topic I entered, however, yielded only "Under Construction."

That was the status of the internet in July, 1995. By the time a few Georgian faculty and institute scientists would visit the U.S. and use its developing system, perhaps internet elements would be available in Georgia.

There was no limit to Georgian hospitality, and that often made it difficult to keep on schedule. Determined to see one more of the Education Ministry or Agriculture Ministry schools, I had set aside two hours for the one closest to Tbilisi, for both the visit and travel time. To my school host, however, hospitality was far more important than any schedule, and it would have been an insult to not accept. On my right is the school director and on my left, my interpreter, Magda Magradze, and my driver.

* * * * *

After two weeks visiting universities, institutes, schools and any private sector people I could reach, I had drafted some recommendations and wanted to get reactions from key people on how they might be accepted.

Just a Terminal in My Office

I had just shared my draft recommendations with the president of Georgia's Academy of Agricultural Sciences. He said he agreed that some consolidation of the eighteen research institutes scattered around Tbilisi, Georgia, should occur and that they should be linked with the city's two agricultural universities. However, he did not agree that a computer terminal for the then infant internet system should be located in each of those locations.

"Just put a terminal in my office," he said, "I'll pass along to the scientists what they need to know!" It was more residue of the Soviet paradigm, that all information comes from the "central office." It was consistent with what he had told me my third day in the country, that after private farms models were designed by scientists, the Ministry would implement.

It was also consistent with what the head of the Plant Pathology Institute had told me, that before the Soviet break-up, all scientific journals had been received in Moscow, translated there, and sent on to his Tbilisi institute.

My recommendation to establish internet downlinks at the two universities and key research locations would be a step in the process in breaking the Soviet tradition and paradigm.

By that time Maglakelidze and I had tapped the vice president of the Academy, Dr. Robert Andguladze, as my successor and the one who would take the lead in achieving any recommended changes in the system that the World Bank would help finance. My next step was to share my draft recommendations with all the research institute directors, university rectors, and ministry department heads. Of course, Andguladze would be with me in the meeting. With risk of misinterpretation due to translation, there would be need to elaborate, clarify, or explain. Most important, these people deserved to hear my recommendations directly from me.

To my first several recommendation, for the Bank to finance scientist travel to the U.S. or western European universities and research institutes, some for graduate study, and to finance subscription costs of scientific journals, there was enthusiastic agreement. All were eager for young scientists—and also for themselves—to experience research programs in the U.S. or Western Europe.

What brought several up off their chair was my recommendation to re-locate several of the institutes to that new and largely un-occupied Agriculture and Biotechnology Research Institute building, the large, new building that then housed only a director and some potato research. Some rapid comments: "My industry would not accept that." "Our institute is a tradition!" "Our institute would no longer be independent."

That last objection told me that he did not consider that there could be three or four separate institutes in one structure, each with its own director. Each of Georgia's research institutes had long been in separate buildings and locations. Only after clarifying that point and, especially, after describing the internet and that priority for connection should be first at the two universities and the large and new biotechnology building did I see some positive head nodding.

From then on, it was largely vigorous debate *among* those present. From some, "We must face reality!" "There is not the money for the duplication we have." "But my industry will be upset, will not support combining." "There is so much tradition in our location."

Perhaps that debate was the most reassuring to me. Enough of the stronger institute directors recognized the reality of their limited funds, both at the time and for the foreseeable future. Should the World Bank accept my recommendations and provide a substantial loan, I believed these people would work constructively with my counterpart and successor, Andguladze. However, his task would not be easy. So much tradition!

My last day in Georgia was Thursday, July 25. I had to put my recommendations into short paragraph form by two o'clock so my report could be taken for copying (missing parts of the office copy machine still had not arrived). I would take the original with me and also leave copies for Maglakelidze and Andguladze. I then took time for a hot dog and coke in the recently established "office buffet." The fresh, chewy bread was fantastic and the mustard was potent. Loaded with horseradish, the mustard would keep my nostrils clear for a week.

There was much left to do, briefing and farewell visits with people who had been helpful, and I distributed to my driver and others the nine bottles of wine, scotch, and bourbon given me during institute and country visits.

Late in the day I would have some unexpected visitors.

Now Georgia Must Compete

I had tried to get a session with representatives of privatized corporations, to get their suggestions, but Tata had not been able to schedule it; most were too busy. However, Jumbar Cholabargia, who I had met several days earlier, had called to say several private sector representatives would like to meet with me at six o'clock. Also the biotechnology institute director had asked for a meeting at seven.

Cholabargia had with him presidents of both a "wine and tea exchange" and a local accounting firm. They told me they were determined to start a private "society" to protect the consumer. They told me that Georgian consumers were getting "ripped off," that gasoline varies from good to bad, that some damages engines. Wine ranges from good to lethal. Not only does the consumer need protection, wine and other exportable items must exceed the competition's quality if Georgia is to develop a good export market. Georgia now had to compete with wines from Italy, France, and other countries; the republic had lost its captive market of other former Soviet republics.

Their society would contract with a private firm to set up and run a product analysis laboratory. They would promote, convince Georgians they needed such a product quality lab. Financing would come from society memberships and fees charged processors and marketers. Could I help? They would work night and day with me if I could help.

I could only respond that I admired what they were about and that I fully agreed on the need they had outlined, but I only had one night left. I was thrilled to hear their enthusiasm, wished them well, and perhaps I could incorporate their concept into my report to the Bank. (I did.) They also told me the country needed a demand-driven extension education program and that Georgia needed to reduce the number of state-financed research locations, already the major thrust of my recommendations. However, Cholabargia "threw a wrench in my gears," told me something I had not learned. He said there was a Georgia law declaring research institutes to be "State treasures," not to be combined or privatized. I asked Magda to track that.

The Biotech director, my last visitor, had with him the young researcher working with virus-free potatoes and a copy of a proposal they had made to Monsanto. They were seeking marketing rights in Georgia and surrounding states for a virus-free potato line Monsanto had developed. The proposal offered the Institute lab as a place to reproduce the material (for a fee, of course), and they wanted my endorsement of the idea.

While editing this section I recalled that Bill Loughmiller, a globally-minded potato producer in southern Idaho and fellow member of the Farm Foundation Roundtable, had known and worked with that young Georgia potato researcher and with Monsanto to try to commercialize those virus-free genetic lines. I called Loughmiller for an up-date and got a disappointing report. Though the lines' value was apparent, after Greenpeace claimed genetically modified potatoes were poisonous the Ministry of Agriculture destroyed the demonstration plots and the effort died.

Cover the Bales Before the Rain

I was back in Iowa for the third cutting of alfalfa. To produce the quality that dairies demand, it should to be harvested at about twenty two days of growth. It then should be baled as soon as the sun and wind have dried it sufficiently that it will not mold in the bale, yet not so dry that the more nutritious leaves will shatter. In June, July, or August, that is likely between five and nine p.m. on the first or second day after mowing/windrowing. If there is risk of rain, the bales then need to be stored under cover.

Olsen and Rick Pellett owned a "large-square" baler, which packed the alfalfa windrows into seven-hundred-pound bales that measured three by four by five feet and that were bound with three strands of nylon twine. I paid that partnership a per bale rate for their equipment.

Research had shown that by spraying a tiny amount of propionic acid onto the stream of alfalfa as it entered the baler, the alfalfa could be baled at slightly higher moisture content without risk of spoilage. That might save a day of drying and risk of rain damage. Olsen and Pellett had devised a system for monitoring the alfalfa windrow moisture content and adjusting the fine spray of propionic acid accordingly.

Olsen would run the baler, my cousin, Clair Acker, or I would load the bales onto flat-bed wagons with the 5140, haul the bales to the farmstead, and stack them in a large open-end barn or, when the barn was full, outside stacks. When evening dew formed on the windrowed hay, baling would stop for the night; Olsen would then help haul and stack. With one hundred twenty five acres of alfalfa and perhaps four cuttings between June and September, we would have more than six hundred tons stored and for sale the following fall and winter.

It had cooled early that day and by four o'clock Olsen was in the field with the baler and by eight o'clock the settling dew had forced him to stop; it also appeared that rain was on the way.

Several of Shirley's classmates, two from out-of-state, had come out to our home to plan a class reunion and, their planning completed, all had come up to watch the stacking. One from Washington State was himself in the cattle and hay business, the locals had not earlier seen such large bales, and a Philadelphia woman was simply inquisitive.

Olsen and I could use their help, handling a more than hundred-pound canvass to cover the just-completed stack, six bales high, four bales wide, and perhaps fifty feet long. To cap off the stack, Olsen had added one row of bales down the center.

Olsen leaned an extension ladder against the end of the stack, issued instructions, and four of us climbed to the top.

We first took a moment to enjoy the view. On the ridge divide between the East Nishna Botna River and its Troublesome Creek tributary, we could see at least twelve miles, a panorama that included four other counties, Pottawattamie to the west, Adair and the lights of Adair city to the east, Audubon County to the north, and even a corner of Guthrie County to the northeast. Farmstead security lights were beginning to dot the countryside for miles in every direction.

Using the tractor's front-end loader, Olsen hoisted the tightly folded canvass up to us. It has been folded in such a way that, once in the center of the stack, it could be unfolded toward the ends, then its full length unfolded to each side. That may appear simple, but working twenty five feet in the air, it would not be an easy task. And, by that time there was sheet lightning to the west.

Collectively, the four us rolled the folded-up canvass off the loader and dragged it to the center of the stack. Olsen then climbed the ladder to join us. He put two of us on each side of that center row of bales, to unfold the canvass first to one end, then the other. Gradually and tediously, so no one would fall or get pushed off the stack, we then unfolded it from the center line to let it drape about half-way down each side of the stack.

Back on the ground, Olsen and I secured the canvass edges with ropes tied to heavy pins thrust into lower bales, cinching each rope down tightly to keep wind from getting under the canvass.

Shirley and her crew had left for our home. I would join them for a ten o'clock dessert and to hear, as the rain pelted the side of our house, their satisfactions from helping cover the bales before the rain.

Part of the 625 tons of alfalfa harvested in 1995, hauled in from the field by Clair Acker, who helped us considerably during the crop season. Half of the hay was stored in this old converted barn, the other half in stacks of the type described.

Did our Cows Make Money?

When we returned to the farm in early 1993, Shirley had said she wanted to enjoy watching some cows and their calves grazing. We bought a small herd, twenty six cows, at the Massena auction later that year. When Olsen agreed to join us, we leased his cows and he would manage the combined herd at the farmstead where he lived, a mile north of our home. Most of our pasture land was adjacent to that farmstead, and Olsen had earlier built cattle-working facilities. Unfortunately for Shirley, watching the cows and calves would be limited to the times she would be at that farmstead to help with them or other farm activity, such as that late evening stacking of hay bales.

Ranchers in the Kansas Flint Hills, Nebraska Sand Hills, or the West River country of South Dakota generally follow the adage, "always leave half the grass." If one over-grazes, lets the cows eat all the forage down to the soil surface, there is no "manufacturing plant," no leaves where photosynthesis can capture sun energy and carbon dioxide to produce new growth. Olsen had suggested a rotation grazing system, where the pasture is divided into paddocks small enough that the herd would graze the full grass growth down half way in three to seven days. For our thirty six head, that meant thirteen paddocks of about three acres each.

When the animals had consumed about half of the growth, they would be moved to the next paddock. Depending on rainfall, soil fertility, and mix of grass species, the herd may get back to that first paddock in twenty to forty days. The animals would have grazed each paddock's limited area more uniformly; re-growth would also be more uniform and higher in volume. Research had demonstrated that up to thirty five per cent more beef produced per acre—more cows or more weight gain on their calves—could be achieved with the rotation system than with a single, open pasture.

Fencing for the lane and between paddocks was a single wire, electrified at low voltage. Paddock gates were also a single wire, electrified by a metal clip to the wire that bordered the lane. If the grass in one or more paddocks was not needed during the grazing season, it could be harvested for hay or "banked," left standing for grazing during the fall and winter.

A critical issue in rotation grazing is water supply for each paddock. Where a rainfall-capturing pond exists, it might serve three or four paddocks. For water in paddocks along a ridge, without access to the ponds, Olsen found a light-weight plastic water tub he could drag from paddock to paddock. At each location he connected it by a "quick-couple" valve to a plastic pipe extended along the ridge from a barn hydrant. When it was time to move the cows from one paddock to another, he would disconnect the hose, dump the water, drag the tub to the next paddock, and re-connect.

To move the cows, he would simply unhook the electric-wire gate, drop it to the ground, and walk to the next paddock, the cows following and sometimes even running toward what they knew would be lush forage.

How about the calves after weaning? Our business plan called for selecting the most promising herd replacement heifers, based on their weight at birth and later, and their dam's record. We would manage them separately to grow for breeding at about fifteen months and calving at two years of age. The steers and the balance of the heifers would be fed grain and forage for harvesting at about eleven hundred pounds.

Midway through our first feeding season, a friend asked, "Where can you find a buyer who will bid on such a small number when they are finished?" Most Corn Belt feedlots then had a thousand or more on feed at any one time.

Fortunately, we did receive a good sale price that year. However, our feeding operation was hardly an economic unit. Labor and overhead cost for thirty-five was not competitive with those thousand-head operations. The second year we sent our calves to a custom feedlot and the third year we sold them after weaning to a feedlot operator.

At the end of the year, I analyzed the data for each enterprise, corn, beans, alfalfa, and the beef herd, including not only expenses and income by enterprise, but also the time that Olsen, some part-time help, and I devoted to each enterprise. For alfalfa or the beef herd, for example, that time included loading alfalfa trucks, moving the cows among paddocks, and hauling hay to the cows in the winter. The "employment cost" of hours not accounted for, such as equipment maintenance or clearing the farmstead of snowdrifts, was allocated to each enterprise in proportion to other input costs.

The cow herd's bottom line was not good. I recalled a comment that good friend and another academic turned farmer, Ralph Neill of Adams County, had made to an audience at Iowa State University, "Anyone that thinks they have been making good money on a cow herd has not been keeping records."

There was no way I could show our cow herd, even with Olsen's good management and rotation grazing, to be profitable. Arithmetic could not make it happen.

Hence, a question to Shirley, "How badly do you want to see those cows?"

However, we did not sell the cows. I recalled an economics lesson from Iowa State's Dairy Professor Art Porter my senior year, "If you do not have another market for your available labor, you should assume no labor cost for the next enterprise." We had no alternative market for either Steve's or my available labor, nor did we have another market for the pasture acreage, land not well suited for cropping. We kept the herd as long as we operated.

CHAPTER X

FROM FARMING TO CHICKENS AND CHINA

"This time, along side the more commonly encountered fermented eggs, were lamb tendons and pickled sections of rooster combs. In this case, the eggs were not quartered or whole fermented eggs that I had been served earlier; rather, the egg yolk and white had been cooked and molded in a container, then fermented, and sliced.

I had no problem in partaking; it is simply a matter of attitude and reality. People of this area consider these items to be delicacies and have been eating them for years. Beyond that, the tendons and combs are simply animal protein, with about the same chemical structure as the strips of connective tissue in a beef roast."

When we returned to the farm in January of 1993, we had compared the financial effect of starting Social security payments at sixty two vs. sixty five. Delaying to sixty five or later supported our desire to farm our own land. In late summer of 1995, enjoying our third year back on the farm, we did another calculation.

We were in good health and enjoyed both the physical and mental challenges of farming. We especially appreciated the working relationship with Steve Olsen and felt good about our operation. Considering weather challenges, drainage problems on some bottomland, and some of our hill ground's limited productivity, we felt good about crop yields. In our first year handling the total acreage, we had achieved our goal of six per cent return on equity. Based on grain and hay sales to date, we would likely beat that six per cent the current year and believed that ten to twelve per cent return in later years was possible.

However, I had been drawn into several other activities, the month in Belarus, then a week in Costa Rica with an Iowa State project, and

I had just returned from the Republic of Georgia. I had been asked to serve on an advisory group for the Iowa Department of Economic Development and my data on county by county sales value per farm acre had put me on the road to speak at Farm Bureau, Extension, and economic development meetings. These activities suggested another calculation was in order.

If our future farm earnings were the same in future years as in our first year of full operation, it would negate any social security payments. Beyond that, I would continue making deposits *into* the social security program, then at nearly twelve and a half per cent of earned income. However, cash rent for land was "passive income," not requiring deposits into the system.

At the same time, other operators were bidding strongly for rental land. In terms of dollars, it was a "no brainer," a significant financial advantage to close down our farm operation, sell our equipment and cattle, and rent the land to others.

It was a disappointment, but a reality, and we shared that reality with Steve. We would plan to close down our operation at the end of the next year, 1996, but if he found another opportunity earlier, we could close down at the end of the current year, 1995.

In late 1996, Steve would join his brother, Keith, who was assuming the fuel business of my long-time friend, Delmar Patterson, and I began the process of selling our equipment, disposing of the cow herd, and arranging for cash rental of our land.

An Egg Production Cooperative

In late 1995, Dan Brawe, a salesman for a farm supply cooperative in Massena, about twenty miles southeast of our farm, had asked if I would meet with a group considering an egg production business. His cooperative was furnishing the mixed ration for an egg-layer unit north of Massena and Brawe had been commissioned to find local corn producers and community leaders that might establish another. Brawe's cooperative could sell more mixed ration and, in turn, use more locally-produced corn. I had been telling any group that would listen that we could increase farm dollar volume and area employment by producing more livestock and poultry, so accepted Brawe's invitation.

The following Tuesday I joined the group for breakfast at the Snack Shack on the north edge of Massena. Included in the effort were farmers Pat McCurdy, Frank Jones, Jr., Dwight Bower, Bob Tichnor, and Fred Kay, bankers Henry Russell and Bill Amdor, John Deere dealer Don McCunn, and Gary Maas, owner of AgriCareers, an agricultural personnel business. In later weeks, Norman Mills, retired from a career in feed sales and part time CADCO staff member for our local Rural Development Action Committee, would often join us.

What this group had in mind was far larger and more complex than my mother's three hundred White Leghorn layers. She had paid me ten cents per day to carry buckets of corn from a storage bin to those layers morning and evening. Every Saturday afternoon fifteen-dozen or thirty-dozen cases of eggs would be in our Ford sedan's trunk or back seat as we headed to Atlantic. One case would be exchanged for groceries at Lester Baron's Thrifty store at Third and Chestnut, the rest sold for cash at Joe Moore's Produce on Walnut Street.

This enterprise would be a "closed cooperative," with members making an up-front investment and delivering corn for the birds in proportion to their ownership interest. In traditional farm supply and grain marketing cooperatives, membership is open to any party that buys from or sells to the cooperative and "unit ownership" is determined by each party's dollar volume of business. I was fascinated, and it soon became an every Tuesday morning breakfast at the Snack Shack. We had much to learn about the egg business, a host of issues we could not then foresee.

The most likely market for the eggs appeared to be forty miles down the road at Lennox, Iowa, at the largest egg "breaker" in the world. We drove to Lennox, watched six circular machines that would cut open each egg and let yolks and whites flow to separate pathways, short of the speed our local Atlantic Bottling Company fills Coca-Cola cans. Products leaving the plant ranged from thirty-gallon tins of whites or yolks to plastic packages of seasoned soufflé mix ready for cooking. We talked with management about a possible marketing contract.

We found and studied historic egg and feed prices, eggs production per hen, and facility costs. The data suggested a unit large enough to be efficient, perhaps a half million or more layers, could average fourteen per cent return on equity over a twenty-year period.

We would need six to seven million dollars for construction, the first flock of birds, and other start-up costs, and we would need at least forty per cent of those dollars up-front. This should be a worthy investment for local corn producers. Far from Iowa's corn processing plants or Missouri River export loading docks, per-bushel corn prices in the area were ten to fifteen cents lower than at those locations. There should also be others willing to invest in a business that would provide more local employment.

In time, we decided to proceed, and each of us wrote a check for five hundred dollars to cover legal and other organization costs. The next step was to write a business plan, to guide us as the initial board of directors and to assure investors and a lender that "we knew where we were going."

Why a "Closed Cooperative?"

In the process we learned that Iowa law did not allow more than ten owners in a closed cooperative. Apparently the law had been designed for family-owned farms or businesses. We would need far more investors than ten.

Being a cooperative was important, in that most cooperatives do not pay state or federal income taxes directly. Rather, income and expenses are each passed through to members in proportion to their ownership. We contacted individual state legislators about getting that Iowa law changed and, with the help of the Iowa Association of Cooperatives, lobbied legislative leaders. Once they learned what we had in mind and why existing legislation was a road-block, they amended the existing law and the amended law was signed by Governor Terry Branstad.

The next question: "Were we *certain* the Internal Revenue Service would allow a closed cooperative to enjoy the same tax treatment as traditional cooperatives?" We had only assumed that. We employed a Des Moines tax attorney to interpret IRS regulations and concluded that we should seek a "private letter ruling" to that effect from IRS. Maas, our attorney, and I, flew to Washington and, accompanied by one of Senator Charles Grassley's staff, made our case to IRS staff. This appeared to be "new ground" for IRS, and staff response was negative.

We pondered asking our Iowa Congressional delegation to pressure IRS for that private letter ruling, but our friends in the Iowa Association of Cooperatives discouraged that. Both IRS and Congress were receiving complaints from corporations and individually-owned businesses that traditional cooperatives were unfair competition because they, per se, did not pay income tax. By making it a major issue for our closed cooperative, there could result IRS or Congressional back-lash against traditional cooperatives and the latter might lose their tax treatment feature.

Our attorney continued to search IRS' extensive regulations and interpretations, and eventually found a statement that for certain new business structures, organizers could *choose* among certain options for tax treatment. It was referred to as a "check the box" option. We chose to "check the box" that would let the income and expense pass through to owners. The egg cooperative would provide each investor a K-1 form, showing their share of the business' income and expense, to accompany each investor's personal return. The cooperative, per se, would file a return but pay no income tax.

Money: Investors and a Loan

For a long-term loan, Russell had worked to put together a consortium of nearby banks, but could not get to the dollar level we needed. We talked to Farm Credit and a major Des Moines bank, and the latter gave us a letter of commitment, pending sufficient investor commitments.

We then prepared for what would become more than fifteen information meetings for potential investors in Cass and adjacent counties. We did a test run with a small group of local lenders, cattle and corn producers, and feed salesmen, people with no experience in the egg business. Their candid feedback would help us refine our presentation.

Before scheduling those meetings, however, I suggested that we members of the steering committee should first make *our* investment commitment. "Whoa," one said, "I'm willing to borrow money to invest in farmland, but I'm not so sure I want to borrow money (as some other of our potential investors would need to do) for this venture."

"But our feasibility study shows there could be a fourteen per cent long-term return. If we have not committed to invest, how can we encourage others?"

In short order, we each made our commitment, most from ten to twenty five units (shares) at twenty seven hundred dollars each. And, after investor meetings during the fall and winter, and personal follow-up with attendees by steering committee members, we had raised two million, seven hundred thousand dollars.

Decisions

We had more decisions to make. What genetic line of layers should we use? Who would raise the pullets for us? Where could we build the facility?

In the years since I had carried corn to my mother's Leghorns, poultry geneticists had had more than sixty generations of birds in which to select ever higher-producing lines of layers. Breeders had developed diverse lines within the Leghorn breed and crossed lines to achieve hybrid vigor in both eggs produced and bird livability. We drove to Johnston and Dallas Center, Iowa, to talk with Hy-Line geneticists, flew to New York State to see Babcock's facilities and hear their geneticists' sales pitch, and visited with two others. Five companies then provided virtually all the egg-producing lines used in the U.S.

We would buy our genetics in the form of pullets raised by an intermediate party, and asked the Babcock people during our New York visit, "If we buy your genetics, where would our pullets be raised?"

Their response surprised me, "The Nelsons, at Manhattan, Kansas." I had known the Nelsons, long in the Manhattan hatchery and poultry business, from my first time at Kansas State, thirty years earlier.

In time, we signed a several-year contract with Babcock for their genetics, and with Nelsons to raise Babcock pullets to eighteen weeks, deliver and place them in our barns. Babcock would provide Nelsons with male and female parent line chicks, which the Nelsons would raise and mate, then hatch the fertile eggs to yield the pullets that would become our layers.

We scoured the area for at least forty acres on which we could build six-hundred-foot barns without costly dirt movement, close to a paved road, and with an adequate water source. It had to be more than twenty five hundred feet from a residence or, if not, we would need a signed waiver from the residence owner (an Iowa requirement for intensive animal operations).

In time, we signed an option for sixty acres four miles southeast of Massena at a price more than double then current land values and pending our finding adequate water. The sixty acres would not only accommodate the five barns and packing building we planned, there would be room for expansion.

Obstacles

Our effort to start that egg business would encounter more obstacles. In fact, potential obstacles seemed to appear on a regular schedule. Test wells for water at our optioned site were disappointing. We considered piping water, but test wells up to a mile away were as dry. The only other sites that met our criteria, near paved roads and level enough on which to build had been rejected; they were too far from Massena and this was a Massena area idea and project.

Someone suggested a reservoir, and calculations showed that annual rainfall to an adjacent drainage area *could* provide the water we would need. We negotiated and signed an option for sixty nearby acres where a reservoir could be built. However, we then had to consider another question, "Could droppings onto the reservoir water by migratory or other fowl bring disease to our expected six hundred and fifty thousand layers?"

I called poultry, migratory bird, and veterinary scientists, from California to North Carolina, and gained sufficient confidence that, with normal water treatment, the reservoir water would be safe. (At this writing, early May, 2012, with an apparent contagion of bird flu in a number of Iowa flocks, there is media speculation that migratory birds may carry the flu virus.)

Several neighbors to the planned site appeared one morning at our steering committee meeting, deeply worried about flies and odor that could reach their homes from the planned operation. We had checked out other layer operations and had found that any fly or odor problems were limited to the site, itself, and easily controlled. We had also checked with entomologists who told us how far flies would venture from their food source, rarely more than a hundred feet. However, the neighbors' concerns remained.

I told the group that if they would invite any interested neighbors to one of their homes some evening, I would be pleased to describe the project in detail, listen to any concerns, and answer questions. I lived twenty five miles from the site; there was no need for committee members living in the neighborhood, or involved in a Massena business, to get into what might be an intense and emotional session.

Committee member Gary Maas, who lived about eight miles from the site and whose business depended on clients statewide and beyond, had joined me, and it was a rather emotional meeting. To the assembled group, this was a new concept, a feared incursion to their neighborhood. It would be both a large concentration of animals and a business structure foreign to the community, mostly one hundred-sixty-acre or slightly larger farms, each with its own animal enterprises. Though we answered every question, we knew that only time would bring acceptance.

Our committed lender, the Des Moines bank, was acquired by a larger bank and the loan commitment letter was withdrawn. We went back to our Farm Credit contact, Nate Burnham. (Burnham had grown up on a farm near Griswold and his grandfather had been Griswold's superintendent and basketball coach during my high school years.) Burnham and his colleagues repeated the proposition they had made earlier, and committed to a long-term loan.

With financing in place, we could now contract with an Iowa builder, one that had built many comparable facilities. We could also contract with that local farm supply cooperative, by now expanded and re-named Twenty First Century, to receive member corn and to mix and deliver a complete ration to our bins on the site.

We wondered when another obstacle might appear and, sure enough, one did. We were alerted to a Mormon Trail publication that suggested our site might be on the exact route of the Trail.

We could not afford objections being raised on that issue after construction was underway, so we had to check it out. Fortunately, Cumberland's mayor, a respected local historian, learned of our problem and produced a map showing that the trail made a significant jog about four miles southeast of Massena

Though we had assumed we would sell our eggs to the breaker plant at Lennox, we discovered that we had set our sights too low. The wholesale price for shell eggs, for the one-dozen and two-dozen cardboard containers on display in supermarkets, is consistently higher.

We found and negotiated an agreement with a larger shell egg producer that was already supplying retailers and that could handle more eggs.

Though putting our eggs at a higher price level, we would, in time, find that monitoring and maintaining that agreement would be the most time consuming and complex of any of the issues we had faced or would face. The reader will find more about that experience in a later section.

A Half-Million Eggs a Day

Though it had taken more than three years from formation of the steering committee, construction equipment was now on site for what would be SouthWest Iowa Egg. We were ready for a formal groundbreaking.

When new businesses are formed, the venture's written prospectus for potential investors usually shows the number of initial ownership shares *granted* the organizers, those who had the idea, invented the product, or spent time and money to hire legal help and clear other hurdles. In the case of SouthWest Iowa Egg's prospectus, that was not the case. For our steering committee and, now, board of directors, the satisfaction of the business in operation would be sufficient reward.

Governor Terry Branstad at the podium for the SouthWest Iowa Egg groundbreaking, August 29, 1998. On the stage were our steering committee, plus representatives of the Iowa Department of Economic Development, the Farmers' Electric Cooperative of Greenfield, Land O'Lakes Cooperative, Farm Credit Services, and other entities that had been helpful.

Though there would be construction and start-up problems, normal in any business, I would, in time, watch in the packing room of SouthWest Iowa Egg a sixteen-inch wide windrow of eggs from five barns, each barn six hundred feet long and holding more than one hundred twenty five thousand hens. The eggs would have rolled out of the birds' tiered cages onto narrow, moving belts, down endless "escalators" to that wide gathering belt. The eggs would move toward the packing building and six sets of mechanical fingers that would lift rows of six eggs and place them into indentations on a thirty-egg cardboard flat.

The flats would then be stacked seven high, nine stacks on a plywood "square," and three squares stacked on a pallet. The loaded pallet would then be wrapped in what might be called heavy-duty Saran wrap, moved by fork lift into a cooler and, in time, to an eighteen-wheel semi. Every second day, an eighteen-wheeler would leave the site with more than five thousand dozen egg — and perhaps a nervous driver.

I had called Sheriff Ken Jones to alert him to a potential problem at SouthWest Iowa Egg. Our newly-hired manager had had a disagreement with an engineering consultant, felt the consultant had not delivered satisfactory work, and had refused to pay. As chairman, I had agreed to be part of a meeting to negotiate a settlement, and then had been told the consultant was "coming with a gun to insure agreement."

Jones told me he would drive to Massena and at the scheduled meeting time he would be in his car in the church parking lot a quarter mile away. I should call his cell phone if our meeting got tense.

In the end, there was no need to call Jones' cell phone. We rather quickly reached a compromise in the consultant's fee, our manager wrote him a check, he departed, and I called Jones to thank him for his support.

Personnel problems are not uncommon in any venture, and all board members were generous of their time when personnel or other problems developed. More than one special board meeting was called, and I recall one that went well into the night. Don McCunn spent days and partial days away from his farm equipment business, helping coordinate construction work. When our first manager departed, Dwight Bower stepped in temporarily, taking time from his farm operation.

In time, we recruited Rich Hall, our former Cass County Extension director, as our manager. A native of the Massena area, Hall had the personality and ability to work well with people. He also had solid connections in animal agriculture and with Iowa State University that would be helpful. That Hall knew little about chickens, I considered a plus. By that time, we had experienced barn and packing room workers on board and Hall could learn about chickens, eggs, and current technology. He would soon hire an experienced industry consultant, perhaps for a day a month, one who could tell Hall what worked and did not work in other units with which he consulted.

China: Ring Roads and Turtle Soup

In 2001 I was asked by the United Nations Development Program to review a "Dryland Agriculture" project in China's Ningxai Autonomous Region, an arid region far northwest from Beijing. An "autonomous region" is the same as a province, except that the Number Two leader is a chairman rather than a governor. (The party secretary is Number One in any case.) The term, autonomous region, acknowledges that, largely because it has a high proportion of an ethnic or cultural minority, that region has a bit more autonomy in its operations. Ningxai has a large proportion of Moslems.

I was joined in the effort by Iowa State seed scientist, Dr. Yuh Yuan Shyy, and I share in the following some notes from my 2001 log and recollections. What we would see would be far different from my 1979 or 1985 China experiences.

We were met at the Beijing airport by a Mr. Gu with an SUV and we drove by way of a tree-lined, multi-lane airport freeway to the "third ring," the third of four and soon to be five muti-lane traffic rings around metropolitan Beijing, (At this writing, 2015, seven rings are shown on a Beijing area map.) The ring roads are filled with fast-moving autos and buses in three to four lanes each direction.

None of the single-story structures comprising both businesses and homes that I had seen twenty three years earlier were in sight, and there was certainly no card playing or visiting under the lights that brightly illuminated the freeway.

We traveled west on the third ring perhaps eight kilometers to Beijing's Friendship House Complex Building Number Two, a hotel. It had been built by the Russians when they were providing technician help to China in the 1950s. Shirley and I had stayed in this same building in 1998, and she had recognized it then as where she had stayed with her People-to-People group in 1980. The building had been recently redecorated and was finely furnished. The streets of the complex were tree-lined, the grounds' lawns mowed and otherwise beautifully maintained.

It was not only the ring roads that were full of traffic, the road past the Friendship House Complex was four lanes each way and the same was true for adjacent, two-lane service roads on each side. The service roads allowed both autos and bicycles, and traffic was heavy enough that during the rush hour the only way to cross these several roads was to use a pedestrian overpass. One evening I wanted to eat at a McDonald's directly across the near-by ring road, but the only way I could get there was by way of a pedestrian overpass a half-mile to my right. I chose to eat at the hotel.

Notes from the Ningxai Region: I had spent the morning visiting dryland farm operations and sheep and goat ranches, impressed that the sparse vegetation had allowed considerable erosion, and we returned to Ling Wu city for lunch. We were in a private dining room with three young waitresses in neat red and gold flowing dresses. One napkin folded to a peak indicated where the guest of honor should sit and, apparently, I was that guest.

No alcohol was served with the meal, only water and orange soda. As expected in this largely Moslem area, no pork would be on the menu. Before us was an array of twelve dishes, some that I did not recognize.

Not understanding the language and reticent to ask, I was never certain if those unfamiliar items were to provide additional "honor" or to simply see if a U. S. guest would partake. Such was not uncommon. This time, along side the more commonly encountered fermented eggs, was what appeared to be a gelatinous seafood item, but turned out to be lamb tendons and pickled sections of rooster combs. In this case, the eggs were not quartered or whole fermented eggs that I had been served earlier; rather, the egg yolk and white had been cooked and molded in a container, then fermented, and sliced.

I had no problem in partaking; it is simply a matter of attitude and reality. People of this area consider these items to be delicacies and have been eating them for years. Beyond that, the tendons and combs are simply animal protein, with about the same chemical structure as the strips of connective tissue in a beef roast.

I did notice that, though the shrimp and roasted lamb plates had been picked clean, there were plentiful amounts of those other delicacies still on the serving plates as they were removed from the table.

Near the end of the meal I was asked if I liked turtle soup. "Sure," I said. Within minutes we were all served a small bowl of turtle soup, but only the honored guest got the shell and the privilege of feasting on some of the softer tissue around the shell's edge. It was only more gelatinous "cartilage."

After that came a bowl of noodle soup, very spicy, and then the suggestion of a fifteen-minute rest. Our hosts disappeared and I took advantage of a soft chair to relax and let my meal "digest."

From Rice to Meat and Milk

In the 1970s and 1980s I would class China as a "developing country," and peoples' diets reflected that. As in most other South Asia and some West Africa developing countries I would later visit, it was a plant-based diet. It was rice in South Asia and cassava in West Africa. Meat, milk, or eggs were rare.

We had watched Taiwan and South Korea develop and intensify their agriculture after WW II and their diets shift, over time, to include wheat and animal products. So would diets of the Chinese. In a later visit to China with leaders of the Kansas legislature, in May of 1985, I would see initial movements in that direction. In that visit, my Kansas State dean of veterinary medicine, Dr. Jim Coffman, and I looked over a state farm fence at about two dozen thin cows of largely Holstein breeding, each chewing away at a rather coarse grass hay. We had been told by Henan Province officials that a major provincial goal was to increase milk consumption, especially among babies, and our visit to this farm and dairy herd was to illustrate the present state of affairs.

We had also visited Henan Agricultural University to check out any mutual value in a university-to-university linkage and, in the process, had visited the university's livestock research and teaching facilities near the campus. It had three thousand chickens, including both layers and broilers, but only ten Holstein cows. We were told that all of the research animals had been moved out and lost during the Cultural Revolution. The cows we were seeing had apparently been obtained within the previous two years.

The universities had also lost a good many professors during that Revolution, most sent to labor in the country side. By the time of our visit, those that had survived and retained their professorial skills had been "rehabilitated" and were back in the classroom.

As we had watched Taiwan and South Korea develop and intensify their agriculture after WW II, and their diets shift over time to include wheat and animal products, so would Chinese diets.

It was now late August, 2001. Dr. Shyy, our local host, Mr. Ming, and I drove to a five thousand-cow Holstein dairy, a state-owned business at the northwest edge of the city of Yinchuan, Ningxai Region, and called the National Pingjipu Cow Factory. We visited one of four operating units, cows averaging about twenty thousand pounds of milk annually, the cows milked in a double-ten milking parlor (ten cows on each side of a worker pit). Cows were penned by their production level in an open shed, fed corn silage, alfalfa, and a concentrate mix, the silage dumped from a horse-drawn cart onto a slab between the stalls and pushed to the feeding trough by hand.

We watched loose corn fodder being chopped on site by five electric-powered stationery cutters and blown onto an open stack, then packed by a track tractor. At each cutter, two men were throwing the corn stalks off from a flat-bed wagon, a third man feeding them into the cutter. It was similar to how silage was made on my home farm in the 1930s and early 1940s, except our standing corn stalks had been mechanically cut and tied in bundles. These corn stalks had been cut by hand and loaded loose on the wagons.

The dairy bought the corn fodder from nearby individual farmers. For the five-thousand-cow dairy, plus the farmers who produce the corn fodder, there were about six thousand workers. Employees at the dairy were secondary school graduates, and earned the equivalent of thirty dollars per month.

We were told the dairy was profitable, the equivalent of about five hundred fifty dollars per cow per year. The milk was sold to a city processor (also likely state-owned) under a long-term pricing arrangement. Ninety per cent was consumed as fluid milk, the balance as a slightly cultured product. We were served some of the latter, rather refreshing and understandably popular during the summer months.

The only similarity to collective or state farm visits one or two decades earlier was the office hosting room, with overstuffed couches and chairs against all four walls. However, there were no doilies.

The next day we would visit what I interpreted to be a private, five-hundred-cow dairy, in a walled compound on top of one of those barren hills in Ningxia Province. We entered a cement courtyard covered with loose alfalfa hay, a cart at the far end was filled with finely-ground alfalfa, and across a low wall/fence were many large Holstein cows. We walked through a double-forty stanchion barn; a foot-bath depression in the entry was dry and apparently un-used. We noted a portable milking machine and buckets being washed, and were told the annual production per cow was estimated at about fifteen thousand pounds. I did not ask why the production was only estimated; a direct question is often interpreted as a challenge, so it is best to just listen.

I asked about grain or silage; alfalfa provides plenty of protein but cows cannot eat enough to get the energy for high production and I considered the fifteen thousand pounds too low for the size and type cows we had seen. The owner said they had exhausted their corn silage supply and the new crop was not yet harvested. He then had a worker bring a bundle of wheatgrass, stored elsewhere. It was lower in protein but higher in energy than alfalfa. They grind the wheatgrass, mix it with alfalfa, and soak the mix with water to achieve more consumption. It was a good strategy under the circumstances.

We were about to leave when the owner asked if his workers could ask some questions. The questions involved quality, fluid vs. manufacturing milk, and alcohol, but I had difficulty with interpretation. Eventually, they led us back to the milk tank room, showed us a test tube with tiny specks of coagulated milk that stuck to the side of the tube. It appeared to be evidence of mastitis, a bacterial infection of the udder that causes milk to coagulate. I told them what I knew from my own farm experience, and how to detect it prior to attaching a milker. (We used a cup with a screen on the top, squeezed a few squirts of milk into the cup and the screen caught the coagulated particles). I also mentioned "somatic cell count" of milk, a routine measurement that discloses the likelihood of infection before it appears in the milk. I urged them to contact a veterinarian or dairy specialist for advice.

Farm communes operate a variety of businesses, often adding value to grains or other plant materials. In this case, one crop was mulberries, the raw material for silk. The workers are delivering bags of mulberry leaves to the commune's silk-worm factory.

After the Professors Came Back

In my visits to China, from 1979 through 2001, I would see the step-wise re-establishment of higher education as a recognized societal need, plus emergence of capitalistic elements within an overall Communist political structure. It would mean investment in universities and research institutes, and sharply increased farm productivity.

My 1979 exposure to higher education in China had been limited. Our trade group was often met at railway stations by students from "colleges of tourism," who were seeking conversations in English. Generally, we were the first people they had seen for whom English was the first language. They wanted to hear English being spoken and they wanted to try out their English on us. Later, I had arranged brief visits to two Beijing universities, and was led by a campus host past rather bare classrooms and laboratories, the latter with the most basic equipment, perhaps microscopes, balances, and titration devices.

I saw little evidence of capitalism in that visit, either in shops or in collective farm and manufacturing businesses. However, in a train trip up river from Beijing to the countryside I shared a seat with a professor of wheat production, who described a system in some regions where, once a collective farm or individual farmers had met their quota, they were free to sell any additional production to processors. Wheat yields had increased sharply.

At Henan Agricultural University in 1985, we had walked through chemistry labs, clean and well equipped, plus a computer room, with sixteen minicomputers and printers that were available for use by students and staff. The Henan Academy of Agricultural Science was even more impressive, with five hundred scientists in ten research institutes and two hundred acres of land.

By 1998 there had been further progress. At Huazhong Agricultural University in the city of Wuhan, the doctorate degree was being offered in fifteen disciplines and the masters' degree in thirty two, spread among the liberal arts, economics, agronomy, forestry, animal science, and molecular biology. Of twenty three hundred staff, eight hundred thirty were full-time scientists and teachers, and included elected members of the National Academy of Science and the National Academy of Engineering.

That university had exchange programs with universities and research institutes in seventeen countries, including Japan, the United States, and Western Europe. As we visited with research faculty in the China Agricultural University in Beijing, we learned of their global exposures. Among them, they had degrees from universities in the U.S., Germany, Scotland, and Canada.

English for Beijing's Olympics

For my 2001 visit to the country, the little time I was in Beijing was in the UNDP project office. I would not see much of Beijing until my last full day, when I would submit my expenses and be paid, the latter to be in the form of a travelers check.

I turned in my report at the UNDP project office and was given a form to take to "the bank" for payment. An English-speaking young woman said she would accompany me to the bank. We hailed a taxi, headed west on the ring road to what appeared to be Beijing's northwestern outskirts, then south. We passed many banks, so I asked, "Is there a special bank we needed to go to?"

"Oh, yes," she said, "the main office of the Bank of China, in the city center." That bank apparently had the UNDP account.

"Why the long way around?" I asked.

"The driver tells me there is a big traffic jam between our office and city center."

We were among tall, impressive buildings all the way, from Georgian architecture to curved and other dramatic designs, seemingly hundreds of new apartment buildings as high as thirty or forty stories. Our destination, the Bank of China's main office, was perhaps the most dramatic structure I had seen, with light yellow marble inside and out, including the floor, walls, and benches. Its atrium was the full ten stories.

I submitted my signed "payment form," handed my passport to be copied, and was told that the form I had brought indicated cash, not a travelers' check. To get a travelers' check, we would have to go back to the project office for another form. "No way," I said, "I'll take the cash."

I was directed to a second counter where a clerk counted out thirty new U.S. hundred-dollar bills, a fifty, and three ones, plus a paper sack to hold it.

The return trip to the project office was more direct, through an older section of traditional one-story homes and businesses, the businesses facing the street and the homes in the back, my memory of 1979 Beijing. These structures, some already vacant, were soon to be removed and replaced by more of the new and dramatic construction. I was told the vacated residents had been assigned a unit in a new apartment building and the shop-keepers would find work in a nearby business or in construction.

My guide asked the taxi driver if he had learned his English. Because the 2008 Olympics were to be in Beijing, taxi drivers had been instructed to learn English. He responded, in rather understandable English, "I'm studying."

CHAPTER XI

TIME FOR MORE ENCOUNTERS

"All of the homes in the area appeared to be three to seven thousand square feet in size, most on about one-acre lots, and some surrounded by a security fence. Though this house was rather new, many of the homes in the immediate community clearly pre-dated that 1996 legislation. A clue to that puzzle came from one of the local guests, who told me the community had once been the state's Agricultural Research Institute. No further inquiry seemed appropriate."

While having dinner with Dr. Keith Huston at the Cosmos Club on Massachusetts Avenue NW, soon after we had arrived in Washington in 1986, he asked why I had agreed to wrestle with the federal bureaucracy. "You've had enough good experiences," he suggested, "Why not just retire and enjoy life?"

Huston, a professor of dairy cattle genetics, had been my college curriculum committee chairman and a valuable adviser during my time as K-State associate dean. He had later been experiment station director at the U. of Minnesota and by 1986 was representing the north central station directors lobbying USDA and Congress.

"But I am enjoying life." I told Huston. Regardless of bureaucratic frustrations, the global development work was satisfying.

Huston got my attention, though, and for a few day I pondered, "Was I being selfish in accepting or seeking such new and different jobs?" Was it fair to my wife, Shirley, when we could have retired to the farm or to some "retirement community?"

I had not pondered long. Her evident enjoyment and satisfactions in this new-to-us Washington environment, working three days a week in the White House Volunteer office, taking lessons in calligraphy, and playing the guest role at foreign embassies related to my international work told me that she, too, was enjoying life. We would have six rewarding years in Washington.

After Washington would come our farming operation and even other encounters and experiences would follow. In regard to those "other encounters and experiences," now free from the farm duties, I could not resist. In this next case, I had been asked to chair a group charged with "Re-inventing Agricultural Education for the Year 2020."

Vocational Agriculture in Philadelphia

It was five o'clock in the livestock barn's classroom; the instructor had dismissed his last class of the day and was ready to leave. However, his students were not heading home; they were out checking on their calves and lambs. Perhaps thirty minutes or an hour later, they would head to the bus stop on Henry Avenue for their travel home, some to distant sections of Philadelphia.

During my university years, I had been in Midwestern high schools when classes closed at four o'clock, and one did not want to be in front of the exit. Not so at W.B. Saul School of Agricultural Sciences, one hundred thirty acres in the Roxborough section of Philadelphia, just inside the Schuylkill Expressway and bordering Fairmount Park. As the horticulture and meats instructors had told me earlier in the afternoon, their students were never ready to leave the campus; they had to be reminded that their parents expected them home for dinner.

This school, part of the greater Philadelphia School District, had six hundred sixty students and forty two instructors, eighteen of which taught agriculture subjects, from animal production to horticulture to meat or milk processing. The rest taught math, English, and other courses. Seventy six per cent of the students were active participants in FFA. Both their meat science and landscaping teams had won state championships. Five hundred fifty people had attended the previous year's FFA banquet.

Five years earlier, in my USDA science and education role, I had met a few W.B. Saul graduates while visiting USDA's Eastern Regional Research Center, a mile or so across the Park in Philadelphia's Windmoor suburb. In quizzing several scientists that day as to what had enticed them to food science, the work of that center, several had told me about W.B. Saul. One was a Saul graduate, working as a lab technician. Another was a Saul alumnus on a summer internship from her college work at Pennsylvania State University.

That USDA research center, by the way, developed the enzyme supplement, lactase, which allows lactose-intolerant people, those who do not produce sufficient lactase themselves, to enjoy dairy products. It is one of four regional "commodity utilization" laboratories established in the early 1940s, during Henry Wallace's tenure as USDA secretary.

W.B. Saul was hosting a faculty conference for faculty of urban schools of agriculture, including similar schools in the Chicago, Milwaukee, Minneapolis, and other metropolitan areas. Our 2020 group was learning more about such programs and their potential.

With continued decreases in farm population, historically the source of many vocational agriculture students and, eventually, agricultural scientists and business professionals, recruiting able young people into agricultural disciplines was vital to U.S. agricultural competitiveness. We needed some of those urban students to fill its ranks.

W.B. Saul and the conference discussions suggested both need and potential for more such schools, plus some form of vocational agriculture in traditional urban high schools, such as Des Moines, Wichita, Denver, or Omaha. In the final report of our "reinventing agricultural education for the year, 2020" working group, one of seven needs highlighted was: *"Leaders — who see the awesome potential for agricultural education in all schools —. This means Chicago, Detroit, and Dallas, and it means Garden City, Kansas and Garden City, New York, (both about 25,000 population). —There just are not enough young people to staff the agriculture, food, fiber, and natural resources positions. More important, few subjects excite and motivate students the way that live animals, growing plants, and business experiences do. For those who fear city kids are at a disadvantage, remember: most rural students have never planted corn, most have never fed a calf, most have never packaged meat, and most have never trimmed a hedge."*

The W.B. Saul School of Agricultural Sciences had been named for an attorney who had pressed for this school's establishment during his years as chairman of the Philadelphia Board of Education. Saul understood student motivation, he understood job opportunities, and he believed that urban students should not be denied opportunity to pursue a vocational program of potential high interest.

Privatizing in the Ukraine

I would return to Eastern Europe again, this time as a collaborative professor for Iowa State University and part of a team that would lecture at a school in Kiev, Ukraine. A bonus in this case was the chance to work with Iowa State's then rather new director of international agricultural programs (at this writing, associate dean for both instruction and international programs) one David Acker. Though we would find no evidence of common lineage, and though he uses the soft "A" for Acker, in him the Acker name is well served.

Along with Acker, Economist Stan Johnson, who would soon become Iowa State's vice provost for extension, others of the Iowa State lecturers, and some of Kiev's elite, I was sampling from a table spread of caviar on bread, olives, eggplant, fish strips, and a variety of salads in one of Kiev's largest and more opulent private homes. At a roll-in bar in the next room we could have our choice of beer, wine, champagne, vodka, or orange juice. It was early September, 1996.

During World War II, Ukraine had been overrun by the Nazi's in fierce fighting, lost thousands in battle, then was re-captured by Soviet forces and, after the end of WWII, fully dominated by Moscow. Only five years before our visit, Ukraine had achieved independence from the former Soviet Union and the republic was working its way to a market-oriented economy. Western countries, especially the U.S., were trying to help. However, Iowa State had had a formal relationship with the National Agricultural University of the Ukraine (NAUU) since 1988, and Johnson had been Iowa State's lead person.

The focus of these ten days in Ukraine was a one-week "Ensminger School," the brainchild of one M.E. Ensminger, then well up in years but with whom, forty years earlier, I had served on American Society of Animal Science committees. Ensminger had authored a series of animal science textbooks, and then dedicated his later years to offering livestock short courses, Ensminger Schools, in developing countries. Though his academic links had been elsewhere, he had chosen Iowa State to be the eventual repository for his papers and, in return, Iowa State had agreed to perpetuate his legacy, including the schools and perhaps revise and continue some of his books. I had been invited to be part of the faculty for this school, to lecture on how a private farm works.

Ukraine had recognized the necessity of moving state-owned land and businesses to private ownership, not only for pride of ownership but so real estate could be used as loan collateral. Especially in a capital-short former Soviet republic, loans were essential in order to buy inputs, hire labor, and make production happen. It had taken time to debate all related issues and not until early 1996 had the Ukraine parliament approved such legislation.

Our host had been the director of science at the National Agricultural University of Ukraine and, I had been told, was then one of the wealthier persons in the country, involved in farm management, custom farming operations, and construction. All of the homes in the area appeared to be three to seven thousand square feet in size, most on about one-acre lots, and some surrounded by a security fence. Though this house was rather new, many of the homes in the immediate community clearly pre-dated that 1996 legislation. A clue to that puzzle came from one of the local guests, who told me the community had once been the state's Agricultural Research Institute. No further inquiry seemed appropriate.

Because I was then helping develop the egg production business, I had asked to visit the university's poultry research farm and learn the status of Ukraine's poultry industry. I would see nutrition research underway and learn that links had been established with several U.S. suppliers of genetic lines, both layers and broilers. Most interesting was that the research farm was also in the process of privatization, and our host, an assistant professor of poultry, was to become one of the major owners.

I drew no conclusion regarding the appropriateness of these privatizing arrangements. Each of the former Soviet republics was working toward privatizing in their own way, within their own political and economic environment. Some had tried giving every citizen a voucher, that to be used to purchase either a property or a share in a property, perhaps a manufacturing company.

My several encounters simply illustrate the circumstances in former Soviet republics in the early 1990s. As in any circumstance, opportunity comes to those who are aware and who may be in an advantageous position.

Political Temptations

In my first days as USDA's assistant secretary for Science and Education, I had learned that Congress had included in the Department's budget several million dollars to help speed the movement of new technologies from ARS' research labs into commercial use. The money would go as grants or forgivable loans to private businesses that would commercialize the technology, and perhaps develop new or higher-value agricultural products. Congress had stipulated that a board appointed by the administration and by Congressional leaders would guide the grant and loan program.

I had seen programs of this type before and their records were not good. First, a politically appointed board will tend to make political decisions. If Senator X has appointed you to such a board and one of the senator's campaign donors seeks a grant or loan for their private business, there is a tendency, perhaps an obligation, to urge approval. Or, a grant application may come from a donor to a president's election or re-election campaign and the White House may "weigh in" on the need for the application to be approved. The financial feasibility or functional merits of any grant or loan proposal may be secondary.

More than one fund using federal or state tax money and similarly structured had dissipated in relatively short time.

My ARS staff were distressed that the work of analyzing proposals, recommending approval, and monitoring performance, had not been delegated to their agency, where the technologies were developed. Instead, it was being handled by staff in the Secretary's office.

I suggested to my ARS staff that, with such a political structure, they were fortunate to not be assigned that responsibility. ARS staff should be fully supportive, provide information, share data, and provide any expertise, but this respected research agency need not risk the taint of political folly. (Within a few years, the money would dissipate, with little to show.)

Now, a half decade later, the Iowa legislature was considering how it might help Iowa cattle producers purchase a closed beef processing plant at Tama, Iowa. The legislature was considering another loan or grant.

Recognizing the failure of previous ventures that had been under political control, Iowa's 1998 legislature chose a different model. It authorized establishment of a private corporation, the Iowa Agricultural

Finance Corporation (IAFC), to be guided by a *private sector* board. Provisions included that investments be in Iowa and that agricultural producers should be beneficiaries of the investments. The state would provide the corporation (borrow from the state's Road Use Tax Fund) twenty five million dollars "seed money" at zero interest, and the Iowa Department of Economic Development was charged with identifying seven people who would establish the corporation and serve as initial board members. There would be no political appointments.

I was impressed that a political body, a state legislature, would deny itself political control of such a fund.

Would the Corporation get established? Would it attract other investors? Would Iowa producers become co-owners and beneficiaries of value-added ventures? Would the corporation and its operation remain free of political pressure or interference? Who would be the seven people?

Venture Capital in Pork and Beans

It was December a year later and we were in a sparkling clean, refrigerated room, in a non-descript building in Sioux City's industrial park just south of the airport. Two officers of Cybus Capital, investment advisers hired by IAFC, other IAFC board members, and I were watching a white-frocked crew working in close quarters among stainless steel tables and conveyors breaking fresh pork carcasses into cuts. Earlier in the day we had been fifty miles up the road at Sioux Center, where those carcasses from "specification" hogs had been processed. As in the beef business, where "Certified Angus Beef" had achieved recognition as superior quality, Berkshire hogs and others that were part of what was known as the Niman Ranch production system had achieved somewhat parallel recognition. Packaged product from these hogs would bring a premium at the retail level, and some of that premium would be captured by both the processor and producer.

Not long after adjournment of that 1998 Iowa legislature, I had been one of thirty or more Iowans who had received a letter from the director of the Iowa Department of Economic Development asking each 1) to suggest several Iowans who should be considered to help establish IAFC and serve on its first board, and 2) if you should be one who was later asked to serve, would you be willing to do it. I had responded with several names and, though my experience in venture capital was limited to the modest amounts I had put on the table for then developing SouthWest Iowa Egg and a hoped-for ethanol plant in the area, I had answered "yes" to the second request.

In early fall, Jack May, president of Kent Feeds, Jeff Plagge, a bank president at Waverly, Wayne Seaman, CEO of West Central Cooperative, Leslie Miller, vice president of a Knoxville bank, Steve Morain, Iowa Farm Bureau general counsel, Tom Urban, former CEO of Pioneer Hybrids, and I met in the Iowa Farm Bureau board room, Des Moines to start the process of establishing the corporation. I had known three of the group, Urban, as a member of President-elect Clinton's USDA transition team six years earlier, May through his work with FFA, and Seaman through a Carroll County development group.

With Urban and I elected chair and vice chair, and Morain as secretary, our board rather quickly made three decisions, 1) we would seek private capital to supplement the state's loan, 2) we would link with persons who had demonstrated success in venture capital, preferably Iowans, and 3) IAFC, per se, would have but one employee, to handle essential board decisions and functions. Within a few months we had filed articles of incorporation with the Iowa Secretary of State, gained commitments for eighteen million dollars of private money, most from major agricultural businesses, banks, and organizations friendly to IAFC's function, and contracted with Cybus, a three-person Des Moines group, to advise on and monitor investments.

We had answered the first two questions above; the corporation was established and had raised some private money, though not as much as we had hoped.

Next question: Would Iowa producers become co-owners or beneficiaries of value-added ventures? Yes, but it would not be easy, and there would be both successes and failures. We sought growers who might have a value-added venture underway but that needed capital to expand or perfect their operation, and we found a family at Grinnell that was growing organic soybeans, producing tofu in a converted garage/storage building on their farm, and distributing the tofu to natural food stores in the area.

Their product response was good, but to expand and develop a broader product line and sales to a wider area, they needed both capital and linkage to an established, broader-line organic foods business. Our capital fund helped bring that about. A new company, Wildwood Harvest Foods, was formed, a new Grinnell plant was built to produce a broad line of organic soyfoods, dairy analogues, such as sour crèmes and yogurts, as well as probiotics, soyburgers, and hot dogs, and vegetarian mayonnaise.

The pork processing business at Sioux Center and Sioux City, a company called SiouxPreme Pork, was a different case; it had been operating profitably for more than thirty years. What made it appropriate for IAFC investment was that an established network of niche producers provided most of the hogs to SiouxPreme and both the company and the producers would benefit from the business' expansion. In the process, both the IAFC fund and the producer network became part owners of an expanded SiouxPreme; both could benefit from the greater volume and, likely, increasing share of the pork market.

Would IAFC and its operation remain free of political pressure and interference? With twenty five million dollars of state money having been provided and some individual legislators remaining opposed to the IAFC concept, that was probably too much to expect. Most important, some legislators' desire to help finance the repurchase of the Tama beef plant had started the original legislative discussion, the broader-purpose IAFC had resulted, and the beef plant *had not met* our financial advisers' criteria as a prudent investment.

Several legislators had continued to press for IAFC to invest in the Tama plant, while also publicly criticizing one or more of the investments we had made, and we were called to a rather intense legislative hearing. After that hearing and several meetings with both key legislators and beef industry leaders, we eventually "negotiated" (Urban had resigned from the board and I had become chairman) an arrangement whereby IAFC would be excused from the first three million dollars of scheduled repayment of the state loan, IAFC would "loan" that three million to the beef plant organizing group, and the legislature would "instruct" the Iowa Department of Economic Development to assume responsibility for (repayment of) that three million.

Founding legislation had stipulated a seven-year limit on IAFC board membership, so my service would end in 2005 and Paul Hill, a leader of the Iowa Turkey Growers Cooperative in its purchase of West Liberty Foods, and who had later joined the IAFC board, had become chairman.

In addition to the two businesses described above, we had made investments in an organic bakery, a crop genetics company, and a company that had developed a system for recovering animal wastes. As expected, we had seen both successes and disappointments. To lower our costs, we had shifted the management and monitoring of our investments from Cybus to persons handling a rather parallel capital investment program of Iowa Farm Bureau.

In the ten-year interval to this writing, early 2015, successive board members, led by Hill and then Reginald Clause, who I had recruited to join the board because of his experience studying and nurturing value-added startups while on the Iowa State University Extension staff, found more ways to enhance the positive aspects of the 1998 legislative intent. The original investment fund was linked not only with Farm Bureau's fund, but with two others to form what is now called a Rural Vitality Fund and a complementary Rural Vitality *Processing* Fund. The two funds, with different parameters, provide a broader field for investment while encouraging more agriculturally-related entrepreneurship. Also, the larger capital amount allows spreading risk among more invested entities.

Though IAFC no longer maintains an office and staff, it continues as a corporate entity, with a three-member executive committee of the board involved in each investment and continually tracking investment status and valuations. The corporation is on track to continue repayment of the loan at the originally prescribed one million dollars per year.

What about the Tama beef plant? It had closed again after that IAFC "loan" and less than eighteen months of operation, and remained vacant for much of a decade. According to media reports at this writing, it has attracted new investors, the Iowa Economic Development Authority has approved four million dollars in tax credits, the city of Tama has committed to rebate up to $3.6 million in property taxes over the next ten years, a $48 million dollar renovation has been completed, and the plant re-opened for business in late 2014.

Midwest Harvest appears to be doing well, and the organic bakery, Rudi's, has been purchased by a holding company. SiouxPreme is now a part of Natural Food Holdings, a holding company of Hilco Equity

Parters. The sale of SiouxPreme to Hilco gave IAFC a sizeable profit, money that let IAFC make other investments and also meet equity capital demands of some current investments. Available cash is critical in order to provide equity capital as invested companies face ups and downs in their business and/or need to expand.

The reader can learn more about the present status of these companies, as well as the two Rural Vitality funds, via their web sites.

A Devious Idea

Becoming a farmer after university and Washington careers had led to some work with the National Association of Conservation Districts (NACD), several task forces or working groups. Since purchasing our first farmland in the early 1960s, we had built more than seven miles of terraces and had established a five acre tract of "rare and declining species" of grasses and forbs and a wildlife food plot. We also had more than two miles of grass buffer strips along Troublesome Creek and drainage tributaries. Conservation efforts beyond our farm were of personal interest.

Along with Bill Richards, Ohio farmer and, during my time in USDA, chief of the Soil Conservation Service (now Natural Resources Conservation Service), and other conservation leaders, I was in a Denver hotel conference room discussing the Conservation Title of the Farm Bill before Congress, the several proposed programs to which NACD and its state and county member organizations might put their lobbying efforts.

Our focus had gotten pre-empted by a bureaucratic problem in Washington, a plan by Secretary Dan Glickman that Richards felt would make the job of his former agency more difficult. Glickman had announced that, instead of a budget and finance office in each of the thirty plus USDA agencies, they would be combined into a smaller number, a budget and finance office in the office of each of five under or assistant secretaries. NRCS and the Forest Service reported to the assistant secretary for conservation and the money for both agencies would be handled in that assistant secretary's office.

Instead of the NRCS administrator supervising that agency's budget and finance decisions, his or her allocations or expenditure approvals would be dependent on the opinions of a staff member in the undersecretary's office. I understood the problem; in both government and universities I had seen far too many "central office" people with control of funds or processes, while the operating unit head was responsible to "make programs happen." Instead of helping the unit head do their job, central staff can become "gate-keepers."

I had known Glickman from the time he was first elected to Congress from Kansas, knew him to be deliberate and sincere. I could also understand how some efficiency expert commissioned by the Clinton White House had convinced him to consolidate offices. The chances for NACD to stop his plan seemed remote.

Over the noon hour, Richards and I dreamed up a devious thought. We might encourage Glickman to go further, move *all* budget and finance operations into one central office, reporting directly to the secretary. Should he do that, expand his proposal to one central office, there would result many more objections, more than from only NACD. Even if such a single central office did come to pass, its control of all financial processes by all agencies would not last long.

AID had had such a central office but there had resulted enough delay in decision-making that, in time, financial judgments had been "delegated" to re-established finance "staff" in operating units. Unit heads could again run their show.

I have no evidence that our suggestion, endorsed by our NACD colleagues, deserves credit for stopping Glickman's consolidation. I was not involved in the debate and consideration within USDA, but NRCS at this writing still has its own budget and finance office.

25 x 25; What is a Quad?

In early 2004 I was asked to join an effort sponsored by the Energy Futures Coalition, a non-partisan public policy group located in Washington, D.C. The Coalition had noted the energy-conserving benefits of zero or minimum tillage and saw the earlier-mentioned NACD as a vehicle to get agriculture involved in national energy policy. It seemed to me that the U.S. should develop all its energy sources, certainly including wind, solar, geothermal, and such products as ethanol and biodiesel. The latter would help the market for corn and soybeans and renewable energy could help reduce atmospheric pollution and so it merited my joining the effort. In the next six years we would learn much about renewable energy.

In late September of 2005, and Shirley and I were in a ten-year-old solar-heated building at the U.S. Department of Energy's (DOE) National Renewable Energy (NREL) Laboratory on the edge of Golden, Colorado. A research group manager, Nancy Carlyle, was telling us that this building's 1995 technology and design were thirty per cent more energy efficient than most current construction. Among the building's features were deep insulation and a long roof overhang above the south windows. The overhang limits radiant heat in the summer months when the sun is overhead, but allows radiant heat in the winter when the sun is lower to the south horizon.

By no means was the south roof overhang new technology; a barn built at Iowa State's swine nutrition farm during my early faculty years was so designed. However, double-pane windows that admit radiant heat but minimize escaping convective heat were new. Because so little fuel-generated heat was required, the electric lights were the building's major energy user.

We next listened to Lab Director Mike Pacheco tell us that, though ethanol from cellulosic materials was not then financially feasible, developing conversion technologies would make it feasible in six to ten years. (In the month of this writing, September, 2014, Iowa's first two cellulosic ethanol plants were dedicated.)

Research focus was largely on the fermenting organisms, searching for those most efficient in converting to alcohol the five different sugars that comprise starch or cellulose and, through genetic engineering, trying to increase their efficiency. Soil-borne fungi were among those being studied. That is logical; they produce the enzyme, cellulase, which breaks down post-harvest crop residue.

Our host cited 1970 data showing production cost of corn ethanol at four to five dollars per gallon, while, at the time of our visit, Brazil was producing corn ethanol for seventy to eighty cents per gallon. Pacheco also told us that, though major oil companies may consider ethanol a competitor, they were following the NREL research. Every major U.S. oil company but one had visited NREL's bio-energy research within the previous year.

Our companions on this visit to NREL were the other members of our group, the 25 x 25 steering committee. The name, 25x25, reflected the goal that by the year, 2025, twenty five per cent of U.S. energy consumption might be from renewables, solar, wind, bio-energy, and geothermal. Though geothermal cannot be technically defined as renewable, it is usually included because it contributes little to atmospheric pollution. We had learned enough about these energy sources to believe that the goal was feasible.

We would next drive north to another DOE facility, the National Wind Technology Center near Boulder. We would stand beside sections of the eighty-meter towers and several seventy-seven-meter blades that would become commonplace in western Iowa in the decade ahead. NWTC Director Dr. Robert Thresher and his colleagues would tell us that then current technology would allow capturing about forty eight per cent of the kinetic energy of wind. Their research on blade design, rotating speed, and other features was focused on getting closer to sixty per cent capture, considered the theoretical limit.

Thresher suggested that wind could provide twenty per cent of the country's electricity needs, compared to one-half of a per cent in 2005, but that would require both improved technology and continuation of the federal tax credit for wind energy investments. Without that tax credit, wind turbines could not compete with existing fossil fuel-generated electricity. Most of the latter was from depreciated plants, allowing a lower per kilowatt rate.

Wind energy has another handicap; wind is inconsistent but electricity consumption is consistent. Meshing the two is not easy.

Nine months later we were on a grassy knoll in the southern Kansas Flint Hills, standing among seventy wind turbines. Our rancher host and his neighbors were pleased with the turbines, especially their annual payments for the acre or so of grazing land required for each turbine, space for the turbine base, and service roads. The installation had brought more employment to the area, first for construction and then for turbine and sub-station maintenance.

Their major problem had been gaining approval by the county commission. Residents had objected to the turbines destroying the open grass country landscape and also feared that the turning blades would kill migrating birds. Objections had been sufficiently intense that the local sheriff had to be on hand to insure an orderly commission meeting.

We learned in grade school that energy is measured in BTUs, British Thermal Units. DOE's Energy Information Agency told us that in 2005 the United States was consuming 100.5 "Quads" (a quadrillion or a million million BTU) and that by 2025, domestic use was expected to be 117.7 Quads. For the 25 x 25 goal to be achieved, nearly thirty Quads would need to be supplied by renewables.

For the year, 2013, renewable sources had provided about 9.3 Quads of the U.S. energy use. Iowa was doing its share, with more than a dozen ethanol plants in operations, perhaps as many wind turbine projects, and more planned. However, for the country, there was still a long way to go.

CHAPTER XII

TRUTH AND CONSEQUENCES

"Beyond that return on equity for an individual investor, SouthWest Iowa Egg, is on solid footing, all debt has been retired, the business has a capacity of nearly nine hundred thousand layers, and has money in the bank".

There would come, of course, the physical limitations of age, and completion of some major projects would give us time for leisure travel, biking, golf, bridge, writing, or, in Shirley's case, more painting. It would also be time to reflect on and assess the outcome of some encounters. In this last chapter are some items I simply want to share with the readers, the items ranging from embarrassment to a self-critique and, of course, they include some satisfactions.

Deer Poachers?

Troublesome Creek Valley has a generous share of the deer population. On a winter day in the early 2000s I watched from the roadway as a line of sixteen white-tails ambled across a field of bean stubble. It is not uncommon for several to wander through our farmstead any season of the year and we once found a young fawn nestled against the base of a tree near our machine shed and shop.

Though I recognize and respect hunting as a sport, and give family and friends permission to hunt on our land, I am not a hunter and do not look kindly on those who break the rules, especially those who cut fences or leave deep pick-up tracks in fall-tilled fields. Hence, my alarm this winter day.

First I saw a red pick-up moving slowly west past our farmstead, with what appeared to be a pair of antlers resting on the top of the tail gate. Perhaps five hundred feet from the road, I was clearing our drive of the previous night's four-inch snowfall with a rear blade on my little Ford tractor. It was cold, about twenty degrees, the wind was strong, and, though the sun was shining brightly, I had on my "never-offs" (insulated coveralls that my neighbors told me that "once you put them on in the fall you never take them off until spring").

"They must have had a good hunt," I thought. I hope it is "they"; it appeared there were more deer carcasses in the pick-up than the limit of one per hunter.

A few minutes later, as I was headed toward the shop, I saw the pick-up going slowly back east. "If they have their limit, why would they be headed back east?" I wondered.

I put the tractor away, shut off the shop lights, and headed toward the house, then stopped. That pick-up was now where it should not be; it was in the middle of our harvested soybean field, about a half mile northeast of the farmstead. I watched it move along a shallow drainage-way and then it headed back south, toward the road.

"They must be after more deer," I thought, and that raised my blood pressure. Our land was posted, no trespassing or hunting without written permission. We saved the hunting for sons-in-law and a few neighbors and friends.

I watched from the family room window. About five hundred feet short of the road, the pick-up turned to the left, out into another section of the crop-land. My blood pressure went up a bit more. Our land is rented to others, but it offends me and there is some cost to the tenant from tracks across cropland in the yet unfrozen soil. Next spring there will be vigorous weeds and foxtail in those very tracks. The pick-up wheels will have packed the soil around ever-present weed and foxtail seeds, provide a perfect environment for germination when the ground warms in the spring.

I deduced the encroaching hunters, still assuming more than one, had spotted the three young does that I had spooked out of the timber while walking late the day before. Across the road from that field, a sliver of native timber separates the road from the creek, good shelter for wildlife.

Now the pick-up was stopped mid-field, and I could see the driver out along side. Had he shot a deer? I stepped outside to see more clearly. Was he eviscerating a deer on the spot?

I keep handy an 800 number to report poachers, rushed into the house to make a call. I had no desire to confront. Anyone who would poach is not the type I would care to confront in the field.

I punched in the number and got a recorded message, "Punch 1 to report poaching." I punched 1, but the recorder kept playing. I dropped the phone, found the number for the local DNR (Department of Natural Resources) office. A pleasant young lady gave me two pieces of information, 1) The 800 number is no longer funded, and 2) the cell number for local conservation officer Eric Sansgaard.

I reached Sansgaard on the second ring, told him what I had seen. "I'm a long way from your place," he said, "Try to get their license number and call me back."

By this time the pick-up moved again and Shirley was watching with her binoculars, "He's down close to the road, but appears to be stuck."

"Great!" I said. "I'm glad he is. I'll drive up, see if I can 'help,' and get his license number."

As I drove up the road to the east I was reciting what I would say, "Got a problem? Hunting on posted land, you have two problems. And, with a pick-up full of deer and only one of you, it appears you have three problems."

In truth, I had not planned to use those last two sentences. I would only suggest that I would call for a wrecker (and, unsaid, Sansgaard). As I got closer, it appeared to me he was in rather deep snow. He had not been aware of a mostly filled-in bayou, a centuries-earlier route of Troublesome Creek. The smooth snow surface had belied its depth. He was in deep. At least, he could not escape.

About the time I was feeling that satisfaction of a poacher stuck in deep snow, I spotted PELGROW on the pick-up door. My mind "pulled up short." It was also soil sampling time. This early snow had not stopped our local fertilizer dealer's men from doing their job, taking soil samples for our tenant. A clean-cut young man was standing by the cab holding a spade and a phone.

How about those deer antlers I had seen thirty minutes earlier from my tractor? They were the handlebars of a four wheeler. And what I thought must be more deer? A couple spades and soil probes tied to the four-wheeler's deck.

"Got a problem?" I asked.

"I guess I do. I didn't realize how deep the snow was.

"Can I help?"

"No. I've called the office and they are sending out another truck and a tow rope."

Back at the house I dialed Sansgaard, "The poachers got away before I could get the license number. And, there is no evidence that they got a deer."

Two With no Suits

On a Sunday night four decades earlier I had arrived in Manhattan, Kansas, where the next morning I would begin a new job as associate dean of agriculture, but I had arrived without a suit. I had left my suit bag in a hall closet at our house in Ames. This time, Shirley and I would arrive in St. Louis for a FarmHouse Fraternity recognition program and *both* of us would be without our suits.

Before departing for St. Louis and the fraternity conclave, I had driven the two miles to feed daughter LuAnn's dogs; we exchange that task when the other party is traveling. It was a beautiful Wednesday morning in Troublesome Creek Valley, heavy dew gave sheen to the corn and beans, and I watched two young fawns dance across the road toward the timber. The only thing that marred the pleasure of that short trip was, on return and within a quarter mile of home, I spotted what appeared to be a garbage bag alongside the road. It was not uncommon to see a couple old tires or, once, even a TV set in a road ditch, dropped off to avoid paying the county re-cycling fee. A garbage bag was even more offensive.

As I pulled into the garage I saw Shirley had placed her bulging carry-on bag beside my suitcase. "She must be traveling light," I thought, but had long marveled at how many items she could get into a carry-on bag. I tossed the bags in the trunk and we headed to St. Louis. We were looking forward to an enjoyable drive through southeastern Iowa, then along the west side of the Mississippi river toward St. Louis, country we had not recently traveled.

Mid morning, as we drove along Highway 34 south of Des Moines, it struck me: I had forgotten to gather my suit bag from the closet. We were too far along to consider returning for my bag, but I had packed a pair of dark gray trousers and several dress shirts. Perhaps a fraternity brother of my vintage would be at the conclave and I could borrow a sport jacket and tie.

Or, perhaps Ottumwa had a Salvation Army store. From the time our grandsons were in junior high, their favorite past-time when they came to visit was an hour or more in Templeman's, a local "used anything" business that occupies a former auto agency building on Walnut Street, or the local Salvation Army store. While they picked through stacks of records or CDs, or looked for outlandish T-shirts at Salvation Army, I would wonder through the men's clothing racks. A few weeks earlier I had spotted a near-new, gray, pin-strip suit, almost identical to one in my home closet and marked only ten dollars. "I could keep that in our Florida condo," I thought. It had fit perfectly.

At a Burger King on the edge of Ottumwa I asked a cute, young waitress if the city had a Salvation Army store and she gave me directions. Once in the store, I found a hardly-used navy sport jacket, my size, and on the tie rack a black tie with a thin gold stripe. For six dollars, five for the jacket and one for the tie, we had a relaxed drive on to St. Louis.

When I clicked open the trunk at St. Louis' former Union Station, recently converted to a hotel and convention center, Shirley exclaimed, "Where's my bag?" I pointed to her carry-on.

"Not that one," she said, "my suit bag. I had laid it on the car trunk before breakfast."

Now I understood; it was that "garbage bag" on the roadside. I had not seen it on the trunk when I had gotten into the car, and it has slid off on my way to LuAnn's.

St. Louis' Salvation Army store would not accommodate Shirley's need. The suit she found the next morning at a local shop cost a bit more than my sport jacket and tie.

Was the suit bag still along the road when we returned Saturday evening, three days later? No luck. I called all the neighbors, especially those upstream who travel Troublesome Creek Road. None that I talked to had seen it, and I left messages on answering machines.

It would be late Sunday night that we got the call, from neighbors Jim and Ginnie Jordan, back from week-end travel. He had spotted the bag and taken it home. It had no identification and he had wondered why anyone would dump such good clothes off on the side of the road.

Now Shirley has an even fuller closet.

Another Home on a Golf Course

Advancing age could someday bring the need to move from our farm home and suggested we should investigate options. With our links to Iowa State University and having lived seven years in Ames, we tried to rent a unit at the Green Hills retirement community south of the campus for a winter month. Finding no rentals, we purchased a one-bedroom unit on the eighth floor of Green Hills' high rise and with a wonderful view of the countryside. We would encounter at Green Hills more than thirty residents with whom we had a linkage, from former instructors and faculty colleagues to mothers or fathers of former students.

It was an enjoyable month, with coffee, lunch, or dinner visits and playing cards with long-time friends, convenient van trips to theatre performances and basketball games, and nearby bus service to university seminars. At the end of the month, however, we headed back to the farm. We had found Ames' February north wind as biting as during my student and faculty days.

The next winter we tried a month in a rental unit in Ft. Myers, Florida, and by the end of that month had purchased a small, two-bedroom condo in a developing "over fifty five" community, now called Pelican Preserve, complete with a theatre, pool, exercise and craft rooms, and dining facilities in a town center. Though we retained the Green Hills unit for a year, thinking we might use it as a base for campus events, our winter attention had shifted to Florida.

Our two-bedroom ground floor condo on the east side of Ft. Myers overlooks the ninth tee and fairway of Pelican Preserve's nine-hole Egret course, one of three nine-hole courses that meander through Pelican's communities. Beyond is dense timber and between the tee and our lanai (a porch in Iowa terminology) is a small lake with its own alligator.

After fifty years we again had a home on a golf course. The first eighteen months of our married life had been in half of a Quonset, the half that faced what was then the first fairway of Iowa State's Veenker Golf Course. Though it had limited space and on Sunday mornings we might hear the rat-a-tat-tat of a golf ball rolling down the Quonset's corrugations, the price had been right, eighteen dollars per month. This Florida condo costs us a bit more.

We are often asked why we chose Ft. Myers. Our twin grandsons had been born prematurely and had spent their first five months in Ft. Myers Lee Memorial Hospital nearly two decades earlier. Shirley had spent many weeks with them during that time, and had become acquainted and impressed with the area and the climate. Further, we prefer Florida's higher humidity and green vegetation over the arid southwest.

In the first years of ownership, we would head to Florida after Christmas. But, with one daughter having a unit on nearby Captiva Island and the other daughter purchasing a unit in Pelican, celebrating both Christmas and Thanksgiving in Florida has become the norm. However, late winter anticipation of budding apple trees and forsythia blossoms, and fresh, bright green bluegrass emerging from the snow at the farm and, especially, our deep appreciation for the Atlantic, Iowa, community, draws us in early April back to the farm and Troublesome Creek Valley.

After establishing our modest winter home in Florida, my goal had been to become a "bogey golfer," to average one stroke over par. Pelican Preserve's three nine-hole courses, as well tended as home town Atlantic's two courses, provide plenty of water and sand challenges. I initially declined buying membership in Pelican's Golf Club and would, instead, pay green fees for the limited times I expected to play. I soon found another retired professor, one Paul Mattson from Northern Michigan University, Marquette, who had joined the club and had a golf cart, and I could play at a reasonable rate as his guest.

I had played little golf since the early 1970s at SDSU. Director of Finance Wes Bugg, Engineering Dean John Lagerstrom, Pharmacy Dean Ray Hopponen, and I would sneak off to Tyler, Minnesota's nine-hole course on summer Wednesday afternoons and I would score forty five to forty eight most outings, bogey or close to bogey on the par-thirty six course.

At Nebraska I had been on a course but once, and played little our eleven years back at Kansas State. During my Washington assignments I did not even investigate golf courses. There was no time and the green fees were, to me, "out of sight."

After renting our Iowa land to others, I had chosen to get back to the game, bought friend Ray Underwood's near-new cart when he gave up the game, and dusted off my clubs. I even took a couple lessons from former Atlantic high school coach, Dale Allen.

In time, I would settle into Monday and Wednesday mornings through the spring, summer, and fall with a retiree group that includes accountant Hal Gronewold, home furnishings Floyd Heithoff, pharmacist Allen Fann, and bridge builder Keith Harlan.

A word about the clubs I had used for nearly fifty years: I purchased the set in early summer, 1958, from Professor Tolbert McRae, who I considered the "grand old man" of Iowa State's Music Department. During my 1948 Freshman Days, McRae had introduced us new enrollees to Iowa State's Alma Mater. Seven years later, after we had returned from two years at Oklahoma State, McRae had led us in singing the Alma Mater at the academic year's opening faculty convocation.

At a Rotary luncheon meeting early summer of 1958, McRae had heard me mention that I was interested in learning golf, but needed clubs. "I'm getting new clubs," he said, "At my age I need a more flexible shaft. If you would like to stop by this evening, I'll show you my old clubs."

McRae lived just two blocks down from our home on Storm Street and had the set laid out on his sidewalk when I arrived, the grips resting on the lower step. I do not recall the price, but it seemed reasonable and I agreed. Then, he added, "On one condition, that you let me give you a couple lessons."

After the next two Rotary meetings, McRae and I met on Iowa State's intramural and ROTC drill field west of the armory (now the site of the College of Design) and he showed me the basics of how to swing a golf club.

Neighbor Gene Schertz, on detached service from the army quartermaster corps to get a degree in food science, also gave me considerable help, and I played several Sundays with him and Walt Woods, long time friend, neighbor, and fellow animal scientist.

In the intervening years I had made but two additions to my bag, a telescoping ball retriever that Shirley gave me and a fifty nine dollar driver that Coach Allen advised after his first lesson.

One of Florida's cold and windy January days, with three enjoyable partners on the seventh fairway of Pelican Preserves Egret nine. To my immediate left is Paul Mattson, retired professor of engineering mechanics at Northern Michigan University, Marquette, then Prem Taneja from Toronto, a native of India and who has traveled the world for Coca Cola and Novartis, and Wayne Paling, a farmer from near Dresden, Ontario, Canada.

If one keeps at a game long enough, with or without skill, some good things will happen. In my second year playing with Mattson, on the par 3 Number Three of the Egret nine, my ball found its way from my five-iron on the tee directly into the cup. And the same would happen two years later, par 3 Number Three on Heron's nine.

Though, at this writing, I have managed a bogey forty five or better on a few nine-hole rounds, I have yet to achieve an eighteen-hole bogey round. If I maintain my present skill level until I am ninety five, perhaps I will achieve a more common goal among retirees, "score my age" on eighteen holes

Pompei and Warsaw

Shirley and I did plan more travel, one international trip and also extended travel within the U.S. most every year. All is broadening, but it is often the misfortunes or mistakes that make a journey memorable. In this case, we had bid daughter LuAnn adieu at the Rome Airport for her flight back to the U.S. after several days in Venice and Rome, and we would take a mid-morning train to Switzerland.

As our train was leaving the outskirts of Rome, I struck up a conversation with a fellow passenger and, noting his dark complexion, asked his destination. His response got my attention, "I'm on my way home to Tunisia." Tunisia? I had misread the track number for our Switzerland train.

We quickly grabbed our timetable and map, saw that we were on our way toward Naples and that Pompei was just beyond. "We've not seen Pompei," Shirley said, "Now is our chance."

An hour later we stored our bags in a Naples station locker, purchased a liter of water at McDonald's, and boarded a local train to Pompei. In forty minutes we were walking the streets of the village that had been buried by up to twenty feet of ash from Mt. Vesuvius in 79 A.D. and remained buried until excavations between 1600 and 1750. Centuries under the ash had preserved the rich colors of the frescoes on wall remnants of Pompei's homes and shops.

We had had a bonus. We would return that evening to Rome, and take a night train toward Switzerland.

Another surprising experience: With daughter Diane, Shirley and I were on our way by train to Warsaw, Poland. Diane would return to the States from Warsaw; Shirley and I would continue through the Baltic countries to Leningrad.

Our first travel days had been in Hamburg and points north visiting Shirley's German relatives and we had arrived about noon at Berlin's Hauptbahnhof station to connect with a Warsaw-bound train. European trains are always on time and, though the time-table showed we had twenty minutes to change trains, we were apprehensive. We checked with other apparent Warsaw-bound travelers to be sure we were at the right track for boarding.

I stepped to a kiosk to buy sandwiches, encountered a long line of hungry travelers and, just as I returned to Shirley and Diane with the sandwiches, an east-bound train pulled in on that track.

A few years earlier we had failed to quickly get off a train in northern Germany, the door closed and the train had proceeded. We had to get off at the next town and return to our destination an hour later. This time, I was not about to tarry. As the last person stepped off this newly arrived train, we three grabbed our bags and rushed on.

We were barely inside when the door closed! No one else had gotten on! I tried the door and it was locked. The train began to move. There was no crew in evidence and, except for the three of us, the car was empty. We were soon speeding along through a residential area. I rushed into the forward car, and on to the next. There was not a soul.

After perhaps ten minutes, our car made a sharp turn off to a siding, and we came to a stop—in what appeared to be a rail car yard. We heard a click, tried the door, and it slid open. However, we were on an elevated track, and six feet off the ground.

Across the yard we spotted a track crew at work and I yelled to get their attention. Though I could not understand their German language, their facial expressions said it all, "What are you idiots doing up in that empty train?"

Two smiling young men rushed over, helped lower our luggage and us down to the ground. They then led us across a battery of tracks and up a stairway to an adjacent inter-urban platform. Ten minutes later, we boarded a local train back to Hauptbahnhof, where we ate our sandwiches and waited for a six o'clock train to Warsaw.

Those track workers would have a good story to tell their families that evening.

Good Research Ten Years Ago

From the early 1980s, my latter years in the K-State presidency, I have been part of a Farm Foundation Agricultural Roundtable, a self-perpetuating mix of about two hundred academics, industry leaders, and farmers and ranchers who gather twice a year to focus on agricultural issues. The Roundtable had its roots in the Eisenhower presidency. He had asked a friend, one Dana Bennett, to put together a small group to serve as a sounding board on agricultural issues. I had had the privilege of knowing Bennett during my associate dean years. As a philanthropist, he had funded a number of workshops for college of agriculture associate deans/directors of instruction. After Bennett's death, the Chicago-based Farm Foundation had become the "organization base" for the Roundtable.

Shirley and I find every meeting of the Roundtable's diverse membership informative and stimulating. At the June, 2003, session in Birmingham, Alabama, for example, a dean of agriculture asked one of the presenters, an Alabama farmer faced with environmental concerns from suburban neighbors, what kind of help he needed from the universities. The farmer's succinct response was, "Good research information ten years ago." His response was right on target, and prompted me to write a brief piece on the issue, to be available when I might have the opportunity to share it with the right audience. It could have been titled, A Self Critique, and here is a condensation.

A Self-Critique

Why did not the nation's agricultural research and extension system, including both the land grant universities and USDA, anticipate the need for environmental research information, earlier devote resources to gathering the data, and mount data-based extension education programs for both producers and the citizenry?

We had known years earlier that high levels of phosphorus run-off from increasingly large feedlots and intensively cropped land often found its way to streams and lakes and prompted bothersome algae blooms. We also knew the U.S. citizenry was increasingly concerned about environmental issues.

I was a player in this system for many years, an animal scientist, a dean, an experiment station director, and a director of extension. I also headed, for a brief time, USDA's agricultural research and extension system as Assistant Secretary. I know now that I did not do enough to prompt needed research.

Yes, there have been good research and education efforts in this arena, and I could cite them, but they have been far too little and far too late. Had we, in the research and extension system, been far more perceptive and far more aggressive in our resource allocations and program decisions, we could have provided the data to guide producers in locating or relocating, sizing and/or designing their animal units and cropping operations for positive environmental effects. We could have also helped producers' bottom line; surplus phosphorus going to the streams is a waste.

Research could have also provided objective data for state legislatures and agencies, county and city commissioners, as well as to the general citizenry, on which to base guidance and regulations. Angry neighbors and lawsuits are a waste of both emotional energy and money.

Since returning to our Iowa farm and involved in putting together a large egg production complex, I have given this issue more thought. Repeatedly, I have recalled a stairway conversation, about 1972, with my beef Extension specialist, Jim O'Connell, at a South Dakota Cattle Feeders convention in Sioux Falls. I was then SDSU's dean and director and we had just listened to a discussion of feedlot run-off problems and the fear of state regulations. I suggested that we should be collecting nutrient run-off data from existing feedlots and use the data in educational meetings and publications. If producers had the data, they could more wisely plan new construction or renovations. We could even devise guidelines for feedlot design and operation.

His response: "If we collected those data, they would just prompt those regulations. Nobody in this business wants state regulations. And, what if the new regulations were different from our guidelines? Then we would be at fault for misleading."

Yes, I have replayed that conversation, *with embarrassment*. Why did I not reallocate funds and assign O'Connell and other staff to gather such data and implement an aggressive educational program?

And, why were those cattle feeders not asking for data and guidelines?

I believe there are three major reasons we were not ahead of the game on environmental issues. I will use animal science as an example; there are parallels in other disciplines.

1. Animal management, including housing, manure management, and animal care, were at the bottom of the prestige scale in university's animal science departments. Nutrition, genetics, reproduction, and muscle biology were the prominent disciplines and brought more acceptance and prestige in the scientific community.
2. The industry, at least the more vocal leaders, did not want the data. Note that stairway conversation with O'Connell. Perhaps he feared implementing my suggestion could risk his job—and mine.
3. As animal scientists, we often feel need to protect our industry from outsiders, the "activists" and regulators. Or, perhaps we thought the issue was short-term and would go away.

As industry or university leaders, we need to insure that our agricultural research and education systems are ahead of the game on future, as well as current, issues. I suggest:

1. To industry leaders: Seek the information, the data that will assess or quantify an emerging issue. Press your university experiment station and Extension staff to initiate needed work. It is better to have the facts early.
2. To faculty: The job of faculty is to "seek the truth and teach the truth as we see it in our discipline of training," the very definition of academic freedom. With credible data from the university, your industry can do a better job of "protecting itself." If a university department related to an industry, whether it be animal science, civil engineering, or accounting, is not forced from time to time to defend the academic freedom of a professor for advancing data or a concept that may make some in their industry uncomfortable, its faculty may not be thinking enough "outside the box," collecting data on potential problems, or adequately challenging industry practices and habits. They may be *risking* their industry. Witness the late 1990s problems

in the accounting profession, accounting practices exposed in the Enron melt-down.

In this time of higher public sensitivity to and demanded accountability for food safety, animal welfare, and impact on the environment, it is critical that facts be established and available *early* to decision-makers.

We are fortunate to have gifted people in our U.S. agricultural research and education system. They need our support in focusing their talents and their limited resources on the issues that will help keep the private sector U.S. agriculture ahead of the game.

The Seaman Knapp Lecture

The right opportunity to share those thoughts came that fall. Annual meetings of the National Association of State Universities and Land Grant Colleges (at this writing, Association of Public Universities) include an invitational lecture named for Seaman A. Knapp, considered by many as the "Father of Extension."

Though it had been seventeen years since I had left the university, I was invited to give the Knapp lecture at the 2003 annual meeting in New Orleans and my audience would be university deans, provosts, and presidents. That was the right audience and my piece, "Good Research Ten Years Ago," was ready.

Though I titled my lecture, Knowledge, Wisdom, and Freedom, most of the body of the lecture was that piece on the preceding pages. I show here only the brief introduction, intended to set the stage.

"The university is based on three premises:

- Academic freedom, the freedom for each faculty member to "seek the truth and teach the truth as they see it in their discipline of training." (Sidney Hook's well accepted definition of academic freedom)
- You shall know the truth and the truth will set you free. (John 8:32)

- Wisdom is strength; knowledge is power. (Carter Burgess, Chairman of American Machine and Foundry, at the dedication of baking equipment his company had provided the Grain Science Department at Kansas State University about 1965)

Your task, as a president, provost, or dean, and the task of those you lead, is to help free individuals, and society as a whole, from the constraints of limited knowledge, the constraints of limited concepts, and the constraints of limited vision."

RDAC: Output and Impact

In Chapter I, I described the formation of a local Rural Development Action Committee (RDAC) our first year back on the farm, its purpose, and some of its initial committees. The reader may wonder the eventual impact. There have been several, direct or indirect. One of the early and more direct impacts was on the state's beef industry. Relative to dairy, poultry, and swine, the U.S. beef industry in the early 1990s was losing market share.

Dairy Herd Improvement Associations (DHIA) had led the animal industry in speeding production increases and improving product quality. Beginning in the first half of the previous century, DHIA technicians visited member farms monthly, recorded evening and morning production of each cow, and took milk samples for butterfat and other qualities. Data helped producers decide which cows to cull and which offspring to keep and breed. Not only did those herds increase production per cow, *national* average production per cow climbed every decade.

Concentration in broiler, egg, and swine production, and the improved genetics that these species' shorter generation time allows, had also brought rapid production gains and more consistent product quality.

There had been no beef industry program comparable to DHIA and, with one calf per cow per year, the species lacked the speed with which selection could increase production or quality. The beef industry risked losing more meat market share.

A Precision Beef Alliance (PBA) of calf producers and feeders was formed in 1995 largely by Rich Hall, Randy Euken, Bill Pellett, Varel Bailey, and, especially, Iowa State's southwest area livestock specialist, Darrel Busby. It flourished rapidly, gained members, and, in time, Hall left his county extension position to head the Alliance. The Alliance implemented precision measurement systems in members' herds and feedlots, took some of the Alliance-identified product to the retail level, and generated enthusiasm state-wide.

However, two developments made continuation of the Alliance, per se, financially infeasible. The enthusiasm the Alliance generated appeared to lead the larger membership Iowa Cattlemens' Association to start what would be a competing program. And, the very effectiveness of PBA's measurement systems appeared to prompt a few producers to think, "Why not do this myself, rather than pay a fee to an association?"

The product quality focus and precision measurement systems *do live on* in a variety of forms, by individual seed stock producers and in what is called the Tri-County Futurity, a program earlier underway and which had provided some of the data on which PBA's system was established. The Tri-County Futurity at this writing involves more than three hundred herds and eight southwest Iowa feedlots that market more than seven thousand cattle per year.

Another early and direct RDAC outcome was SouthWest Iowa Specialty Crops (SWISC), a business formed in 1995 by twenty three local farmers as a joint venture with SunRich, Inc., of Hope, Minnesota. Several of us had planted a "waxy" corn variety in 1994 and had sold the grain for a twenty cent per bushel premium and saw more potential. This new business, led by local producers Gary Muller, Garry Pellett, and Delbert Westphalen, would seek more high-value crop opportunities. One of the most promising efforts was the growing of a soybean variety to be exported to Japan for soymilk and tofu, or harvested as green pods and shipped to the east or west coast for specialty markets. Craig Huff, native of the Anita area, managed the operation for the growers and investors, and including first-stage processing and perhaps some packaging.

As one of the twenty three investors, I contracted to grow and to sell that year at harvest nearly forty six hundred bushels of Number One grade LS-201 soybeans at $1.40 above the Chicago Board of Trade

November futures price. Though the higher price received per bushel did not in every case offset the lower yields of some of the lines, the business gave local growers the experience of growing and processing identity-preserved crops.

Later, in 2001, growers encountered a virus that stained the coating of the company's contracted beans, making them unacceptable to their Japanese buyers. After repeated efforts to shift to other products, the judgment was made in 2004 to liquidate SWISC. However, a number of the growers continued to grow higher-value or special-value crops, such as high-oil corn, oleic soybeans, and white corn. Some producers, including David Denne and others mentioned earlier, joined another, parallel effort, Iowa Quality Producers Alliance.

In more recent years, genetic engineering has allowed changing the make-up of the corn kernel, the bean, and even the vegetative portion of the plant so that they may yield, or be converted more efficiently to, a higher value end product. While editing this section, January, 2015, I received a letter from Southwest Renewable Energy, an ethanol plant south of Council Bluffs, telling its investors that by growing and delivering corn that had been bioengineered to express the alpha amylase enzyme in the corn kernel, one would receive a forty cent per bushel premium. That enzyme allows more efficient conversion of the corn kernel starch to ethyl alcohol.

The 1993 Iowa legislature had allowed formal establishment of "Agricultural Areas," their purpose to protect crop and livestock producers from lawsuits as long as their operations were consistent with other laws and regulations (such as distance from residences for intensive animal units). Defined and approved Agricultural Areas could encourage more livestock and poultry operations in our county, and RDAC took on the task of educating and promoting. Ray Underwood, retired marketing director for local feed manufacturer, Walnut Grove, led the effort with both publicity and public meetings in Anita, Massena, Griswold, and Atlantic.

Seven neighbors, Shirley, and I filed in early 1996 with the County Recorder a Certificate of Resolution establishing an Agricultural Area that covered about thirty nine hundred contiguous acres, and it was approved by the Cass County Board of Supervisors. We were not the first in the county to file; by that time, nine Agricultural Area applications had been approved by the County Board.

The 1993 law was eventually voided by the Iowa Supreme court on the grounds that it imposed constraints on a citizen's right to sue for redress, so our established "agricultural areas" had no validity. However, perhaps the process elevated some local producers' sensitivity to neighbors' interests and comfort.

A late 1990s effort to establish a local ethanol business did not "get off the ground." An ethanol committee gathered enough positive data on local grain supply, ethanol price trends, and ethanol plant operating margins that several of us put in seven hundred fifty dollars each to employ an adviser and to finance a series of information meetings for potential investors. Though that effort came up short, several of the RDAC group would be early investors in what became Southwest Iowa Renewable Energy just south of Council Bluffs and/or Amaizing Energy at Denison, Iowa. In the case of the latter, a second plant for Amaizing Energy was planned for north of Atlantic. Construction began, but was interrupted by a shift in the economics of the ethanol industry. At this writing, there appears potential for that plant to be completed and join SIRE and Amaizing Energy, as well as other ethanol plants in a hundred mile radius, in providing a stronger market for area corn.

There was more. Several who were growing or interested in vegetable production, including Dave Armentrout, Bob Anderson, Kathy Swinnerton, and others studied the potential for "critical mass" production in the area. Bernie Havlovic, the Wallace Foundation, and the local Master Gardeners' group brought attention to vegetable production with the Armstrong Farm's "high tunnel" system, which allows a longer vegetable growing season. Deb Schuler worked with Iowa State on a class for young people to become rural leaders. Pat and Linda McCurdy, banker Chuck Edwards, and local veterinarian, Dr. Keith Leonard, were among others who played leadership roles.

RDAC's swine committee, led by Leonard and Rick Pellett, attracted a North Carolina company to consider developing swine breeding and growing operations in southwest Iowa. Our committee told the company it would help them get established in this area, including co-sponsorship of producer interest meetings, *if* they would work with the committee in choosing sites and adhere to guidelines we had developed to minimize negative impacts on nearby residents. However, the company would not agree to local involvement in site selection or the guidelines.

The reader may wonder if Milk Unlimited, a large dairy established southwest of Atlantic in the late 1990s, had its roots in RDAC. Not necessarily, but RDAC's efforts may have encouraged leaders of the Cass-Atlantic Development Corporation and the County Board of Supervisors to solicit or respond to the organizers' interest in the county and help the organizers find a good location.

At this writing, early 2015, Milk Unlimited's thirty five employees handle thirty five hundred cows, milking two or three times per day in a "double thirty" milking parlor, with the milk routed directly through a rapid chiller to a waiting tanker. Four 6,200-gallon tankers leave the site every twenty four hours toward a Des Moines processing plant. Milk Unlimited produces a portion of its needed corn silage on its own land, but it also purchases tons of corn and silage from nearby farmers.

The same relationship could be suggested for SouthWest Iowa Egg. Though not traced to RDAC's list of committees, perhaps county officials were more helpful in supporting this venture, and perhaps more farmers and others who invested had been influenced in part by RDAC's parallel activity.

Nearly twenty years have elapsed since those first breakfast discussions in Massena's Snack Shack about a potential egg business. The Snack Shack is long gone, but SouthWest Iowa Egg is flourishing. Following is a brief summary of the years since the 1998 groundbreaking. In 2001, after six years with the effort, most as chairman of the steering committee or board, and with President Frank Jones, Jr. and Manager Rich Hall in charge of the operation, it was time for another to take my place on the board. I would retain share ownership, deliver corn quarterly, and have continued pride in the business.

An aerial photo of SouthWest Iowa Egg. Note the reservoir that catches and supplies most of the water for the 625,000 birds at that location.

Southwest Iowa Egg at Sixteen Years

At this writing, early 2015, SWIE has twenty eight full-time or part-time employees, all local residents. Three have worked fifteen years, virtually from the time operations began, and most of the others have been with the business five to ten years, either at the site southeast of Massena or at the two hundred fifty thousand bird unit north of Massena that SWIE purchased several years ago.

Long term debt has been retired, there is cash in the bank, and the business' eggs have an excellent reputation in the shell egg market, some eggs going as far as California and even some product to Japan.

Perhaps Manager Rich Hall's and the board's most serious challenge in the early-years had been monitoring and enforcing our initial marketing contract. As organizers, we had learned that selling and pricing eggs is far different from selling and pricing grain or livestock. First, there is no daily price gathering and reporting by USDA. Instead, a private entity, Urner-Berry, polls egg buyers and sellers each day and declares the "Urner-Berry price" for each egg class, such as large white shell eggs or medium-size breaker eggs.

We had contracted our eggs to a larger egg business, one with the experience, packaging facilities, and retail relationships we did not have.

Our agreement was called a "window contract," rather common in the business and designed to share price risk. As long as the Urner-Berry (UB) price the day of delivery to their packaging facility was within a price range specified in the contract, (such as between thirty and forty cents per dozen), SWIE would receive that price. If the UB price that day was above the range, we would receive a price half way between that UB price and forty cents. If the UB price was below the range, we would receive a price halfway between the UB price and thirty cents. There was an additional feature, too detailed to describe but providing that certain price departures outside the price window would be maintained in a credit or debit ledger and, periodically, the debits and credits would be balanced to zero.

It was this latter feature that brought disagreements. More than one meeting between parties focused on contract interpretations and disparities in the ledger. The issue eventually came to a head because we both used the same auditor. An amount we were calling a credit, an asset, in our accounts (so, presumably, a debit or liability in the other party's account) was *also* being shown in the other party's yet un-audited books as an asset.

In time, SWIE was paid a significant lump sum by the other party and the contract was terminated. By that time, Hall had sufficient experience and contacts in the industry to develop other marketing arrangements.

Yes, the business is profitable, though there have been both profitable and money-losing years. As we planned the business, data from well-managed egg units suggested we might average fourteen per cent return on equity over a twenty-year period. Following are my calculations at the end of the business' sixteenth fiscal year, September 30, 2014. They assume no profit or loss on corn "delivered" and that a later seven-share purchase was at the initial $2,700.

In December of 1998, I had purchased ten equity shares at twenty seven hundred dollars each plus a voting share at one hundred dollars. I later purchased from others seven more equity shares. Through the close of the sixteenth fiscal year, I had received $80,597 in dividends plus $3,465 for selling my "manure rights" to other parties.

The sum, $84,062, divided by sixteen years equals $5,254. That figure, divided by the cost of the seventeen equity shares and one voting share, $46,000, equals an *average* of 11.42% per cent cash return *per year.*

There is more. At the end Fiscal 2014, the equity value of each share was $4,866, an increase of $2,166 from the initial $2,700 cost. That figure, divided by sixteen years and by the original share cost, is another five per cent *per year.*

Though the high corn and soybean meal prices from 2011 through 2013 resulted in several egg business failures, or egg businesses taken over by others, SWIE survived to enjoy fiscal 2014, when egg prices continued strong and grain prices had dropped.

Beyond that return on equity data shown above for an individual investor, SouthWest Iowa Egg is on solid footing, all debt has been retired, the business has a capacity of nearly nine hundred thousand layers, and has money in the bank. (At this writing, late May of 2015, a bird flu virus has decimated several flocks in northwest Iowa. That illustrates one of the business' risks and the board's wisdom in retaining money in the bank.)

Though I carry much satisfaction and pride in having been involved at the beginning, major credit for this record of profitability goes to Manager Rich Hall, successive members of the board, and the long-time and dedicated local employees. Credit for the business' existence should go also to the many area residents, ranging from area retailers to local widows to a retired minister, in addition to corn producers, citizens who were willing to risk some of their money to help establish an area business that would employ more local people.

The entrance to SouthWest Iowa Egg, after several years of operation allowed spending some money for some fencing and a welcoming appearance.

A Seventy-Year Sideline

From the time I learned the typewriter keyboard in a junior-year typing class, writing has been one of my enjoyments. The following year, Wiota Superintendent Arnold Christ suggested I start a column, "Did You Know That?" for our school's monthly mimeograph, *The Wiota Owl*, and I would later use that same "handle" for weekly newspaper columns as a summer 4-H youth assistant in nearby Audubon County.

To earn extra income during graduate school and early faculty years, I submitted short pieces on livestock topics to Farm Journal, Successful Farming, Feed Age, and other farm and feed industry journals. Publishing my graduate thesis research in Animal Science and Nutrition scientific journals, as well as *Agricultural and Food Chemistry*, was satisfying, as well as an obligation. I could say the same for a series on curriculum and academic advising that I wrote for the *Journal on College and University Teaching*.

My largest effort in those years was a textbook, *Animal Science and Industry*, put together while teaching the freshman courses at Iowa State. Virtually every evening for a year, I would play with our daughters until their eight o'clock bedtime and, from eight o'clock to ten, I would be at my desk writing. Over the next three years I would refine and use dittoed and printed versions in my classes, and the book would be formally published by Prentice Hall in 1963, soon after my departure for Kansas State.

However, from the time I moved to South Dakota State as dean until closing down our farm operation thirty years later, except for speeches and two up-dated editions of the textbook, there had been little time for substantive writing. The only pieces I recall from those years were a piece on our SDSU course reduction efforts in *College and University Management*, the future of AID's agricultural programs in an agricultural economics journal, *Choices,* and sections on agriculture and livestock for the *World Book Encyclopedia.*

After our farm operation, I found time to get back to the keyboard, by then a computer's keyboard, where my revisions and edits would be on a display screen instead of on paper.

About that time, my animal science textbook needed another revision, what would become the seventh edition. The fourth through sixth editions had been handled by two professors at Purdue University, and I sent word that, because they had been doing the recent revisions, it was time to remove my name from authorship. They declined, wanted to keep my name on the book, at least as a junior author. When I agreed, the next e-mail from Purdue was, "Which chapters would you like to revise?"

Now closer to the livestock and poultry business, I felt comfortable re-writing the poultry and dairy chapters and revising three or four others.

That seventh edition would be the last. By 2013, one Purdue co-author had long retired, the second had moved to a deanship at another university, and both technology in the animal sciences and the structure of animal production suggested a new approach. Successors to *Animal Science and Industry* will be done by a younger generation and may even be a "virtual book," with initial availability to students and continuous revision via web sites or other internet "vehicles."

After Ralph Titus, the long-time "radio voice" of Kansas State University, had led me, in the early 2000s, through the first of several oral history sessions covering my presidency, he encouraged me write a book, to share some of my thoughts, some do's and don'ts, with those who might be heading to a presidency. A month later, at a Farm Foundation Roundtable meeting, I mentioned the idea to fellow Roundtable members, Ohio State University trustee Jim Patterson and Purdue University Regent John Hardin. One responded, "It's needed." The other, "Do it!" And each followed up with content suggestions.

The result was 204-page *Can State Universities be Managed? A Primer for Presidents and Management Teams,* published in 2006 as part of the American Council on Higher Education Series on Higher Education. The limited market for such a book did not justify a promotional budget and the Council made clear the author carries responsibility for letting people know about it. Consequently, I would check web sites and the Chronicle of Higher Education for names of people chosen, or on a finalist list for a presidency or provost position, and e-mail a note alerting them to the book. Responses have been most rewarding, among them:

From a finalist for a presidency in Texas: "Thanks! I do have the book and am reading it—very helpful!"

From a newly-named president in Indiana: "I've already purchased the book and find its content very informative! Thank you!"

A more recently named president, who had earlier obtained the book, told me that when, as a candidate, he was invited back by a board of regents for a second interview, the implication being that he would be offered the job, he called his wife, "Get out that book, let's read it again."

Next was work on my memoirs and, in this book's introduction, I described the memoir sequence. People often ask how I chose the title, *Two at a Time*, for the Kansas State book. Many things in those eleven university presidential years seemed to happen in pairs. For example, gaining legislative approval and money for a new university building project is a major task, and it does not happen every year. However, in each of my first and last years in the presidency, the Kansas legislature authorized *two* major building projects for Kansas State. And, for each, there were stories of political intrigue, both on campus and in Topeka, which I could tell. That fact, and other cases of dual events, made the title logical.

The title for *From Troublesome Creek* appeared in my mind during one of those 2 a.m. sleep interruptions. The title of this book, *Back to Troublesome Creek,* is a logical follow-up.

More than a Gold Watch

During my high school years, relatives and family friends might ask what I wanted to do in life. I was then uncertain and had been considering several areas of work. However, my response might have included—at least I carried in my mind, "One thing I do not seek is a gold watch for thirty five years in the same job."

I respect years of service and, in fact, during my time as Kansas State president I established a recognition program for both years of service and outstanding service. For me, however, to be in one job, one office, one location, or on one assembly line for an entire career did not seem enticing.

The farm was then giving me so many varied experiences. It seemed there was a new or different task every week, perhaps seeding oats or harrowing ahead of the corn planter, and the types of tasks differed from season to season. I would use a variety of tools or equipment, work with cattle, sheep, hogs, horses, and chickens, and, as we traded work with neighbors or, as part of a threshing or silo-filling "ring," we worked on different farms and could enjoy different vistas as we worked. I could not envision a life without multiple experiences.

By no means do I minimize the varied exposures and experiences one can have in a life-time business or a long-time career with one employer. A bank lending officer or an accountant will work with multiple businesses, encounter new and unique issues in each. As laws or regulations change, they must adapt and their perspectives change. A retailer must adapt to new merchandise and new technologies. A life-time farmer or rancher has both the experiences I had in my youth, but also the challenges of new technology and changes in market demand.

Though I spent a third of a century in higher education, I had varied teaching assignments, formally advised hundreds of students—each with their individual skills and goals—, played administrative roles at all levels, and had the privilege of serving at universities in five states. Life and work in Washington, D.C., with four different assignments in two federal agencies or departments, was a challenging series of experiences. My agricultural development work on four continents was a bonus.

When we returned from Washington to operate our farm, friends and neighbors of earlier days asked, "Why would you want to do that?" For me, it would be a challenge, another new and exciting experience.

I also acknowledge that there are trade-offs in life. Those of us who move often and travel much miss the security and support that comes with continuing close relationships, whether it be a church, neighbors, or extended family. In that, however, my wife, Shirley, and I have had good years back in our home community. We have established and re-established such relationships, have watched a generation of young people mature, and feel an integral a part of the community.

The many experiences, some of which are described in these three memoirs, have been more than a gold watch.

Printed in the United States
By Bookmasters